Unidentified demonstration, probably April 3, 1968.
Photo by Mehdikhonsari, provided by George Abbott White.

The Resistance

BY

Michael Ferber

AND

Staughton Lynd

BEACON PRESS   BOSTON

And perhaps the great day will come when a people, distinguished by wars and victories and by the highest development of a military order and intelligence, and accustomed to make the highest sacrifice for these things, will exclaim of its own free will, "we break the sword," and will smash its military establishment down to its lowest foundations. Rendering oneself unarmed when one has been the best armed, out of a height of feeling—that is the means to real peace, which must always rest on a peace of mind; whereas the so-called armed peace, as it now exists in all countries, is the absence of peace of mind. One trusts neither oneself nor one's neighbor and, half from hatred, half from fear, does not lay down arms. Rather perish than hate and fear, and twice rather perish than make oneself hated and feared—this must someday become the highest maxim for every single commonwealth too.

From Friedrich Nietzsche, *The Wanderer and His Shadow,* used as an introduction to the first leaflet of the Resistance

Episcopal minister burns card, Sheep's Meadow, New York, April 15, 1967.

Contents

Preface   ix
Glossary   xv
Chronology   xvii
1   Resistance and Its Precedents   1
2   Burners and Returners, 1960–1965   9
3   Black Courage, White Caution   29
4   We Won't Go   47
5   Sheep's Meadow   68
6   David Harris and the Palo Alto Commune   78
7   CADRE   92
8   New England Resistance   104
9   The Call to Resist   116
10   The Resistance, the Pentagon, and Stop The Draft Week   126
11   Life in the Resistance   149
12   Community-Based Resistance   164
13   Sanctuary   186
14   The Ultra Resistance   201
15   The Corporation as Target   222
16   The Resistance Mentality   242
17   The Politics of Resistance   277
18   Epilogue: UNDO   291
Index   297

Preface

As an expression, "the movement" still enjoys wide currency in America, but it no longer refers to an existing entity. Until 1968, perhaps, someone "in the movement" could travel almost anywhere in the country and with little trouble find a group that would recognize him as one of its own. They might be in different factions, and stay up late arguing, but they would still be intuitive comrades; he would have friends, food, and bed. Now, two or three discouraging years later, it is no longer correct to speak of a single movement, and if we do in the latter parts of this book it should be understood as referring to a set of movements, some overlapping, some mutually exclusive, many hostile to one another. The very survival of the expression and idea of a single movement, however, points to a strong urge that American young people still feel, perhaps more than ever, and certainly still in growing numbers. It is an urge to make plans and theories, organizations and life styles, dreams and "trips" that will take us out of the murderous wasteland of America. Its existence may remain our only hope.

A movement founded on the idea of rebellion rather than obedience, it is said, is bound to fall apart through an endless series of internal rebellions, and a movement made up mostly of young people, with no memories and experience, will be all the more likely to break up. If unity is preserved it will be only on its lowest common denominator, the inarticulate herd instinct visible at

Woodstock in 1969 and Georgia in 1970. Perhaps so. But at least
one of the problems in the larger movement is of a specific and re-
mediable sort: the ignorance of history, of precedents and experiments, successes and failures. We are not referring to the ignorance of Hitler and Pearl Harbor with which conscientious
objectors annoy draft boards, or of the Depression with which
hippies irritate their fathers—but of what happened during their
own lives, during the last two or three decades.

George White, presently at work with Paul Garver on a history
of SDS, told us "There aren't a hundred people in the country
who know what has happened since 1960." We agree. It is to increase that number that we have written this book about one
main group or tendency in the movement, the draft resistance. It
is not a hopeless goal: even without written histories some wisdom has accumulated from generation to generation (a generation these days being about two years). Despite the pressures to
drop out or seek refuge in doctrinaire cell groups, for example,
large numbers of new activists are struggling to stay relevant, responsive, and open, and this in part because of the example of
those who preceded them. There are signs that the broader movement has come to see Scientology and Krishna Consciousness,
conspiratorial Stalinist sects and affinity groups of "trashers" as
only so many ways of giving up the struggle. The opposite danger,
itself made more likely by ignorance of the past, is to remain as
idealistic "liberals," periodically outraged by events but unable to
sustain an initiative to bring events about. It is for the new activists that we have written this book. In the next few years they will
be making decisions crucial to the fate of this country.

This book, more than most, bears signs of the process of its
composition, not all of them happy. The authors differed in age,
temperament, experience, and (occasionally) political judgment;
we lived a thousand miles apart; and we had very different relations with the draft resistance movement and the draft itself.
Staughton Lynd, now a historian, applied for and was granted
1–AO status (noncombatant within the Armed Forces) in 1953–4.
An early advocate of mass resistance to the draft for Vietnam,
Lynd has nevertheless, because of age, been no more than sup-

porter, observer, and friendly critic of the Resistance. Michael Ferber, a graduate student in English, has been a resister himself, and an organizer of the first large draft card turn-in in Boston. What Ferber lacked in perspective he filled with passion; what Lynd lacked in intuitive understanding he attempted to extrapolate from other kinds of experience. But we were not always able to make up for each other's shortcomings, and some have remained in the text. The chapter on the New England Resistance and the excursus on "resistance epistemology" were left entirely to Ferber, but others, though jointly written, still tend somewhat toward one bias or the other.

We also went about the writing in the opposite order from what our differing roles in the Resistance would seem to dictate. A protagonist, or "informant," usually provides raw data for an historian to interpret, but with us it was reversed. Out of impatience with the protagonist's procrastination the historian wrote most of the first draft, relying primarily on documents, and then the protagonist, impatient with the historian's prose style, rewrote it, trying to add that sense of the right relationship of things which, we both feel, only he who has experienced them can provide. We fell into this pattern by accident but, for all its problems, we recommend it to others.

For a large part of the book, however, we were not so much its creators as its midwives. The Resistance is a decentralized national network, so we tried to decentralize the authorship of its story. We invited every group in the loose federation called the Resistance to send us old newsletters and leaflets, and asked eight or nine of them to make tape recordings. The taping sessions varied a great deal from group to group, but typically they became occasions not only for recollection but for exploring and resolving personal and political differences, a process that we think was more important than any use to which we may later have put the tapes. If the completed book provokes similar occasions, in fact, it will fulfill its highest purpose.

We have many individuals to thank. Paul Lauter and Florence Howe shared their clippings, unpublished manuscripts, and diaries, which were especially helpful in illuminating the genesis of draft resistance sentiment within SNCC. Karl Meyer of the *Catholic Worker* provided files of peace journals of the early 1960s, and David Mitchell dug up much old correspondence of the End The Draft movement. Brent Kramer volunteered correspondence of the national SDS committee on the draft which functioned, or at least met, in the summer of 1966. The Reverend David M. Gracie sent clippings and leaflets about the December 1966 conference which gave birth to the Detroit Resistance. Judy Longley had similar material for the antidraft union formed at Michigan State University a few months later.

Norma Becker of the National Mobilization Committee shared a key letter from Steve Hamilton concerning the origin of Anti-Draft Week. Marty Jezer of WIN not only sent along letters from We Won't Go groups as they formed in the spring and summer of 1967, but read and criticized much of our first draft. So did Gene Keyes, Rick Boardman, Lawrence Wittner and (from prison) David Harris. George White shared material from student newspapers and his own participant observations of the Ann Arbor draft board sit-in of October 1965. The staff of the national Resist office kindly let us ransack their files one weekend, and we drew heavily on the material collected by Alice Lynd for her book *We Won't Go*. WIN and George White were among our sources for pictures.

Many others went out of their way to help, including Richard Hathaway, Dave Kenney, the New York City and San Francisco Resistance office staffs, Bob Langfelder of Santa Barbara Resistance, Larry Gara (a World War II resister), David McReynolds and Tom Cornell, fellow draft card burners, Dick Freer of St. Louis Resistance, and Joe Neal.

We hope all those who helped will feel as they read it that this is their book, too.

We owe a special kind of thanks to four persons:

to Neil Robertson, who joined with us in conceiving the book and had the painful experience of not being able to take part in its completion;

to Wicki Edwards (now Ferber) and Alice Lynd: not only is it abundantly true that without them the book would not have been

Signing complicity statement at Town Hall, January 14, 1968.
Photo by Maury Englander.

Glossary

ACLU	American Civil Liberties Union
AEL	Applied Electronics Laboratory (at Stanford University)
AFSC	American Friends Service Committee
AWOL	Absent Without Leave
BDRG	Boston Draft Resistance Group
CADRE	Chicago Area Draft Resisters
CCCO	Central Committee for Conscientious Objectors
CNVA	Committee for Nonviolent Action
CO	Conscientious Objector
CORE	Congress Of Racial Equality
ERAP	Economic Research and Action Project (of SDS)
ETD	End The Draft
FOR	Fellowship Of Reconciliation
IRS	Internal Revenue Service
IUC	Inter-University Committee on War and Peace
JOIN	Jobs Or Income Now
M2M	May Second Movement
MFDP	Mississippi Freedom Democratic Party
NAACP	National Association for the Advancement of Colored People

NC	National Council (of SDS)
NCCEWV	National Coordinating Committee to End the War in Vietnam
NER	New England Resistance
NSA	National Student Association
PISS	Prisoners' Information and Support Service
PL, PLP	Progressive Labor, Progressive Labor Party
SANE	Committee for a Sane Nuclear Policy
SCLC	Southern Christian Leadership Conference
SDS	Students for a Democratic Society
SMC	Student Mobilization Committee
SNCC	Student Nonviolent Coordinating Committee
SPU	Student Peace Union
SRI	Stanford Research Institute
SSS	Selective Service System
STDW	Stop The Draft Week
TCDIC	Twin Cities Draft Information Center
UNDO	Union for National Draft Opposition
VDC	Vietnam Day Committee (of Berkeley)
WDRU	Wisconsin Draft Resistance Union
WIN	WIN magazine (originated by Workshop In Violence)
WRL	War Resisters League
WSP	Women Strike for Peace

Partial Chronology

May 1964 The May Second Movement publishes the first We Won't Go statement

April 17, 1965 SDS sponsors the first mass protest against the war in Washington, D.C.

July 1965 Blacks in McComb, Mississippi, call for draft resistance

September 1965 Trial of David Mitchell begins in New Haven

October 15, 1965 First "International Day of Protest": David Miller burns his draft card in New York City, and a sit-in takes place at the Ann Arbor draft board

December 1965 SNCC executive committee supports draft resistance

May 14, 1966 First of three Selective Service examinations on college campuses protested by SDS

June 1966 Carl Oglesby and Stokely Carmichael issue joint statement condemning all forms of national service

August 25–26, 1966 Draft resistance conference in Des Moines, Iowa

October 28–30, 1966 Eastern Conference on Noncooperation with Conscription

December 4–5, 1966   We Won't Go conference in Chicago

December 14, 1966   Bruce Dancis tears up his draft card, which led to the call for mass draft-card burning on April 15, 1967

December 1966   SDS National Council supports draft resistance

January 20, 1967   Excerpts from the Selective Service "Channeling" memorandum are published in *New Left Notes*

April 15, 1967   More than 150 persons burn their draft cards at Sheep's Meadow in New York City, and in San Francisco David Harris calls for the mass return of draft cards on October 16

September 1967   "A Call to Resist Illegitimate Authority" is published

October 16, 1967   First national draft card turn-in

October 20, 1967   Draft cards turned in on October 16 are presented to the Department of Justice, and Stop the Draft Week reaches a climax in Oakland

October 21, 1967   Teach-in with the troops on the steps of the Pentagon

October 27, 1967   First action of ultra resistance: Father Berrigan and three others pour blood on draft files in Baltimore

December 4, 1967   Second national draft card turn-in

January 1968   Dr. Benjamin Spock, Rev. William S. Coffin, Jr., Michael Ferber, Mitchell Goodman, Marcus Raskin are indicted for conspiracy

April 3, 1968   Third national draft card turn-in

November 14, 1968   Fourth and last national draft card turn-in

May 19–21, 1970   Founding conference of Union for National Draft Opposition at Princeton, New Jersey

Selective Service sit-in, Ann Arbor, October 15, 1965.
Photo by Andy Sacks, provided by George Abbott White.

Tucson, Arizona, December 4, 1967.
Photo provided by Peace and Freedom Association, Tucson, Arizona.

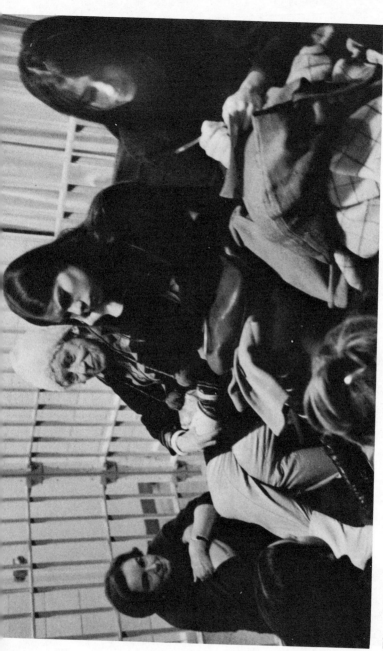

Women in detention cell after arrest for sit-in at induction station, December 5, 1967. Photo by Diana J. Davies, InSight.

Sheep's Meadow, New York, April 15, 1967.
Photo by Diana J. Davies, InSight.

Stop the Draft Week, October 1967.
Photo provided by WIN magazine.

Anti-Memorial Day March, Madison, Wisconsin, May 31, 1969.
Photo by Mickey Pfleger, provided by George Abbott White.

1968 SDS Convention, East Lansing, Michigan.
Photo provided by George Abbott White.

Card burner supported by Father Daniel Berrigan of Catonsville Nine.
Photo provided by George Abbott White.

Whitehall Street, New York.
Photo by Diana J. Davies, InSight.

At Sheep's Meadow, April 15, 1967.
Photo supplied by WIN magazine.

First New York Resistance support demonstration for induction refuser. Photo provided by WIN magazine.

December 4, 1967.
Photo by Diana J. Davies, InSight.

October 16, 1967.
Photo provided by WIN magazine.

December 4, 1967, St. Evangelist Church.
Photo by Diana J. Davies, InSight.

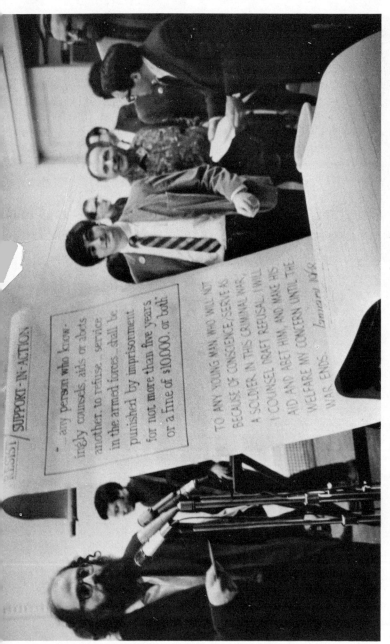

Support rally for Spock, Coffin, Goodman, Ferber, and Raskin, Town Hall, New York. Allen Ginsberg on left, Bruce Dancis to right of scroll. January 14, 1968. Photo by Diana J. Davies.

Paul Goodman sends cards from April 3 turn-in to Attorney General Clark.
Photo by Louis Salzberg.

Resistance and Its Precedents

RESISTANCE

The word "resistance" joined the antiwar movement in the spring of 1967. Greg Calvert of the national office of Students for a Democratic Society (SDS) had been popularizing the phrase "From Protest to Resistance" in speeches around the country, and it soon became the movement's governing slogan. A large number of activists that spring felt they had moved into a deeper and riskier commitment, a move that warranted a new term to replace "dissent" and "protest." And when David Harris, Dennis Sweeney, Lennie Heller, and Steve Hamilton met in March to plan a mass draft card turn-in for the fall, they named themselves, simply but audaciously, "the Resistance."

The terms "resist" and "resistance" have a long history in political thought. They were the words John Locke used to name the beginning of a revolution or "dissolution of government" (he used the word "revolution" only occasionally):

> When any one or more shall take upon them to make laws, whom the people have not appointed to do so, they make laws without authority, which the people are not therefore bound to obey; by which means they come again to be out of subjection and may constitute themselves a new legislative as they think best, being in full liberty to *resist* the force of those who without authority would impose anything upon them. (Italics added)

For Thoreau the terms were nearly synonymous with "revolt" and "revolution":

> All men recognize the right of revolution; that is, the right to re-fuse allegiance to, and to *resist,* the government, when its tyranny or its inefficiency are great and unendurable. (Italics added)

But "resistance" was given its present semantic edge largely by the struggle against fascism in occupied Europe. On the new sharpness of the word it is worth quoting Dwight Macdonald, named (though not indicted) by the government as a "co-conspirator" of Dr. Spock's for his support of draft resistance in 1967. In early 1945 Macdonald wrote in *Politics,* the excellent radical journal which he edited, a piece called "Resistance—A Semantic Note":

> Two new terms have emerged in this concluding phase of the war which are not (as yet) devaluated, which retain all their sharpness and moral purity: "collaboration" and "resistance." I think it deeply significant that these are becoming the great political watchwords in Europe today, since they indicate no specific, positive ideology, no aspiring faith, but simply the fact that people either "go along" or that they "resist" . . .
>
> To resist, to *reject* simply—this is the first condition for the human spirit's survival in the face of the increasingly tighter organization of state power everywhere. That this is not a sufficient condition is true: only a general, positive faith and system of ideas can save us in the long run. Such a faith and system are no longer held by significant numbers of people. But they will develop, if they do, from the seeds of "resistance."

Though the New Leftists of the early 1960s had not heard of *Politics* and were only generally familiar with occupied Europe, they could catch the ambience of "resistance" from activists of Macdonald's generation, and from the philosophy of confrontation and moral courage in the writings of Albert Camus and the French existentialists, who had fought against the Nazis.

The term was enriched further by events in France around 1960: early New Leftists were vaguely aware that their French counterparts were engaged in a "Young Resistance" to the colonial war in Algeria. Several thousand young men refused induction into the army or deserted it later, and were probably a major cause of the eventual French withdrawal.

When the founders of the Resistance named themselves, then, they not only reflected the new mood in the antiwar movement but invoked a rich and imposing heritage. Their choice of the term as a name for a new departure in the practice of noncooperation annoyed many in the movement for whom "resistance," if it did not imply sabotage and armed struggle, certainly ruled out voluntary submission to arrest, trial, and imprisonment. (The suggestion of exclusiveness carried in "*the* Resistance," with the article frequently capitalized, only added to the annoyance.) But the early organizers were determined to claim for themselves something more than the tactics suggested by the traditional terms of "noncooperation" and "passive resistance," the latter a misnomer for Gandhi's anything-but-passive *satyagraha.* They intended to be aggressive. They sought to overcome the isolationism of individual acts of "moral witness." They were hopeful they could hinder the induction process to the point where serious pressure would be felt by the warmakers. They were confident that by organizing large-scale aggressive noncooperation they could communicate a spirit of refusal and defiance to a whole generation. And that, they felt, justified the potent name of the Resistance.

PRECEDENTS

On Lincoln's Birthday 1947 some four or five hundred Americans in several cities publicly destroyed their draft cards or mailed them in to President Truman. In New York City sixty-three persons burned their draft cards before an audience of 250. Among the speakers at the rally were Dwight Macdonald; A. J. Muste, the dean of American pacifists and promoter of the massive New York marches against the Vietnam war (until his death in 1967); Bayard Rustin, militant black pacifist, organizer of the Washington March of 1963, and more recently a spokesman for the "left wing" of the Democratic Party; and David Dellinger, draft re-

sister during World War II, editor of *Liberation* magazine since
1956, and in 1969–1970 the senior member of the Chicago Eight,
or "The Conspiracy." That Muste, Dellinger, Macdonald, and
other pacifist/resisters of the 1940s maintained their activism and
devotion to principle throughout the 1950s may be one reason for
the generally open, trusting, unembittered style of the draft resistance groups that flourished in the 1960s. All New Left groups
have felt a generation gap in their traditions, and when (especially
in the late 1960s) large-scale militant actions seemed to have no
effect, the temptations to drop out, take refuge in dogma, or lash
out in futile violence went unchecked in most groups by veterans
with a sense of history and irony. Draft resisters had in their midst
a generation of older supporters, many of whom had undergone
lonely and seemingly useless struggles without giving up; they
served as models of patience and good cheer when youthful faith
and exuberance flagged.

Dwight Macdonald expressed the purpose of the 1947 New
York rally as attacking conscription "by the simplest and most direct way possible"—by civil disobedience, "by refusing, as individuals, to recognize the authority of the State in this matter."

> When the State—or rather, the individuals who speak in its name,
> for there is no such thing as the State—tells me that I must "defend" it
> against foreign enemies—that is, must be prepared to kill people who
> have done me no injury in defense of a social system which has done me
> considerable injury—then I say that I cannot go along. In such a serious
> matter as going to war, each individual must decide for himself; and this
> means civil disobedience to the State power that presumes to decide for
> one.

But the radicals of 1947 were barely felt by a country now gear-
ing its economy and ideology to the Cold War. Congress let the
draft law of 1940 lapse briefly but reenacted it, slightly altered, in
1948. Gone was the opposition that had met the draft in 1940, the
first peacetime conscription in America's history, with words like
these of Senator Vandenberg of Michigan:

> There must have been sound reasons all down the years why
> our predecessors in the Congress always consistently and relentlessly

shunned this thing we are now asked to do. These reasons must have been related in some indispensable fashion to the fundamental theory that peacetime military conscription is repugnant to the spirit of democracy and the soul of Republican institutions, and that it leads in dark directions.

It was hopeless in 1948 to prevent passage of a law that expressed a nearly unified national passion, however manipulated. What this country had done under a similar national passion only thirty years earlier—the massive raids against draft "slackers" or nonregistrants in 1918 and against radicals in 1919—showed to what extent it would violate its best traditions and even its Constitution in order to work its will. Almost routinely the Universal Military Training and Service Act of 1948 was passed, and almost routinely it has been reenacted, substantially unchanged, ever since, just as the Cold War has persisted with dreary monotony since it began in 1945-1947.

There was another, more powerful, challenge to the draft in 1947, directed not against conscription itself but against segregation in the armed forces. When high army officers reported that segregation was "in the interests of national defense," black leaders like A. Phillip Randolph and Bayard Rustin organized the League for Non-Violent Civil Disobedience Against Military Segregation. Randolph told the Senate Armed Services Committee he would "personally pledge . . . to openly counsel, aid and abet youth . . . in an organized refusal to register and be drafted." A poll of college blacks revealed that 71 percent favored civil disobedience to the draft. The NAACP pledged its support. In July 1948, however, Truman signed an executive order to end racial segregation in the armed forces, and the campaign, moderate in aim but radical in means, was called off. But this campaign, like that of the white pacifists, produced leaders (such as Conrad Lynn and William Worthy) who would find themselves spokesmen and supporters of black draft resistance a generation later.

By July 1949 more than forty young men had been sentenced to prison terms for refusal to register. They were supported by a statement entitled "A Call to American Christians of Draft Age" signed by over four hundred clergymen and religious leaders:

For young men we believe breaking with war means: refusal to enlist in the armed forces; withdrawal from armed forces for those now in them; refusal to register or render any service under a conscription act. "Peacetime" conscription, whether for training or service or both, is such a huge and tragic step toward war, dictatorship and catastrophe that we believe it must meet with total rejection. As the early Christians refused to offer a pinch of incense to Caesar's image, so we believe that Christian youth in the United States today should refuse to grant even the "token" recognition of registration to this contemporary evil which means disaster for their country and their church.

That statement was a forerunner of the declarations of resistance to the Vietnam war, of which the most famous would be "A Call to Resist Illegitimate Authority" in 1967.

In 1948 a group of pacifist noncooperators organized themselves into a mutual aid community and began publishing a journal called the *Peacemaker*. Group and journal both served as modest vehicles of continuity through the 1950s. In 1951, for example, the *Peacemaker* carried a statement signed by over two hundred persons entitled "We Say No!" Besides the pledge of noncooperation the statement carried a description of "the trend toward totalitarianism" in the United States. Starting late in 1966 the *Peacemaker* has been carrying a similar statement pledging total noncooperation with the draft. By early 1970 it had gathered over six hundred signatures.

As if they were aware of their historical role, shared by *Liberation* and a few small groups of Catholic anarchists and Quakers, the editors of the *Peacemaker* published a retrospective issue in May 1964, a few months before the Tonkin Bay incident, under the heading "Saying 'No' to Conscription." Three generations of draft resisters were represented: Ammon Hennacy of the *Catholic Worker* who served 32 months in prison for refusing to register during World War I; Wally Nelson and Amos Brokaw who each quit their alternative service jobs during World War II and were imprisoned for doing so (Brokaw ultimately served three terms); David Dellinger who declined a divinity student exemption by refusing to register in 1940 and did several years in prison; the 1951 statement of noncooperation; and two young men, Tom Rodd and David Mitchell. Tom Rodd had been deeply involved in civil rights in the South, and out of his experiences and sufferings there he professed in the *Peacemaker* a belief in universal disarmament and nonviolence. He was later imprisoned twice: once for nonregistration and once for violating parole by demonstrating at a helicopter factory. The story of David Mitchell and his founding of End The Draft in 1962 we tell in the next chapter.

The heritage that the *Peacemaker* exemplified was not broad, but it was deep. It provided some guidance and a few examples of demonstrations and statements, but it also offered more important help for the young men (and women) who would create the new resistance: living examples of the possibility of enduring loneliness, abuse, and privation, and coming through it creatively, affirmatively; the possibility of living a whole life dedicated to resistance and social transformation. For young men facing prison, especially, such examples would be sources of strength. And the movement in general would be deepened and stiffened by the experience of the older men, and made ready to take on the protracted struggle against the war in Vietnam and the draft that feeds it.

Notes to Chapter One

Much of the material in this chapter is drawn from Lawrence Wittner's fine study, *Rebels Against War: The American Peace Movement, 1941–1960* (New York: Columbia University Press, 1969).

The draft card burning of 1947 is described in "Draft Cards Burned: Defy Conscription," in *Why? An Anarchist Bulletin,* February 1947, kindly made available by Larry Gara, and in Dwight Macdonald, "Why Destroy Draft Cards?" *Politics,* March–April 1947, reprinted in the *Catholic Worker,* November 1965.

Longstanding American hostility to conscription in peacetime and to a standing army is detailed in Richard Gillam, "The Peacetime Draft," *Yale Review,* summer 1968; and Leon Friedman, "Conscription and the Constitution: The Original Understanding," *Michigan Law Review,* June 1969. The dubious history of the draft card is discussed in Peter W. Mar-

CHAPTER TWO

Burners and Returners, 1960–1965

The draft card burnings and returnings of 1947 took place on the eve of the passage of a law which would place in jeopardy all young men between the ages of eighteen and twenty-six. However unsympathetic the mood of the country might have been then to antidraft agitation, the radicals of 1947 at least had the advantage of focusing on an event with a collective impact. Once the law took effect, however, each young man had to work out a private relationship with it. The requirements of the Selective Service System had to be met on one's own schedule, a schedule determined by date of birth, by qualifications for deferment, by cleverness at feigning grounds for exemption, and ultimately by race and economic class. Anyone who wanted to organize draft resistance in 1960, when the movement this book describes took its first steps, had to decide how to transform into collective resistance the private reluctance young men felt at being plucked out one by one. He also had to face the fact that those most likely to understand the reasons for collective resistance, the college students, were shielded by 2–S deferments from the agony of a personal encounter.

But an organizer in the early 1960s would have one thing going for him that the pacifists of the 1940s lacked. A new spirit of awareness and energy could be felt in America. The civil rights movement, now several years old and with several victories to its credit, was attracting young white students and spreading to the

9

north. A new young president was talking about a Peace Corps. Fidel Castro and his band of guerrillas had overthrown the corrupt dictator of Cuba. The House Committee on Un-American Activities was in retreat from Berkeley. The silence of the 1950s was ending.

This chapter will deal with the first organizations to sponsor, or at least consider, resistance to the draft in the 1960s, and with the remarkable young men who first entered the lists in what was then a much lonelier struggle than it later became.

PETER IRONS AND THE STUDENT PEACE UNION

The Student Peace Union (SPU) was organized in April 1959 by pacifist and socialist students in the midwest, and by 1960 it claimed five thousand members and twelve thousand subscribers to its *Bulletin.* Groups such as TOCSIN at Harvard and SLATE at Berkeley, and persons later active in SDS such as Paul Booth and Todd Gitlin, were involved in SPU. Its tone—serious, even visionary, but aloof from traditional ideologies—is suggested by the December 1960 issue of the *Bulletin.* There Ken Calkins, a founder of SPU, paraphrased Albert Camus' famous essay "Neither Victims Nor Executioners" in the following words:

> For those who would dare to join him in refusing to become either victim or executioner, Camus outlines a series of consequences which are both challenging and frightening.
>
> He proposes that these rebels join together to form a new living society inside the corpse of the old. The goal of this society will be nothing less than to restore sociability ("le dialogue") among men. The individuals who make up this revolutionary fraternity must be prepared to resist the international dictatorship of violence and lies with their whole beings— their course will not be an easy one.

In an adjoining column Karl Meyer, son of a Vermont Congressman and member of the Catholic Worker group, asserted that American radicals of all varieties were failing to practice what they preached. "What we need are Christians who will practice the program of Jesus; individualists who will practice the program of Thoreau; and socialists who will practice the program of Debs."

Karl was the most vigorous advocate of draft resistance within SPU. "At first we did a lot of street speaking and had a more radical tone," he recalls, "but as more and more students from many campuses were brought in, a more conservative tone began to dominate." Karl was nevertheless permitted to continue his column in the *Bulletin*, entitled "Stepping Up the Agitation." In it he described his own decision to "noncooperate" with the draft by returning his card, an act punishable by five years in prison. "Over the years," he wrote his draft board in 1959, "I have come to the conclusion that I have no obligation to obey the draft act and that I have an obligation to resist it." When his draft board sent him a 4–F (ineligible) classification card, Karl returned that card too. Reminding the board that "at least twenty Jehovah's Witnesses are doing time now at the federal prison in Springfield, Missouri, and more in other prisons, for refusing to comply with the draft," he asked his classifiers to consider whether he should not be jailed as well.

In his columns Karl urged what he termed "total resistance" to the claims of the nation state. Anticipating Marcuse's concept of "repressive tolerance," Karl asserted: "If we resist only up to the limit of resistance that the State will tolerate, we acquiesce in a paradoxical impotence. . . . Protests, petitions, and prudent resistance are essentially worthless to the extent that they are tolerable." He argued that American pacifism fit into four types, of which the first three were repressively tolerated by the state. There was peace education, exemplified by the American Friends Service Committee (AFSC); public witness, exemplified by "Peacemaker projects"; something he called "nonviolent direct part time and summer revolution," exemplified by projects of the Committee for Nonviolent Action, "manned mainly by summer supporters and sunshine radicals on leave of absence from the first phase and the second phase." The fourth phase was "the nonviolent revolution, exemplified by nobody." American pacifism was bourgeois and verbal, Karl insisted.

In the *Bulletin* for April 1961 Karl reported a conversation which suggested that he had begun to find an audience. Two students from Oberlin College, Chris Williams and Joel Sherzer, were "going around trying to sign people up to repudiate their Selective Service registrations and turn in their draft cards." That same month Chris and Joel joined forces with Peter Irons at an SPU national conference at Oberlin. Peter had returned his own draft card the previous fall. At the conference he made a speech proposing a mass draft card return.

Peter Irons' father was a nuclear engineer, closely involved in building plants for H-bomb construction, who had quit the Atomic Energy Commission because of the Oppenheimer incident and McCarthyism in general. "He wasn't politically active," according to Peter, "but he was very much a civil libertarian." During Peter's first year at Antioch College his father died, probably because of his long exposure to radiation. The two had not been particularly close. "But it seems probable that I had picked up from him, very indirectly, his revulsion toward nuclear weapons and his inner agony over his role in developing them." Peter thinks his own experience was similar to that of many of the younger men who later organized the Resistance, in that "most of us had fathers in the professions whose work led to some feelings of guilt or conflict about values which we picked up sort of unconsciously."

Peter is now as he was then a Unitarian, but soon after coming to Antioch he fell in with Quaker pacifists at the college and in the town of Yellow Springs. He became a member of the Socialist Discussion Group and "the informal pacifist group which centered around the Friends Meeting and contained a lot of people associated with the Peacemaker group." He read A. J. Muste's serial autobiography in *Liberation* magazine, Ray Ginger's biography of Eugene Debs, Tolstoy's *The Kingdom of God Is Within You*, and "wound up with a Gandhian pacifism and an admiration for native American socialism and anarcho-syndicalism." He felt a "visceral attachment" to "people like AJ and Debs and the Wobblies." In the fall of 1960, while working in Washington, Peter met Howard University students active in the Student Nonviolent Coordinating Committee (SNCC). When the second SNCC conference was held in Atlanta in September 1960, he drove down and took part. "People who spoke there whom I remember especially include Richard Gregg, Martin Luther King, and Jim Lawson, all of whom tied the civil rights struggle directly to pacifism in the Gandhian tradition." The connections led Peter to action. After returning from Atlanta, he and some friends from Antioch and Howard regularly picketed suburban movie theaters that discriminated against blacks. He was arrested at a bowling alley in suburban Maryland for sitting-in.

In October 1960 he decided to send his draft card back.

> I had given considerable thought to filling out the CO [Conscientious Objector] questionnaire, but my almost passionate First Amendment philosophy led me to reject that, since the religious questions were totally repugnant. . . . I wouldn't fight, as a Gandhian, I felt the need to make a symbolic break with a country which oppressed blacks, and I wouldn't apply for an exemption based on religious grounds. The direction of these vectors led only one place: sending back the card.

Peter was not only one of the first of his generation to return his card, but the first to make the connection between the draft and the whole interlocking system of repressive institutions.

After the Oberlin conference at which he urged the mass return of draft cards, the Antioch chapter of SPU (the largest chapter in the country) printed and distributed five thousand copies of a leaflet Peter wrote elaborating his proposal. The leaflet was entitled "An Alternative to the Draft—A Statement to Young Men."

> Fifteen years ago, [the leaflet began] arguments against cooperating with the draft went something like this: no conscientious man could sincerely contemplate the prospect of possibly having to face another human being in combat, plunging a knife into his belly, or sending a bullet crashing into his face, or blowing him to bits with a grenade.

Feeling this,

> a small minority of conscientious men . . . refused to have anything to do with the draft, and many of them served time in prison for this belief.

But today, the leaflet continued, this argument

> hardly seems relevant, in an era of push-button warfare. We have become so accustomed to the pictures of a missile rising in a graceful arc from the launching pad, controlled from an antiseptic instrument room, and to the thought of the men in a spotless nuclear submarine eating apple pie as they cruise beneath the sea, that we have forgotten what happens at the other end of the missile.

The prospect of a war with weapons of mass destruction like germs and chemicals, and the memory of Hiroshima and Nagasaki, both seem far away.

> War, and the horrible results of war, have become so removed from our field of vision that they seem as remote to young people as a far-off galaxy.

All we can say, Peter concluded,

> is that if conscience and a sense of reality . . . have become lost in a generation whose motto is "I'm all right, Jack," we must stand alone in resisting the coercion, physical and moral, of the draft. We would much rather have company, for wars will cease only when men refuse to fight.

Then Peter described the "small and harassed group" of noncooperators.

> They agree with the nonviolent, direct action methods of the sit-in movement, those students who feel that a law which violates the moral precepts they hold so deeply must be broken, and the consequences accepted.

But beyond this,

> If someone decides to take this stand it is because, in addition to the logical arguments, a responsive chord has been struck within, since for an argument to take root and flower into action there must be fertile

soil in the deepest part of the personality. The refusal to register or the return of the draft card will be but an outward manifestation of a basic pat-
terning of one's life.

The reader was asked at the end to let his beliefs show themselves
in "the crucible in which a man's beliefs, noble or base, are tested
—action."

Chris Williams, supporting Peter's proposal, suggested the idea
of staging the return of 500 draft cards, pledged in advance. (The
goal was later scaled down to one hundred.) Shortly after the SPU
conference, Chris, Joel Sherzer, and Peter issued a statement
which began: "The undersigned are considering returning their
draft cards to the United States Government. Our signatures do
not commit us to this action, but they do indicate our readiness to
publicly affirm our beliefs." The statement then went on to envis-
age a curious process of organizing, one that reflects both their
dedication and their inexperience (and also perhaps a touch of
paranoia):

> In order to keep this statement alive, it should not be relin-
> quished to anyone except a definitely affirmed signer. When it is passed
> to a new campus, there must be direct, personal assurance that it will be
> signed and cared for by at least one person on that campus. Oberlin must
> be notified of the change. All statements in circulation must be returned
> to Oberlin on the date stamped below. At Oberlin, a master list will be
> made containing all the signatures to date. Copies of the master list will
> be mailed to each participating campus for continued circulation. This
> process of revision will be continued every twenty days until June of
> 1961.

In the SPU *Bulletin,* a little later, the trio stated:

> Most students feel that the return of draft cards will not stimu-
> late a moral reexamination unless this action is taken simultaneously by
> a large number of students. Others feel this conscientious action to be
> necessary regardless of its effects. All signers are committed to return
> their draft cards if a certain number of students (named by themselves)
> do so at the same time. In order to clearly define and understand our

ideals and goals, meetings will be held periodically at strategic locations in the country.

Many individuals who do not hold draft cards are in sympathy with our action. These include men who have already taken this action, men over draft age, and women. Because peace is an issue which concerns us all, these people are encouraged to express their opinions concerning the return of draft cards and to write statements to this effect.

"That's as far as it got," Peter commented eight years later. He had served twenty-six months in Danbury prison for draft refusal, getting out in March 1969, too late to see the tremendous expansion of draft resistance in 1967 and 1968 to which he indirectly contributed.

Peter's proposal was a more direct inspiration to Gene Keyes, who remembered it in 1963 and improvised a small-scale equivalent: a pact with his two friends Russ Goddard and Barry Bassin which stipulated that when one of them was arrested for noncooperation the other two would demand immediate prosecution. Like Peter these three men sought a means whereby young men touched by Selective Service one by one could resist it together. "An Arrest of One Is an Arrest of All," declared one of their leaflets, paraphrasing the old IWW motto, "An Injury to One Is an Injury to All." Another leaflet recalled the French resistance to the Algerian war:

> Several times in France recently the gendarmes have tried to arrest draft refusers—only to find ten young men chained together, each claiming to be the intended victim. (Remember the scene in the movie "Spartacus" when the legionnaires are trying to single him out for execution and each of his soldiers yells, "I am Spartacus.")

It had little impact on the larger peace movement, but the three friends carried out their plan as they had intended.

Karl Meyer, for his part, continued to reach people. Among those who trace their radical commitment to Karl's influence is Charlie Fisher, one of the mainstays of the Boston Draft Resistance Group in 1968 and 1969.

DAVID MITCHELL AND END THE DRAFT

David Mitchell was also present at the Oberlin SPU conference and he, like Gene Keyes, remembered the turn-in idea. In September 1965, when the End The Draft (ETD) group with which David was associated urged SDS to support an antidraft campaign, one of ETD's specific suggestions was

> "minimal number" activities, e.g., a minimal number of 500 commitments must be reached before anyone goes ahead with the activity—from draft card burning to total noncooperation (Peter Irons, formerly of SPU, suggested that a few years back).

Concerned about imperialism and the wars it causes, David had joined the Student Peace Union as a freshman at Brown University. Dismayed by the American-sponsored invasion of Cuba at the Bay of Pigs, and especially by Adlai Stevenson's defense of it at the United Nations, he dropped out of Brown and went directly to the SPU national conference at Oberlin. He arrived expecting to work for SPU on the west coast. At the conference, however, David was discouraged by the struggle for power within the organization, and by the lack of enthusiasm for his own belief in unilateral disarmament by the United States. So he returned to the east and, after joining the last American leg of a San Francisco-to-Moscow peace walk, spent the summer of 1961 at the New England Committee for Nonviolent Action (CNVA) project center in Connecticut.

Organized in 1957, CNVA had undertaken projects such as a "nonviolent invasion" of the Omaha, Nebraska, missile testing site and a similar venture by sailboat into the nuclear testing grounds of the Pacific Ocean. The New England affiliate was created in 1960 to facilitate a program of sustained nonviolent civil disobedience against the launching of Polaris submarines at New London. A remarkable array of resisters, including David, Gene Keyes, and Tom Cornell, spent time with New England CNVA during the early 1960s.

Neither then nor at any subsequent point was David a pacifist;

he argued all summer against pacifism at the CNVA farm. He also began to feel, at the farm, that the peace movement had neglected the draft resisters already in jail, and that something had to be done to make their stand more meaningful. "I was in the Peacemaker faction," he remembers, meaning that he sided with those in CNVA more concerned to "take a stand on principle" than to create a "respectable image in the community." The Peacemakers had always been solicitous for the men in prison and their families outside. But, after he was jailed for seventeen days as one of eight men who rowed boats toward the nuclear submarine *Ethan Allen,* David's conviction grew that such symbolic resistance was not enough. One had to take a stand on principle, but one must do it in a way that is politically effective.

After the summer of 1961 David left the CNVA farm and moved to Brooklyn, where in November 1962 he helped to initiate End The Draft. The group took its name from an organization called End the Draft in '63, which was headed by the eminent socialist Norman Thomas and formed to put pressure on Congress before it considered an extension of the Selective Service law scheduled for 1963. David and his friends criticized Thomas' group because it argued against the draft on civil libertarian grounds without opposing the foreign policy of which the draft is an instrument.

Besides taking an anti-imperialist stand before Congress, ETD wanted to be a continuing "subcommittee of the whole movement" on the draft. "There are many different levels in the fight against the draft," ETD declared, and "there are many different philosophies in opposition" to it. Only by bringing all these together in one program of action could isolated acts of witness be transformed into collective power.

For a time it seemed ETD might be able to accomplish this. At its inception ETD included people active in CNVA, in the Congress Of Racial Equality (CORE), and in the Committee for a Sane Nuclear Policy. Difficulties soon arose, however. Like SNCC in the south, ETD was "nonexclusionist": membership was a function of actions, not beliefs, and as long as an individual carried out the work of the group there could be no grounds for expelling him. This tolerant policy was a barrier to certain pacifists, who objected to the inclusion of Marxists, and to certain Marxists, who objected to the inclusion of certain other Marxists. Such feelings might have been overcome had ETD been able to provide a concrete definition of its work. SNCC, in defining its program by the act of voter registration, had transcended sectarian bickering in the south. But ETD's very ecumenicity prevented such concrete definition. David himself, for example, was the only member of the small group to become a noncooperator.

There were also, as there always are, problems arising from personal misunderstandings and hurt feelings. Some members of older peace groups felt that the creation of a new one was an implicit insult to their work. From its side, ETD was not always so ecumenical as its rhetoric suggested. Although it did not insist on a set of specific ways to oppose the draft, it sometimes showed intolerance of ways that were in fact chosen. On May 16, 1964, for instance, twelve young men burned their draft cards at a demonstration in New York sponsored by the War Resisters League, the Committee for Nonviolent Action, the Student Peace Union, and the Catholic Worker group. Martin Boksenbaum of ETD summed up the tenor of their meeting in a sardonic parody:

A pox on everybody's house! Make everything neutral! I don't want anything to do with violence! However, since I feel strongly opposed to violence, I must give people the right to feel strongly in favor of violence. I would consider the matter closed if I had the choice of joining or not joining the army. It's not a question of international criminality nor of the right of the people of Vietnam to self-determination. The basic issue is my right of choice.

One can understand how ETD, with its passionate focus on war crimes and U.S. imperialism, felt obliged to repudiate the attitude that the growing conflict in Vietnam and the draft were acceptable if only everyone were free to choose his own relationship to them. This was the civil libertarian position ETD had rejected in first organizing itself. Martin Boksenbaum's position may have been perfectly sound politically and morally but it was a position which made it difficult to build unity.

David Mitchell himself, it would seem, was somewhat more tolerant. In *Downdraft,* an ETD newsletter that began publication in January 1964, he repeatedly called for a united draft resistance movement. "The draft issue continues to suffer from a lack of concerted opposition," he wrote. "We will never succeed if we are unable to achieve unity among the opposition to the draft." From September 1965 when he was brought to trial for draft refusal until his imprisonment in February 1967, David's attention was necessarily focused on his own case, but he and ETD continued to work for unity in the resistance movement. Recognizing that other peace groups regarded ETD as one group among many rather than as a coordinating committee, ETD sought to form a New York Anti-Draft Coordinating Committee in which theirs would be one of several cooperating organizations. This too failed to materialize. Something of David's cumulative frustration was expressed in a letter to Frank Emspak and Lew Jones of the National Coordinating Committee to End the War in Vietnam (NCCEWV), in November 1965. Again he reiterated his desire for a

> program that supports and builds a movement from *all* individuals who are fighting US militarism by challenging the draft . . . which because it is serious about . . . US crimes, will cooperate and build a united front of groups and individuals to seriously challenge the government, instead of cooperating in one-shot actions, and those only when they can be profitable to their group.

He condemned, in a memorable phrase, the factional spirit which turned radicals into "the guards, goons and hacks of their private churches (groups) and the perfectors of the private property of protest." He confessed that those in ETD itself who had planned to go to a forthcoming NCCEWV convention in Washington had decided not to go because it would be useless, but that he, at least, would have gone were it not for the travel restrictions attendant on his bail.

> I felt Washington this week was worth a try and that regardless of all the pettyness and group conceit and retreat, it was worth voicing the need for coordinated efforts and see if anyone—anyone at all—of the

represented groups, or even just some individuals were ready and felt enough concern.

David was acutely aware, earlier than most, of the divisive tendencies of movements in which individuals have invested their personal identities and pet theories. Draft resistance groups in the years that followed would always be subject to strong centrifugal forces, though it is probably a fair generalization to say that they have tried harder than other groups to overcome them, if only because one of their purposes was to combat the divisiveness of the draft itself.

THE BURNERS

When the bombing of North Vietnam began in February 1965, draft card burning was a more familiar practice than draft card returning. Tom Cornell of the Catholic Worker group burned his first card in 1960. By the time of the mass draft card burning of April 1967 he could say: "My other cards went at various occasions. I think I have the record, having burned ten."

During the first year of the escalated war, card burning was the principal form of resistance, or at least it was the most visible and controversial form. At the end of the year only about a dozen men had been jailed for induction refusal (except for a number of Jehovah's Witnesses, who decline to join political activities), and only the first SNCC refusers and David Mitchell had attracted any public attention. Draft card burning, in contrast, became front-page news from coast to coast. As one veteran resister put it several years later: "With the draft card burnings, and the furor they stirred, a line of demarcation seemed crossed and, looking backward, one realizes that the Resistance was born."

On July 29, 1965, about four hundred war protesters picketed the Whitehall Street induction center in New York City. Up to that point draft card burning had seemed dramatic and radical but, as David McReynolds of WRL recalled, "since no one had been prosecuted, they were not such emotionally charged events." On July 29 Chris Kearns of the *Catholic Worker* burned a card (apparently a borrowed card because he had forgotten his own),

Life magazine ran a picture of the event, and Congress took notice. A week later Representative Mendel Rivers introduced a bill to make destruction of draft cards a crime additional to the existing crime of willful nonpossession. The next week Senator Strom Thurmond submitted the identical legislation to the Senate. In the House debate, Rivers referred to "a vocal minority in this country [who] thumb their noses at their own Government," and Congressman Bray to "a filthy, sleazy beatnik gang . . . led by a Yale University professor" (one of the authors of this book). On August 30 President Johnson signed this carefully considered piece of legislation into law.

"We knew we had to respond," Tom Cornell wrote some time afterward. During August he and Neil Haworth of CNVA talked of burning cards outside the White House at the time the president signed the bill. Thereafter

the idea vanished for a while. Then around late September some of us around the Catholic Peace Fellowship and the Catholic Worker began thinking of it again.

Tom called for card burning in the September issue of the *Catholic Worker*. But the first card burner in defiance of the new law was another member of the group, David Miller. "It was my thought," Tom continued,

that we should do it as a group action, with Dorothy Day and AJ [Muste] presiding for maximum impact and protection as well. Dave Miller was asked to speak at the International Day of Protest [October 15, 1965]. He was thinking of what he should say when he told us (at my apartment, after supper) that he would burn his card instead. I thought this was precipitous of him and tried to talk him out of it. Fortunately, Dave seized the moment.

David Miller had become a radical at Le Moyne College, where he was influenced by, among others, Father Daniel Berrigan (see chapter 14). A concern to "follow the Gospel" led him to work in Natchez, Mississippi, and then to his own parish in a downtown section of Syracuse, New York, to work with black children. He was arrested in September 1963 after participating in several CORE demonstrations. He became first a nuclear pacifist, then a complete pacifist.

> And it was during my senior year in college that I became interested in the Catholic Worker, effectively interested in wanting to go down there, by reading *The Other America* by Michael Harrington. . . . I decided that I was a conscientious objector, but the noncooperator position appealed to me most of all. I was going to go to the Catholic Worker and begin my noncooperation there.

David was Chris Kearns' roommate during the summer of 1965.

David's action on October 15, as Tom Cornell says, made "a fantastic impression," in part because of his personality and manner. David believed that

> given the situation of our society and the innocence of young men who are . . . drafted, it simply would be unfaithful to them, unfaithful to myself, were I not to take such a strong stand against conscription and against war.

He was drawn to a style of protest which communicated "natural, open refusal, in good courtesy, of the draft." Between two long speeches at the October 15 rally he said, before burning his draft card, just two sentences: "I believe the napalming of villages is an immoral act. I hope this will be a significant political act, so here goes." Tom Cornell writes: "The nation saw in David Miller a normal, healthy young man, who could be their son or brother, a Catholic, evidently moved by the Gospel of Christ, admittedly a dangerous document."

To burn a card, of course, was open defiance of the war, the state, and a recently passed law at a moment when tens of thousands of young men had just entered combat in Vietnam. It was reported that Vincent Di Mattina, New York State Commander of the Veterans of Foreign Wars, along with several other VFW officers, traveled from New York City to Miller's home in Syracuse to arrest him. The *New York Daily News* demanded that "Communist-incited beatniks, pacifists and damned idiots who are demonstrating" be tried for treason, and carried a cartoon depicting the draft card burners as rats. David McReynolds, who with Tom Cornell was considering burning his own card, recalls that

> the immediate and massive public response to David Miller's action shocked me and obviously shocked Tom Cornell. . . . (One reason that I absolutely reject the calling of police "pigs" is the same reason that I took part in that draft card burning [on November 6]—an attempt to keep us from placing human beings in the category of animals. The *Daily News* cartoon bothered me a great deal.)

The public and governmental response was not without effect. Tom Cornell remembers that "after Dave's arrest, in New Hampshire, most of the people who had considered burning their cards withdrew."

Three others—Marc Edelman, Roy Lisker, and another member of the Catholic Worker group, Jim Wilson—decided to join Tom and David McReynolds in repeating David Miller's act. With the exception of Jim, who was classified 1–A, all were classified 4–F or overage. A first attempt to burn their cards late in October was called off when at least fifty newsmen crowded so closely around the demonstrators that, in Tom's words, they "made it impossible to carry out the project with any dignity." The demonstration was rescheduled for November 6.

A few days before the November 6 ceremony Norman Morrison, a thirty-two-year-old Quaker and father of three, burned himself to death at the Pentagon. His action was in the minds of the two thousand persons who gathered at Union Square in New York City. A. J. Muste led the crowd in a moment of silence for Norman Morrison and for "the combatants on both sides in Vietnam who are perishing." The Catholic magazine *Commonweal* reported that "seldom does there occur a liturgical ceremony more impressive": counterdemonstrators carried signs reading "BURN YOURSELF INSTEAD OF YOUR CARD" and "THANKS PINKOS, QUEERS, COWARDS, DRAFT DODGERS—MAO TSE-TUNG"; they chanted "Drop dead, Red," "Give us joy, bomb Hanoi," and, when Dorothy Day spoke, "Moscow Mary!" When the five men set fire to their cards a heckler drenched them with water from a fire extinguisher. Unperturbed, they dried the cards off and relighted them. Tom recalls:

> I had hoped to try to remain calm, almost solemn, to communicate the better what we were trying to do. But suddenly, as the flames started to consume our cards and my drenched trousers warmed to my body heat, I heard a voice from the crowd, strong and joyful, singing, "This little light of mine."

At the close everyone sang "We shall overcome."

Leaving the platform at the end of the ceremony David McReynolds

> was hustled with the others into a waiting car. I took it for granted that we were under arrest as we drove away with one police car in front and one behind. . . . It was not until we got to 5 Beekman and got out of the car without the police coming with us that I realized they had provided an escort for our protection. That escort is another indication of the extraordinary tension which was felt not only by us but by the police.

From the peace movement offices at 5 Beekman Street David went home to his apartment.

> A number of friends came by that night and we drank and talked until quite late and what was on all of our minds but what no one put into words was the fear of some kind of attack on the apartment. I think at some point, such as midnight, we all realized that we were keeping vigil together without anyone saying as much and I was rather moved.

Among the onlookers at the November 6 ceremony was a young member of the Catholic Worker group, Roger LaPorte. At 5:20 A.M. on November 9 Roger sat on the landing of the Swords and Ploughshares staircase opposite the United Nations building, poured gasoline from a two-gallon can over himself, and ignited it. He died thirty hours later at Bellevue Hospital. Tom Cornell writes of his death:

> Roger was conscious and lucid for hours. He was not in pain; his nerve endings had been burned off. He spoke to the police and the ambulance attendants, saying "I am a Catholic Worker. I am anti-war, all wars. I did this as a religious action . . . all the hatred in the world . . . I picked this hour so no one could stop me." He spoke to the doctors and to several priests and to a nun. He made his last confession, and received the anointing of the sick and dying. He indicated his desire to live.

David McReynolds adds that the lights went out in Manhattan in the great power failure exactly twelve hours after Roger's immolation.

> I had been quite disturbed by the burning because of the general tension involved—a great deal more tension certainly than on the occasion some years ago when I refused induction and that whole event was a very private confrontation—and I could not help thinking once I realized that the lights had gone out throughout the entire area of the familiar "and darkness fell over the whole land." Both Tom Cornell and I feel that LaPorte burned himself in an effort to absorb part of the violence that he had felt at the demonstration on November 6th. He . . . was absolutely appalled at the chants from the right wing that we burn ourselves rather than draft cards. Perhaps we are wrong and perhaps Roger LaPorte would have burned himself to death in any event but I have never since that date been very enthusiastic about burning things because I know that in a society as tense as this one the flame in my hand can very quickly engulf someone else altogether.

There were only a few draft card burnings between November 1965 and the massive card burning in April 1967.

David Miller and Tom Cornell each began their prison terms in the summer of 1968, David for thirty months, Tom for six. "The draft card," David wrote, "still remains a symbol of forceful, inordinate authority over the minds and hearts of men and women

struggling to love and to be free. I have loved and I am free."
Thinking back to November 6, Tom Cornell wrote:

> I still believe in the words of that day. "We who have dedicated
> ourselves to the war upon war, to the development of nonviolence as an
> effective means to resist tyranny, cannot shrink from the consequences of
> our conscientious acts." . . . I suppose I am glad. Things have worked
> out better than we could have planned. The isolated acts of a handful of
> us two and a half years ago have become a major movement of resistance
> to the draft.

Neither man surrendered voluntarily. David announced that he
would appear at the courthouse at the appointed time, but would
have to be carried into it: "This too is a symbolic act of conscience." Tom said: "I will continue to walk with friends and family, balloons, flowers, and cotton candy, if we can find any, and
maybe liberate two doves when the feds come to take me."

Tom does not regret the fact that he did not attempt to organize
further card burnings.

> I felt that if the tactic was in fact politically right, as I hoped
> and believed it was, then others would take up other forms of expression
> of stiffened resistance to militarism. And so it happened. I would be sus-
> picious of the validity of actions that have to be planned over and over
> by the same people. It's better that things fan out and that people take on
> different styles and forms, involving always larger and more diverse ele-
> ments. Like the Resistance.

Notes to Chapter Two

The story of the Student Peace Union and Peter Irons was put together
with the help of Gene Keyes, Karl Meyer, and Peter. Among the documents they provided were the *Student Peace Union Bulletin,* December
1960, April and May 1961; Karl Meyer to SSS Local Board (January 4
and October 31, 1959); and by the same author, "Bellow It Out!" *Concerned Student,* March 1959, and *Nonviolent Revolution and the American
Peace Movement* (c. 1960); Peter Irons, "Last Thoughts before Going to
Prison," *New Left Notes,* January 27, 1967; the 1961 pamphlet, *An Alter-*

native to the Draft; and a mimeographed collection of nonregistration pledges collected by Irons, Williams, and Sherzer, including their own statements and a joint "Statement" describing the collection process they projected. For the Keyes-Goddard-Bassin pact, see Alice Lynd, ed., *We Won't Go* (Boston: Beacon Press, 1968), 15–32.

David Mitchell was similarly helpful in documenting his efforts as an antidraft organizer. Mitchell's personal experience is recounted in *We Won't Go,* 92–108, based largely on his speech to the We Won't Go conference in Chicago in December 1966 and statements which appeared in *Downdraft.* The present account is drawn from a conversation with him in April 1969, and from letters from Mitchell to Nick Salvatore (June 18, 1967), Salvatore to Alice Lynd (August 13, 1967), and Martin Boksenbaum to Alice Lynd (December 1967). Also the initiating statement of End The Draft, November 1962; *Downdraft,* January 1964, May 1964, January 1965; correspondence between ETD and the Fifth Avenue Peace Parade Committee, Fort Hood Three Defense Committee, Bill of Rights Fund, NCCEWV, and SDS; and *Downdraft News,* November 26, 1965. The ETD memorandum to SDS in which Irons' plan is mentioned is "Suggestions for an Anti-Draft Campaign," September 3, 1965.

The basic source for the section on the card burners is Tom Cornell's account in *We Won't Go,* 33–43, which is drawn primarily from Cornell to Alice Lynd (July 21, 1967) and his "Life & Death on the Streets of New York," *Catholic Worker,* November 1965. This material has been supplemented by Pete Hamill, "The Man Who Burned the Card," *New York Post,* October 19, 1965; WRL leaflet, "Statement by David McReynolds," issued November 6, 1965; CNVA, "News and Editorial Comment about Draft Card Burning from the *New York Times* and *Commonweal,*" November 1965; interviews with James Forest, Tom Cornell, and David Miller in James Finn, ed., *Protest: Pacifism and Politics* (New York: Random House, 1967), 176–192; McReynolds and Cornell to Staughton Lynd (April 14, 1969) and Martin Jezer to Staughton Lynd (August 30, 1969). The "veteran resister" quoted on page 21 is Jim Forest (see chapter 14) in *Delivered Into Resistance,* published by the Catonsville Nine–Milwaukee Fourteen Defense Committee (New Haven: Advocate Press, 1969), 3. David Miller's words on October 15 are quoted in Catherine Swann, "Burning a Draft Card," *Catholic Worker,* November 1965, and the farewell statements by Cornell and Miller in the *Catholic Peace Fellowship Bulletin,* June 1968.

 CHAPTER THREE

Black Courage, White Caution

SNCC, 1965–1966

From its founding in April 1960 the Student Nonviolent Coordinating Committee (SNCC) had been the toughest and most deeply committed civil rights group in the country. It had initiated the sit-in movement, helped the Freedom Rides, organized the Mississippi Freedom Democratic Party (MFDP), and provided most of the manpower for the voter registration drives throughout the south. Its workers, black and white, had been arrested, beaten, and shot so often that in some areas it became the custom for them to say farewell to each other before beginning a new task. Further harassment in the south, and withdrawal of support in the north, could be the only consequences of taking on the issue of the war and the draft. Yet the staff of SNCC became the first group outside the peace movement to express sympathy for draft resistance. In early January 1966 the group published a statement which said, as Julian Bond later described it,

> we had sympathy with those young men who could not respond to the military draft, and that included those young men who burned their draft cards. We sympathized with them, we understood why they did it, and appreciated the act for what it was. We considered it a real and meaningful protest against induction, against the war in Vietnam.

Julian himself was one of the first to suffer retaliation. He had been elected to the Georgia legislature the previous November, but after the statement which he, as a SNCC staff member, refused to disavow, the legislature voted not to seat him. After several reelections and a Supreme Court decision he was finally granted his seat.

It seems clear that SNCC took a stand against the draft because of the severe impact of the war on the black community and because of the desire of that community to protest through the groups that represented it. The escalation of the Vietnam war fell most heavily on young men without college (2–S) deferments. That included most black youth. A year after American Marines in large numbers were landed in South Vietnam, the Pentagon conceded that "proportionately more Negroes have been killed in Vietnam ground combat than other Americans."

By August 1965 every civil rights group was under pressure from below to take a stand on the war. Howard Zinn summarized the situation after the CORE and SCLC conventions of that month:

> The NAACP, through Roy Wilkins, says, "Let's not take a stand." The Urban League says very much the same. CORE obviously has a strong rank-and-file sentiment for opposing American policy in Vietnam, but James Farmer pressured them into silence at their recent convention. The SCLC, at its annual meeting, showed great concern, with James Bevel speaking of using non-violence to somehow stop the war.

Even SNCC moved slowly to take a forthright antiwar position. In 1965 SNCC's main program was a campaign to seat Mississippi Freedom Democratic Party congressmen in the House of Representatives, and for this SNCC needed the votes of moderate politicians which it feared alienating by an antiwar stand.

Individual SNCC leaders did not disguise their hostility to the war. Robert Parris (Robert Moses) spoke at the first antiwar march on Washington in April 1965. The next month Charlie Cobb read a poem at a Berkeley teach-in about

all the dead people
killed by the triggers
we've been taught
it's our responsibility to pull.

The *Nation* quoted a third SNCC veteran in July as saying:

We have to convince the country that civil rights workers get killed in the South because the government has a certain attitude toward killing in Vietnam. The concept that it is all right to kill an "enemy" affects the morality of the country so that people can be murdered here.

Protest against the war, of course, was not yet draft resistance. The first call for draft resistance from within the civil rights movement was a leaflet distributed in July 1965 in McComb, Mississippi, where Moses had begun voter registration work in the fall of 1961. It was written by a group of blacks in the community who met together after learning that a classmate of theirs, John D. Shaw, had been killed in action in Vietnam. John had taken part in the 1961 demonstrations in McComb in support of Brenda Travis, expelled from the local high school for protesting segregation at the McComb bus station. The McComb leaflet listed "five reasons why Negroes should not be in any war fighting for America":

No.Mississippi Negroes should be fighting in Viet Nam for the White Man's freedom, until all the Negro People are free in Mississippi.

Negro boys should not honor the draft here in Mississippi. Mothers should encourage their sons not to go.

We will gain respect and dignity as a race only by forcing the United States Government and the Mississippi Government to come with guns, dogs and trucks to take our sons away to fight and be killed protecting Miss., Ala., Ga., and La.

No one has a right to ask us to risk our lives and kill other Colored People in Santo Domingo and Viet Nam, so that the White American can get richer. We will be looked upon as traitors by all the Colored People of the world if the Negro people continue to fight and die without a cause.

Last week a white soldier from New Jersey was discharged from the Army because he refused to fight in Viet Nam he went on a hunger strike. Negro boys can do the same thing. We can write and ask our sons if they know what they are fighting for. If he answers Freedom, tell him thats what we are fighting for here in Mississippi. And if he says Democracy, tell him the truth—we don't know anything about Communism, Socialism, and all that, but we do know that Negroes have caught hell here under this *American Democracy.*

Reprinted by the state newsletter of the MFDP as well as by the newsletter of the Mississippi Student Union, another SNCC-initiated group, the McComb leaflet became a cause celebre. The State Director of Selective Service announced an investigation; Congressman Diggs of Michigan and Assistant Secretary of Labor George Weaver (both black) condemned it, as did Mississippi NAACP officials Aaron Henry and Charles Evers; even Lawrence Guyot, chairman of the MFDP and a SNCC field secretary, felt obliged to state that the leaflet did not represent the MFDP. The Mississippi press was jubilant. The *Jackson Daily News and Clarion-Ledger* reported that "Draft Evasion Note May Kill FD Party," and the *Natchez Democrat* editorialized: "Must Reject MFDP."

Less eminent black Mississippians associated with the civil rights movement, however, seem to have responded to the McComb leaflet with considerable support. A woman in Natchez heard of the leaflet on the radio and told two sympathetic visitors that "we should get together and have a meeting on that here, that our mothers are against our sons going to this war because they won't give us our freedom." A woman in Rosedale, in the Mississippi Delta, showed the same travelers a poem with the last lines:

> Maybe the people in the Vietnam
> can't register to vote
> Just like us.

Antidraft agitation in Mississippi undoubtedly influenced the crystallization of antidraft sentiment in national SNCC. The SNCC statement was moderate in tone: it expressed "sympathy" for draft refusers and the belief "that work in the civil rights movement and other human relations organizations is a valid alternative to the draft. We urge all Americans to seek this alternative." By August 1966, after the enunciation of black power, SNCC was making the point less circumspectly: "Hell no, we won't go!" Daily demonstrations began at the Atlanta induction center. Twelve blacks were arrested and held in jail fifty-eight days before being released on bond. During their imprisonment at the Atlanta stockade, the ten male prisoners were frequently placed in "the hole," four feet square and seven feet tall, for talking, or for saying "Black Power!" to their fellow prisoners. All but one of the demonstrators were convicted; six received three and a half years for "interfering with the administration of the Selective Service Act": and one, John Wilson, was sentenced to three years on the Georgia chain gang for "insurrection." John later became chairman of the National Black Anti-War Anti-Draft Union.

By the fall of 1966, when white students were beginning to sign We Won't Go statements, induction refusal by blacks had become a widespread phenomenon. In October SNCC chairman Stokely Carmichael reiterated that, if called for induction, he would go to Leavenworth before serving in the armed forces.

SDS, 1965: CONSCIENTIOUS OBJECTION

Stokely and SNCC felt alone and exposed in the struggle against the draft, as they had for so long in the struggle against racism. In seeking white allies, SNCC naturally turned first to Students for a Democratic Society.

SDS had spoken out early against the war. On April 17, 1965, two months after the United States had begun to bomb North Vietnam, SDS sponsored the first mass protest against the war. Song sheets distributed to the twenty thousand marchers at the Washington Monument proposed new antiwar words to songs of the civil rights movement. A suggested verse for the tune "Keep Your Eye on the Prize" ran:

> Only thing that we did right
> Was the day we refused to fight.

SDS president Paul Potter closed the rally with a call to draft resistance:

> . . . we will build a movement that will find ways to support the increasing numbers of young men who are unwilling to and will not fight in Vietnam; a movement that . . . will, if necessary, respond to the administration war effort with massive civil disobedience all over the country, that will wrench the country into a confrontation with the issues of the war.

But SDS did not move to build that movement at once. At the SDS national convention (in June at Kewahdin, Michigan) a foreign policy workshop chaired by Todd Gitlin recommended against concentrating on the war. At another workshop, Clark Kissinger proposed what came to be known as his "kamikaze plan." The plan was to have SDS appeal to American soldiers to desert, and then turn the probable federal indictments into a political forum. Drawing on the experience of socialist opposition to America's involvement in World War I and French opposition to the Algerian war, Clark argued that even if few soldiers deserted, the appeal to desert, presented in full-page newspaper ads and in leaflets distributed at military bases, would have a "salutary shock effect" on the country. The SDS officers who had been indicted would speak all over America about the concept of war crimes as defined by the Nuremberg Tribunal.

There were two reasons for the reluctance of SDS to embark on a resistance program of this kind. The first was the conviction of many members, especially those involved in local community organizing, that the single-issue movement to end the war must become a multi-issue "movement to change America." According to this argument, radicals should forego the hope of influencing the Vietnam war directly, and instead build new constituencies around domestic issues which would have power to do something effective about future wars. This came to be known in SDS as the argument for "stopping the seventh war from now."

The second reason was fear of repression. The Kewahdin convention tabled the kamikaze plan for consideration by the SDS National Council. An accompanying resolution required the National Council to poll the membership by referendum before initiating any program which might be considered illegal and lead to government repression.

At its September meeting the National Council (NC) took up the question. It endorsed a mild program for the encouragement of conscientious objection: tables outside physical examination centers, leaflets urging application for CO ("strictly legal, unlike draft refusal"), debates with military recruiters at high schools. As required by the Kewahdin resolution, these proposals were submitted to the membership for referendum.

Meanwhile End The Draft was badgering SDS. It sent letters to Paul Potter and incoming president Carl Oglesby and got no response. It sent a representative to the September NC with an extensive program, including "an antidraft enlistment day in October (Enlist Now—To Fight the Draft!)," free university courses on "The Individual Under International Law," anti-ROTC activity, mock courts "to try the government for its criminality while the courts are trying individuals for draft refusal," and mass draft card burning and noncooperation. (It was at this point that ETD referred to Peter Irons' proposal to the 1961 SPU conference.) But SDS that year was unwilling to endorse a forthright resistance program.

On October 15 and 16, 1965, about 70,000 antiwar demonstrators went into the streets across the nation. The two "International Days of Protest" had been called by the Berkeley Vietnam Day Committee and the National Coordinating Committee to End the War, not by SDS. Yet on the eve of the demonstrations the Senate Internal Security Subcommittee released a report on "subversive influences" in the antiwar movement which linked several SDS leaders to "communist" organizations. Columnists Evans and Novak reflected a substantial segment of Congressional opinion when they singled out SDS as the main instigators of the protest. In the words of SDS national secretary Paul Booth, they "found the most far-out proposals in a Vietnam newsletter we put out and . . . broadcast them to the world." The events of the next two days only confirmed conservative paranoia. David Miller burned his draft card; three dozen students sat-in at the local draft board in Ann Arbor and were arrested. On October 16 a front-page headline across the width of the *Chicago Sun-Times* cried: "US-Wide Drive to Beat Draft Is Organized Here." The story was based on Paul Booth's description of the program for the encouragement of conscientious objection endorsed by the September NC meeting. The next day the *Chicago Tribune* reprinted a pamphlet circulating in Berkeley entitled "Brief Notes on the Ways and Means of 'Beating' and Defeating the Draft." Ways and means included conscientious objection, demonstrating during the pre-induction physical, refusing to sign the loyalty oath, and feigning homosexuality. The pamphlet was attributed to SDS. Senator Stennis urged the administration "to jerk this movement up by the roots and grind it to bits." Attorney General Katzenbach hinted at an investigation. For a few days, SDSers expected to suffer substantial repression.

In response, Paul Booth and Carl Oglesby issued a controversial press statement. The statement implied that SDS would favor a plan for compulsory national service, provided nonmilitary options were available. Carl and Paul asserted that young Americans wanted to "build, not burn." Until young men opposed to service in Vietnam were permitted to "serve in hospitals and schools in the slums, in the Job Corps and Vista, in the new Teacher Corps," or in SNCC and community organizations, SDS would have no choice but to "encourage every member of our generation to object, and to file his objection through the Form 150 provided by law for conscientious objection."

The reaction against SDS, however, remained only verbal, so the draft program in the winter of 1965–66 proceeded with the encouragement of conscientious objection. The results of the referendum on the program were never clear-cut, but many local chapters went ahead with work on it, and several SDS officers applied for CO status. Lee Webb, the national secretary before Paul Booth, had applied in 1964; now Jeff Shero, Rennie Davis, and others were joining him.

The most significant effort by the SDS national office was the publication in twenty thousand copies of a "Guide to Conscientious Objection." Across its cover ran Bob Dylan's words:

> You don't believe in war,
> But what's that gun you're totin'?

The pamphlet presented moral and legal arguments against the war and outlined the alternatives to induction. A leaflet of Ann Arbor SDS, announcing a rally for Carl Oglesby, also began with the Dylan quotation, and went on:

DO YOU OBJECT TO FIGHTING? YOU MAY BE LEGALLY AND MORALLY RIGHT. Everyone knows how the army thinks about war. But perhaps *you* have some second thoughts—about killing, about shelling civilians, about nuclear gambles. And maybe all the hating and wrecking has made you believe that you cannot, should not, have anything to do with it. We agree with that. We feel that wars weren't made for people, so we are making sure that everyone knows about his legal right to be a conscientious objector to military service.

Another leaflet by the same SDS group, designed for a nonstudent audience, began with questions about the undemocratic character of government decision-making about the war ("*The last time* your Congressman asked you what *you* thought about the war in Vietnam, what did you say?"), moved on to questions concerning the war itself, and ended with questions "about your conscience" ("Are there any circumstances under which you would refuse to fight in a war?") and "about your rights" ("If your conscience gave you any doubts about fighting, do you know how to tell your draft board?").

Most of the young men who were the targets of the SDS campaign were not pacifists—they could not honestly say (on Form 150) they opposed "war in any form"—so they were technically ineligible for CO status. Applying for it, then, was a protest: not entirely symbolic, since at that time it might cost them their student deferments, but not entirely altruistic, since they might persuade draft boards to allow them to do alternative service. By

1966, partly because of SDS, the number of applications for CO began a dramatic rise.

SDS, 1966: *THE CLASS RANK*

During the first half of 1966 the draft became the most intensely discussed issue within SDS. The January National Council meeting suggested that chapters petition local draft boards "demanding that they promise not to use the draft as a weapon of silencing political dissent," and circulate "freedom draft cards" with which draft-eligible men might register their desire "to build, not burn." About the beginning of March chapters began to be concerned with Selective Service examinations scheduled in May and June at 1800 campuses. The tests were designed to rank students according to scholastic ability so that the least successful might be drafted. Lee Webb proposed that SDS distribute a counterexamination at the testing centers, and his proposal became the focus of an important National Council meeting at Antioch in April.

The key issue at Antioch was student deferments. Bill Hartzog, who later served briefly as SDS draft coordinator, urged the organization to tell students to give up draft deferments. Mendy Samstein, who had coordinated the 1964 Mississippi Summer Project, spoke intensely of the recent turn of the civil rights movement to black power and of the need for white radicals "to be serious," to put their bodies on the line as they had in Mississippi to "win the confidence of Negro movement people." The concern expressed by Bill and Mendy and others took the form of an amendment to Lee's resolution (for a counterexamination) which would commit SDS also to urge students to boycott the draft examinations altogether. For those who pushed it the boycott amendment meant a de facto renunciation of the 2–S deferment, since students failing to take the examination might not be granted student deferments.

National secretary Booth moved the boycott amendment. In a subsequent exchange in *New Left Notes* Paul argued:

> If the anti-war movement submits to the exam, with all its implications of preserving the 2–S class privilege for a few students, it will

confirm the suspicion and hope of the administration that our commitment is half-serious . . . that we are willing to have our parades and petitions because we have that 2–S classification that means that other kids have to go off and die.

Opponents of the amendment during the four-hour debate at Antioch stressed that the proposal would "cut SDS off from the bulk of students who will be taking the exam."

The "Booth amendment" carried by a vote of 39 to 29, with two abstentions. A motion to reconsider failed 22–30. So close were the votes and so strong the feelings on both sides, however, that the Council decided to submit the amendment to the entire National Council membership by mail ballot. As submitted to referendum the amendment read: "We are opposed to the Selective Service Exam; we will not participate in it; and we urge other young men not to take it. We do this because we oppose the war in Vietnam." On April 29 *New Left Notes* announced that the amendment failed, 21 for, 61 against, 2 abstentions.

The policy that passed was leafleting (rather than the boycott), but the spirit that passed was militancy. The counterexamination program went forward with great efficiency. Faculty at the University of Michigan, who had originated the teach-in a year earlier, arranged for the Inter-University Committee on War and Peace to co-sponsor the counterexam and helped Mike Locker of SDS in preparing the questions. In final form the counterexam had a factual section on the war and Vietnamese history, a section on opinion questions, and an answer sheet. With the aid of a Wide Area Telephone Service line, the SDS national office distributed a half million copies to a thousand testing centers. Particularly impressive was the fact that the counterexam reached 80 percent of the centers in the south, where antiwar sentiment was weak; eight students at Tulane, for instance, arranged for the distribution of the exam to every center in Louisiana.

Meanwhile, as the first testing date of May 14 approached, sentiment grew against university complicity with the war. Dick Flacks, an SDS founder, organized 142 midwest faculty members to issue an "Educators' Statement of Principle on Selective Service" which condemned "the use of class standing as determined by grades as a basis of drafting students." A group of Brandeis professors were reported ready either to withhold grades or give nothing but A's. Steve Baum, SDS regional coordinator for Chicago, and Earl Silbar, later a coordinator of national SDS anti-draft activity, announced a regionwide demonstration against the tests and the war on May 7 and several chapter demonstrations on May 14. Early in May forty students of the State University of New York at Buffalo sat-in in the president's office in opposition to the university's use as a testing center. More than three hundred students occupied the University of Chicago administration building in a protest "against the rank." Similar sit-ins followed at Cornell, Brooklyn College, Roosevelt University, State University of New York at New Paltz, and the University of Wisconsin. At Bloomington (Indiana) and Dartmouth, students denounced the appearance of General Hershey, national SSS Director. Interspersed with these chapter actions were individual deeds, like that of the non-SDS biology graduate at Chicago who stood up during the exam, tore up his paper, and walked out to applause.

The demonstrators' arguments against the tests, and against university complicity with the war, were three. First, as one group of students put it, "the examination divides students by forcing them to compete for continued protection from service in the war": do well on the exam so the man next to you will be killed in your place. The analogy of the Nazi death camps was not missed, where the strongest and best educated Jews were often spared the fate of the majority. Secondly, in the words of protesters at City College of New York,

> there are other young men who cannot take this test. Many Negroes, Puerto Ricans and other poor guys who do not have the opportunity to go to college. . . . We ask for an end to this system which discriminates between rich and poor, black and white.

Oberlin SDS put into words the third and strongest reason for the protests. It stated simply: "The war in Vietnam is the most important reason why we oppose College cooperation with the SSS."

A first concrete victory was recorded at San Francisco State, where the Faculty Senate unanimously moved that "the registrar not circulate or record class standings" and that "the college not allow its facilities to be used for giving the college qualification test." Another triumph was scored when on June 16 the president of Wayne State University in Detroit announced that his institution would no longer establish class rankings prior to graduation or make rankings available for use outside the university. Several other universities followed suit.

The Selective Service System did not offer the examinations again.

SDS, 1966: HESITATION

SDS action around the SSS examinations, like the march on Washington the previous spring, was a one-shot effort which failed to resolve the question of what long-range program would be effective against the draft and the war. On May 17 Paul Booth reiterated the October position that the Vietnam war should be fought by volunteers, with young men conscientiously opposed to the war permitted to work in "constructive service for democracy." Carl Oglesby added that "a truly American plan for universal national service would not require that the service be under the Federal Government." The national service proposal, already under attack by some SDSers, became even more controversial when Secretary of Defense McNamara proposed a similar plan, and debate raged in the pages of *New Left Notes* for weeks.

Since the 1966 national convention was postponed to August, the National Council met again in Ann Arbor in June. From the discussions there two documents emerged. The first was a joint statement to the House Armed Services Committee by Carl Oglesby, still president, and the new SNCC chairman, Stokely Carmichael. The statement called for abolition of the draft, and finally repudiated national service as "an instrument for stifling whatever social change the government opposes and for controlling the destinies of millions under the guise of humanitarianism." The government had no right to draft its young men for any purposes, military or otherwise.

The second document, a "report from the draft workshop" at the Ann Arbor meeting, once more addressed the central problem of the 2–S deferment. Although ostensibly reporting on the NC's draft workshop, this paper actually summarized one position presented there, that of the Progressive Labor Party (PLP). The position stated that "while we must . . . oppose 2–S as a divisive and class-racial-discriminatory system, we have to do this on the basis of collective struggle against the administration and the government, not by individual sacrifice." Just what, if anything, this meant in practice was not said. How was the 2–S deferment to be effectively "opposed" except by many individuals renouncing it? John Wilhelm of New Haven, a delegate to the Ann Arbor National Council meeting, remembered the draft discussion as particularly frustrating. He had brought a detailed proposal for organizing induction refusals and other antidraft actions, but nobody seemed ready for this kind of work. Three or four proposals were debated, John recalls, yet none of them seemed very different from the others, nor was it clear what the adoption of any of them would mean. In retrospect, John saw this meeting as a first step away from the SDS tradition that there "shouldn't be resolutions unless a person was going to work on their implementation." He was one of the first in SDS to become discouraged with its rhetorical substitutes for action and to look elsewhere for a group willing to work.

After it issued the Oglesby-Carmichael statement and the PLP position paper, the June National Council meeting created an "ad hoc committee for formulation of proposals for a national antidraft campaign." Its members included Paul Lauter, an AFSC staff member in Chicago and a member of the SDS National Administrative Council; John Wilhelm; Earl Silbar and Jared Israel, both of PLP; Steve Weissman, a leader of the Berkeley Free Speech Movement; and Brent Kramer, active in the antirank sit-in at the University of Chicago. The Chicago members of the committee met June 30 without settling on any plan. A letter from Steve to Brent expressed the ambivalence characteristic of SDS at the time. He suggested that SDS obtain pledges from students "that if, say, 3000 people commit themselves, each of the 3000 will refuse his 2–S." This would probably mean jail, Steve went on, but would be worthwhile because it would mobilize support for legislative remedies such as legalizing selective conscientious objection and forbidding the shipment of draftees to Vietnam. But, he concluded, "I'm frankly appalled at the fear of alienating students by raising the 2–S issue. While I don't expect many people to *individually* give back their deferments, I do see students collectively asking that 2–S be abolished." Brent Kramer observed that "the NC kept being too scared to say anything firm" because it feared "that most chapter people weren't ready yet." Paul Goodman, who was urging chapter meetings to come out against the 2–S deferment, estimates that only about one fifth of his listeners agreed.

No one in SDS that summer was able to formulate a program of antidraft action. On the eve of the SDS national convention at Clear Lake, Iowa, Jesse Lemisch articulated a proposal for antidraft militancy. Jesse, a junior faculty member who had joined the sit-in at Chicago, began with a summary of SDS activity on the draft:

> On this important matter SDS has been largely screwing around since last October, when the press discovered that we had a more coherent and subversive plan than any of us knew about. On paper our accomplishments are not negligible: there are the various sit-ins, the Vietnam test, etc. But these are not part of any coherent plan, and, more important, few of us would claim that they even begin to relieve us of the burden of being, vis-a-vis Vietnam, merely white liberals: they are not serious enough.

Jesse was unable to point a way out of this dilemma. He confessed that he himself was not prepared to renounce his teacher deferment. Yet he was clear that, if called for induction, he would refuse. Assuming this combination of sentiments to be prevalent in SDS, he suggested that the organization should not call on students to renounce their deferments but should prepare them, through education, to refuse induction when their deferments were exhausted. The difficulty with this program was that, despite its testing program in the spring, the Selective Service System was drafting very few students or ex-students. To prepare for refusal a constituency which would not be drafted was not to present much of a barrier to the continuation of the war.

The only other concrete proposal to the Clear Lake convention was from Frederick Gordon of Cambridge. He merely resuscitated the idea of applying for CO status on the ground of moral objection to a particular war. This, he thought, would be "something more than marches and petitions" yet "not so radical as to decapitate the radical leadership of the movement (by sending them to jail)." In assuming that SDS was not prepared "to initiate an 'enemy of the state' stand on the draft" Fred was undoubtedly correct. Someone else would have to take the initiative.

Notes to Chapter Three

Julian Bond's comment is from an interview in James Finn, ed., *Protest: Pacifism and Politics* (New York: Random House, 1967), 308. The Pentagon is quoted in "Ratio of Negroes Killed in Vietnam Tops White," *Los Angeles Times,* March 10, 1966, reproduced in a flier by Freedom Draft Movement, Los Angeles, entitled "War Is Good Business, Invest Your Son." For the early attitudes of civil rights groups toward the war, see Howard Zinn, "Should Civil Rights Workers Take a Stand on Vietnam?" [SNCC] *Voice,* August 30, 1965; Courtland Cox, *Nation,* July 19, 1965, quoted in a pamphlet written for the Assembly of Unrepresented People, August 8–11, 1965, "What's Wrong with the War in Vietnam?"

On the McComb leaflet: *Mississippi Freedom Democratic Party Newsletter,* July 28, 1965; conversations between Joe Martin, Paul Lauter, and Florence Howe (August 4 and 28, 1965), reported in an unpublished manuscript by Lauter and Howe; transcript of a conversation between an unidentified woman and three civil rights workers, Natchez (August 3, 1965); Ida Mae Lawrence, "Vietnam: A Poem"; *Natchez Democrat,* August 1 and 11, 1965; *Jackson Daily News and Clarion-Ledger,* August 1 and 8, 1965.

By spring 1966, MFDP candidates had adopted the position Guyot disavowed in July 1965. See the report of the remarks of Rev. Clifton Whitley, MFDP candidate for U.S. Senate, at a prayer meeting on Vietnam in Sidon, Miss., March 26, 1966, in the *National Guardian,* April 23, 1966.

On the SNCC demonstration of August 1966: SNCC press release, March 7, 1967; *Southern Patriot,* November 1966; leaflet called "I Can

Put You in the Hole and You Can Eat Bread and Water till You Die . . . ," put out by Women in Action [fall 1966]; "Another Wild Bust," *New Left Notes,* March 6, 1967; "History of Atlanta Peace Movement, Part VI," *Atlanta Workshop in Nonviolence Newsletter,* April 1969.

On antidraft sentiment in SNCC and the black community, fall 1966: "Carmichael Says He Won't Go if Drafted," *New York Times,* October 29, 1966; "Negroes Resist Fighting a 'White Man's War,'" *National Guardian,* November 5, 1966; "'It's Not Our War!': An Explosive Interview with Four Young Black Men who Have Refused Military Service," *Viet-Report,* November–December, 1966; conversation between Stokely Carmichael and Staughton Lynd (October or November, 1966).

The discussion of SDS here and elsewhere in this book should be understood as provisional. It may be revised in the light of the book-length studies of SDS now in process by Jim O'Brien, Paul C. Garver, and George Abbott White, and others.

For SDS in 1964–65 we drew on the *SDS Bulletin,* May 1964; song sheet and text of Paul Potter's speech for the march on Washington, April 1965; conversations between Clark Kissinger and Staughton Lynd, and David Mitchell and Lynd (May and April, 1969); Lee Webb and Paul Booth, "The Anti-War Movement: From Protest to Radical Politics," unpublished mimeographed paper, fall 1965; statement of Paul Booth, October 20, 1965, at Washington, D.C., press conference; press attacks on SDS antidraft work, especially the *Chicago Tribune*'s story entitled "Berkeley Pamphlets Describe Details on How to Dodge Draft," October 17, 1965, and *Chicago Sun-Times,* October 16, 1965; various SDS pamphlets on conscientious objection; Thomas R. Brooks, "Voice of the New Campus 'Underclass,'" *New York Times Magazine,* November 7, 1965; Paul Lauter, "Report on Ann Arbor Draft and CO Project for Worklist," unpublished mimeographed paper, October 1965; National Secretary's report, *New Left Notes,* June 17, 1966; and the following letters: David Mitchell to Paul Potter (June 9, 1965); Ellen Schneider to Potter (June 10, 1965); Helen Garvy to the editor of *New Left Notes* (January 28, 1966).

The discussion of SDS and the draft in the first half of 1966 is based on *New Left Notes,* January through August, 1966, and on discussions of the Antioch and Ann Arbor NC meetings between Staughton Lynd and John Wilhelm (December 31, 1968), Paul Booth (April 13, 1969), and Paul Lauter (April 19–20, 1969). Also on the following material supplied

CHAPTER FOUR

We Won't Go

In the absence of leadership from SDS, other groups in the white radical movement tried to build and coordinate draft resistance. Their work in the second half of 1966, during which draft calls rose from 30,000 (July) to as high as 46,000 (October), created enough momentum to make a genuine mass movement of resistance a realistic hope.

PACIFISTS AND MARXISTS

One of the few draft card burnings after those of the fall of 1965 was set in motion by David Reed, who dropped out of Harvard in the winter of 1965–66, briefly left the country, returned to join the New England CNVA farm, and decided to resist. He wrote his Milton, Massachusetts, draft board that he intended to return his cards, and then on March 8,

> I returned the cards. About 30 people joined my vigil outside the draft board. The press was out in force; television cameras were even waiting behind the desk in the draft board office.
>
> On March 25, I participated in civil disobedience at the Boston Army Base and was arrested with ten others. While being dragged off military property by two Defense Department Security Police officers, my friend David Benson tore up his draft card. Then, on March 29, two days before our scheduled appearance in South Boston District Court for the Army

47

Base charges, Benson and I received new draft classification cards, both
1–A, in the mail. We decided to destroy these publicly on the steps of the
courthouse before trial. Our friends John Phillips and David O'Brien decided to burn draft cards of their own at the same time.

They all did so, and they were all later imprisoned. David
O'Brien's case became the test case for the Supreme Court on the
constitutionality of the 1965 law prohibiting the destruction of
draft cards. (The law was upheld, seven to one.) John Phillips,
after his release from prison, risked incarceration again by joining
the Chicago Fifteen in burning Selective Service files (see chapter
14).

David Reed and others connected with CNVA took part in a
Peacemakers Training Session held at the Catholic Worker Farm
in Tivoli, New York, in August 1966. The occasion brought together pacifist-oriented noncooperators from a variety of organizations who were convinced that the escalation of the Vietnam
war and the radicalization of the student movement had brought
more men than ever before to seriously consider complete withdrawal from the Selective Service System.

One plan projected by the conferees was a CNVA draft refusers' project, proposed by Martin Jezer, which called for the circulation of a statement of refusal, to be published when it attracted
one thousand signatures:

> We, the undersigned, young Americans who are now or soon
> will be eligible for the draft, now publicly inform you that we will have
> nothing to do with your dirty and illegal war in Vietnam and that if
> drafted into your army, WE WILL NOT SERVE, or if already in the army, WE
> WILL NOT FIGHT IN VIETNAM. In doing so we affirm our solidarity with the
> 25 and more Americans now imprisoned in American civilian and mili-
> tary jails for their refusal to kill Vietnamese people.

The statement ended with what A. J. Muste, in a covering letter to
the CNVA Executive Committee, described as a "youthful,
defiant tone":

> We offer this challenge to our draft-age brothers the world over.
> Beware of old men in uniforms giving orders. Refuse to fight in wars of

aggression. Refuse to die fighting enemies who don't exist. Our elders have screwed this world up but good.

But the Executive Committee did not push the plan, and nothing came of it.

The second project was more successful: a call for a conference on noncooperation in New York City for the end of October. The call was signed by David Miller, Jim Wilson, and David Reed, who had all burned draft cards; Paul Mann, John Cooke, and Chuck Matthei. Listed as supporters of the conference "who in earlier years refused to cooperate with conscription and were imprisoned" were, among others, Wally Nelson, Amos Brokaw, Ammon Hennacy, and Dave Dellinger. Nearly every pacifist group in the east joined as sponsors.

Over two hundred attended the conference. One described its atmosphere:

> The six men who called it were themselves noncooperating which gave an element of seriousness to the affair. It began with each of them telling us why he chose this path. Speaking to others out of one's own personal life, rather than in political abstractions, eventually became the Resistance way of organizing, and this was one of the early examples of it.

Two older men who spoke were A. J. Muste and Michael Scott, a nonviolent fighter against apartheid in South Africa.

A "Statement on Noncooperation with Military Conscription" prepared by David Reed was almost totally rewritten by potential signers at the conference who intentionally excluded COs or holders of any card. *Peacemaker* publishes this statement with the latest list of signers under the title, "Saying 'NO' to Military Conscription, For Draft-Agers Who Have Shunned, or Broken Their Ties To, the System."

> We, the undersigned men of draft age (18–35), believe that all war is immoral and ultimately self-defeating. We believe that military

conscription is evil and unjust. Therefore, we will not cooperate in any way with the Selective Service System.

We will not register for the draft.

If we have registered, we will sever all relations with the Selective Service System.

We will carry no draft cards or other Selective Service certificates.

We will not accept any deferment, such as 2–S.

We will not accept any exemption, such as 1–O or 4–D.

We will refuse induction into the armed forces.

We urge and advocate that other young men join us in noncooperating with the Selective Service System.

We are in full knowledge that these actions are violations of the Selective Service laws punishable by up to 5 years imprisonment and/or a fine of $10,000.

The conference had some impact outside of pacifist circles. One of those who came to it, for example, was Richard Schweid, a reporter from the Boston University *News*. When he returned to Boston and told his editor Ray Mungo about the conference, they published a centerfold spread on draft resistance, a daring act for a student newspaper at that time. (Ray Mungo joined the New England Resistance next year, and the *News* became its most reliable supporter among the collegiate press.)

This initiative by pacifist noncooperators made room only for those who opposed all wars and all forms of cooperation with the draft. Rigidities of a different sort were involved in the draft work emanating from the various Marxist groups.

The Progressive Labor Party, through the May Second Movement (M2M) which it initiated as a broad-based anti-imperialist group, sponsored the first We Won't Go pledge against the Vietnam war (spring 1964). In contrast to the position adopted in 1966 by SNCC and SDS, M2M did not oppose all conscription—"We understand our obligations to defend our country and to serve in the armed forces"—and for this reason the End The Draft group condemned it. But M2M took an anti-imperialist stand as clear as that of SNCC, SDS, or ETD:

Believing that United States participation in that war is for the suppression of the Vietnamese struggle for national independence we see no justification for our involvement. We agree with Senator Wayne Morse, who said on the floor of the Senate on March 4, 1964, regarding South Vietnam, that "We should never have gone in. We should never have stayed in. We should get out."

BELIEVING THAT WE SHOULD NOT BE ASKED TO FIGHT AGAINST THE PEOPLE OF VIET NAM, WE HEREWITH STATE OUR REFUSAL TO DO SO.

But Progressive Labor forfeited whatever chance it might have had to unify the draft resistance movement when, in the fall of 1965, it decided to stop supporting induction refusal. Thereafter its members made use of the draft issue in antiwar propaganda on campus and played a prominent role in discussion of the draft within SDS, but for practical purposes the Party followed the Leninist policy of entering the army and agitating among the troops. This was also the orientation of the Trotskyist Young Socialist Alliance. In the summer of 1966 members of two other tiny Marxist groups, Youth Against War and Fascism, and the American Liberation League, formed the New York Anti-Draft Union "united in a commitment individually to refuse the military draft and collectively to support that refusal by all appropriate means." It accomplished little and does not seem to have survived past October.

THE DES MOINES MEETING

Neither pacifism nor Marxism could organize the thousands of white students who were ready by mid-1966 to say publicly that they would never fight in Vietnam. Most of these students were moral without being pacifist and political without being Marxist. They had expressed their seriousness by sitting-in against the sending of class ranks to draft boards, and now were seeking new directions. Dissatisfied with SDS, CNVA, and the Marxist sects, they created organizations of their own.

In July 1966 a group of young men met in New Haven and drew up the following statement:

> We men of draft age disavow all military obligations to our government until it ceases wars against peoples seeking to determine their

own destinies. On November 16 we will return our draft cards to our local boards with a notice of our refusal to cooperate until American invasions are ended. We fully realize that this action will be considered illegal and that we will be liable to five years imprisonment.

We propose to develop our program August 25 and 26 prior to the SDS convention at Clear Lake, Iowa.

Of the eight men who signed it, one was a longtime worker with CNVA, a second had worked in the SDS national office and belonged to the SDS "anarchist" wing, and a third had made a detailed proposal for antidraft activity at an SDS National Council meeting earlier in the year. They were disappointed in their organizations. Three of the others had organized in Mississippi in the summer of 1964. They had not found comparable work in the north.

The mood of the New Haven meeting was tense. We talked about the moderation and hesitation of SDS, and the dedication and aggressiveness of SNCC. One of those who had worked with SNCC stressed the urgency of finding a means whereby whites could commit themselves as strongly against the war as blacks had against racism. By the end of the daylong discussion, the statement announcing the draft card turn-in was written and hectographed.

From that meeting four or five set out at once to carry the idea across the country. A letter by one of the travelers on July 22 begins:

> We've made our way to Chicago and on up to Madison, Wisconsin. The results of our probes into Detroit have been encouraging. . . . We've been keeping the numbers small, but discussions have been intense.

Small, intense discussion groups were more suited than mass rallies for propagating the idea and the serious personal consequences of applying it. The letter continued:

> Discussion in Ann Arbor clarified another pattern of thinking: namely, that the idea and act [of returning cards] were not political. Per-

sons who say this . . . had to see this idea as a comprehensive political program with organization "guarantees" for its expansion into all levels of the student movement. Until that could be developed, they were unable to see it as a viable political movement. I come at the question from a different perspective.

In the accusation that draft resistance was apolitical lay the germ of the coming antagonism between the Resistance and SDS.

At least one traveler got as far as the west coast, but by July 30 all had returned to New Haven for a second meeting. Their experiences were reviewed carefully, and out of the discussions came the most comprehensive report yet produced on the philosophy, techniques, and problems of organizing draft resistance. It is worth quoting at some length.

> Since the individual commitment to go to jail is the basis of the collective strength of the movement, we talked for a while about the kinds of reasons a person would take such an action. The two basic motivations are personal and political. In the case of the former, the person sees the draft situation as his personal climax with the system—he probably would have done a similar act anyway, but he decides to do it with the group because of the strength that adds to him and the group. A large majority of us, however, would not have taken this act, at least not until after confronted with induction itself. We are arriving at the decision because we feel that we have a political program we can make work.

It would not be an easy task, however.

> [Organizers] have to really go out and *work* to build strong democratic local organizations (or anti-draft struggle committees), that have a common relationship through this and other programs. In the case of existing organizations like SDS chapters, the idea would be to strengthen the movement and deepen the particular group's commitment to change.

With an implicit dig at SDS for its inaction at Ann Arbor in June, the report went on:

We have decided to reject the type of organizing that issues calls to do something, writes magazine articles and prints newspaper ads, and then expects people to act. . . . Only after the basic groundwork is laid over the next few months (i.e., building strong committed local groups by the field staff) will we pull out the stops on publicity. . . . Those of us who travelled west were awed by the size of the country and feel that if there is regional strength and unity this will help in the struggle that is to come.

The report reflected the group's awareness of the limitations of one-shot spectacles. They anticipated the charge that turn-ins are inherently climactic by insisting that

the November launching date is seen as a *beginning*, not as a final goal. It is from this date that the important building has to be done with other constituencies and programs. It was generally agreed that the major *program* that would follow from the collective act of draft defiance would be the organizing [of] a broad range of forms of draft resistance.

It was assumed that those who turned in their cards on November 16 would thereafter become organizers.

The group discussed the need for adult support and gave to Staughton Lynd, then at Yale, the task of organizing it. They also dealt with the merits of different kinds of legal defense:

We can take a civil liberties defense (claiming that we can advocate anything and also that the government is violating our liberties by drafting us to fight their war). We can take a Nuremberg defense (the war is immoral and unjust and it is our responsibility not to fight but to resist). We can also stand mute (and declare that the court is a political tool of the system and could not possibly grant us any justice).

Finally there was talk of women's liberation:

It was noted that there was a vast potential for organizing young women since there was such a vacuum now organizationally and programatically. WSP [Women's Strike for Peace] is mostly middle-aged and programatically fuzzy. SDS, despite occasional rhetoric to the contrary, remains a male-dominated organization. We agreed to raise pro-gramatic possibilities with women we know, but felt it would be up to the women themselves to develop corollary programs to our draft resistance.

There were in fact women's workshops at the subsequent Des Moines meeting and at the We Won't Go conference in Chicago the following December.

The national discussion envisioned by the first New Haven meeting took place on August 25–26. Forty or fifty persons gath-ered in the high-ceilinged meeting room of the AFSC building in Des Moines, Iowa, for a nonstop day-and-night conversation. Participants slept in adjoining offices and ate spaghetti in the basement. The SDS national office was represented by Paul Booth and Jeff Shero, members of opposing factions, who wisely sprawled in opposite corners of the meeting room in order not to bring SDS differences into the smaller group. The participants needed a chance to report on their work before they could debate theory. Dan Angert talked about Antioch, Dan Wood about De-troit. In Tom Bell's recollection there was a quiet, considerate tone to the discussion.

There was tremendous respect for the opinion of each person who spoke and there was virtually no interruption of someone speaking. Everyone who wanted to could express his or her opinion thoroughly. I had the definite sense that the issues were being considered in a deep clear manner and that we moved into a consensus quite naturally.

Two questions dominated the Des Moines discussion. The first was to assess how the government would react to mass draft defiance in wartime. It was thought there would be prosecution for organizing draft resistance as well as for draft resistance itself. There was a dispute over whether anyone should have a list of ev-eryone at the meeting. To Tom Bell, who had spent the summer among underground political activists in Brazil, preparations for the Des Moines meeting had seemed so casual, security so lax, that he had almost stayed away. "There was some of the sense that the next time we saw each other it might be in prison."

The other question was whether the individuals then committed
to public and collective noncooperation should proceed directly
to a single dramatic act, or should first organize others to act with
them. Jeff Shero described this as the choice between "big bang"
and "organic growth." The New Haven meetings had projected a
big bang. The Des Moines meeting, for several reasons, decided
against it.

One reason was that a loose, decentralized structure, which permitted each group to "go public" when it was ready, would protect the resistance movement as a whole from repression. But a
more important reason was that community-based draft resistance unions would be more effective in the long run than demonstrations, however impressive. The unions would pose a real
threat, not a symbolic one, to the draft system. In Tom Bell's
words,

> the unions or communities could reach beyond those who
> would normally respond to a massive demonstration; they would not be
> bounded by the existing movement or by the campus. While a demon-
> stration would rely primarily upon the mass media for its effect, the re-
> sistance communities would establish their own means of communication
> in the locality and would bring events directly to draft-age people.
> Growth of the resistance unions would depend upon their internal dy-
> namic, resting only minimally on reaction to the decisions of others
> within the movement or in national or international politics.

The same line of thinking led to the conclusion that We Won't Go
statements should not say "I won't go into the army" but "I won't
go to Vietnam." In that way the resistance movement would "give
people more room," as one person said at Des Moines, and would
keep the door open for the participation of soldiers, who were beginning to refuse orders to go to Vietnam.

The differences between "big bangers" and "organic growers"
would be felt within Resistance groups in the following two years,
as well as the inherent dangers of each approach. Where the bang
philosophy prevailed, the group sometimes collapsed of its own
hollowness. Where the growth philosophy dominated, the groups
often converted to altogether different work, like GI counseling or

rent control. A balance, in groups that wanted to stay with the draft, would be hard to maintain.

The Des Moines meeting decided not to push any plan for draft resistance at the SDS convention, which followed immediately. There is no question, however, that Des Moines and its consequences had an impact on SDS in rather the same way the McComb, Mississippi, statement of July 1965 impressed the SNCC staff. At the Clear Lake convention, it is true, extensive discussion of the draft produced little in the way of program. But by the end of the year SDS, prodded by its constituents, would endorse a broad range of serious draft resistance actions.

Paul Lauter, who attended the Des Moines meeting, thinks that almost every We Won't Go group in the country in the fall of 1966 was started by people who had been there, and he is probably right. The large groups at Yale, Chicago, and Cornell all resulted from Des Moines, and so did a number of smaller groups, less well known, like the one in Detroit.

Dan Wood returned to Detroit from Des Moines and began to organize an antidraft union. By October about a dozen people were involved, although "older 'new left' radicals" were skeptical. Dan's fundamental problem as an organizer was to make the transition from a We Won't Go pledge to active resistance. "There appears to be little doubt," he wrote in October, that several dozen people could be brought together

> to write their draft boards renouncing the war and pledging not to serve in Vietnam. But behind the pledge there is real ambiguity. Do people see themselves stepping up their commitments if and when the government begins harassment and repression or do people withdraw their step forward?

His first response to this question was "to build simultaneous resistance activities around issues such as napalm/Dow Chemical, tax refusal, draft board sit-ins, etc." Common effort in these activities, Dan hoped, would provide a learning experience such that the antidraft union could become a "struggle committee" of the kind envisioned by the New Haven meetings early in the summer.

Discussion with Dan Angert of the Antioch group led to a specific plan for a sit-in at the Detroit Selective Service Center in late October 1966, drawing participants from Michigan, Ohio, and Indiana. As Dan Wood thought ahead to the action he was also aware that SNCC workers were "still in the stockade hole" as a result of their demonstration at the Atlanta induction center in August, and that some of the students who had sat-in the previous October in nearby Ann Arbor had been reclassified by their draft boards. His plans for the sit-in included a ten-day fast by those arrested, during which others would "organize politically around the defined issue of draft refusal." Energy thus created would be taken back by participants to local groups in the three-state area. Within the context of a sit-in and jail-in, the antidraft union would begin to take the form of a "resistance union, oriented toward direct action."

The sit-in, however, never materialized. When Dan Wood and a co-worker approached David Gracie, an Episcopalian minister, for help in organizing adult support, he discouraged them.

> They proposed sit-ins at draft boards. I told them I thought that was out of the question. Nobody would come. I suggested as a first step holding a city-wide conference on the draft and I promised I would try to get a group of clergymen to sponsor it. For once in my life I made the right tactical decision.

The resulting conference on draft alternatives was attended by sixty draft-age men. It received national press and TV coverage when members of a right wing group, Breakthrough, interrupted the meeting by shouting and throwing a Communist flag on the stage. According to the *New York Times*, "No speaker advocated disobedience to the law." But the *Times* reporter evidently missed the closing session when the ubiquitous Paul Booth asked, "How many of you are willing right now to stand up and say you're not willing to go and fight in Vietnam?" and more than half the audience of one hundred fifty, and all the draftable men, stood up. Thus Detroit chose to avoid a big bang in favor of slow growth. After that meeting, it had a viable group.

THE ANTIDRAFT UNIONS

Three other events in December 1966 helped transform the resistance into a movement. They were the We Won't Go conference in Chicago, the prediction by one hundred "respectable" student leaders of widespread draft resistance, and the endorsement of draft resistance by the SDS National Council.

Early in November 1966 the student newspaper of the University of Chicago, the *Chicago Maroon,* published a We Won't Go statement typical of dozens which followed later. "The undersigned men of draft age are united in their determination to refuse military service in Vietnam, and urge others of like mind to join them." The thirty-two signers included Paul Booth and Brent Kramer, who had been pushing for a more vigorous antidraft stance by SDS.

Shortly afterward, the Chicago We Won't Go group called a national We Won't Go conference for December 4. The conference was a "parallel institution," for the university had already called a draft conference for the same weekend, as its response to the student sit-in of the preceding spring. Financed by the Ford Foundation, closed to the public except for its final session, the university-sponsored conference hardly lent itself to the needs of the incipient resistance. The We Won't Go gathering, on the other hand, brought together representatives of every significant strain of antidraft activity—at a moment when that activity was on the verge of assuming mass proportions.

Besides two representatives of the Chicago We Won't Go group, speakers included Richard Flacks, a Chicago professor and a founder of SDS; John Otis Sumrall, a CORE organizer in Mississippi; Arlo Tatum of the Central Committee for Conscientious Objectors; David Mitchell; Jeff Segal, an induction refuser who later became national SDS draft coordinator; James Bevel of the Southern Christian Leadership Conference (Martin Luther King's group); and Staughton Lynd, who read an article (written at his request by Martin Verlet) on the French draft resistance during the Algerian war. The impact of the conference was due less to specific projects it discussed than to its size and range of representation. Over five hundred attended from dozens of organizations. They brought back to their organizations not only ideas and contacts but a sense of purpose and solidarity within a rapidly growing almost-movement.

The front page of the *New York Times* for December 29, 1966, reported an open letter to President Johnson from one hundred student leaders which stated that "unless this conflict can be eased, the United States will find some of her most loyal and courageous young people choosing to go to jail rather than to bear the country's arms." The *Times* observed that "as elected campus leaders, the students represent a far more moderate university group than the members of the student New Left, whose objections to the war are frequently and stridently demonstrated."

After the Clear Lake convention, the SDS National Council vaguely affirmed that "SDS should organize young people . . . thru anti-war and anti-draft activity." But at the NC meeting at Berkeley in December, it finally adopted a militant and comprehensive antidraft resolution:

1. SDS reaffirms its opposition to the United States Government's immoral, illegal, and genocidal war against the Vietnamese people in their struggle for self-determination.

2. SDS reaffirms its opposition to conscription in any form. We maintain that all conscription is coercive and anti-democratic, and that it is used by the United States Government to oppress people in the United States and around the world.

3. SDS recognizes that the draft is intimately connected with the requirements of the economic system and the foreign policy of the United States.

4. SDS opposes and will organize against any attempt to legitimize the Selective Service System by reforms. The proposals for a lottery or for compulsory national service would not change the essential purpose of the draft—to abduct young men to fight in aggressive wars.

5. SDS believes that a sense of urgency must be developed that will move people to leave the campus and organize a movement of resist-

ance to the draft and the war, with its base in poor, working class, and middle class communities.

> 6. SDS therefore encourages all young men to resist the draft.

To implement the resolution the NC outlined a program of draft resistance unions "united by the common principle that under no circumstances will they allow themselves to be drafted." The unions would try to reach other draftable men by demonstrating at induction ceremonies, pre-induction physicals, draft boards, and recruiting stations, and by circulating We Won't Go petitions. The NC promised to help resistance within the army as well. "We seek to break the barriers placed between us and our brothers in uniform." And though it would not advocate emigration it offered information to those who wanted to leave.

The resolution, Greg Calvert (then SDS National Secretary) recalls, passed after an "extraordinarily long" debate. "I and a lot of other people considered it a turning point for SDS, in that it seemed to us the one clear way to establish radical opposition to the war, to go beyond the liberal phase of dissent." Greg soon tried to summarize this transition in a national secretary's report entitled "From Protest to Resistance." The new program of draft resistance

> talks about the only thing that has given life and creativity to "the movement." It talks about the kind of struggle which has been most meaningful to the new left—the revolutionary struggle which engages and claims the lives of those involved despite the seeming impossibility of revolutionary social change—the struggle which has the power to transform, to revolutionize human lives whether or not it can humanize the societal conditions of human existence. It is the struggle which has offered imprisonment and even death as a way of being free—which says that "this is what a human being must do, no matter what the consequences, because this is what it means to be a human being."

SDS expressed its new mood in two buttons. One said simply "Resist." The other, borrowed from a current third-rate movie called *Not with My Wife You Don't,* said "Not with My Life You

Don't." The main consequence of the Berkeley resolution, however, was that SDS chapters threw themselves into the formation of antidraft unions.

Stimulated by the NC resolution, the Michigan State University (MSU) chapter, for instance, went to work on an antidraft union to "bring the system to a grinding halt by interfering as efficiently as possible with the formal functioning of the Selective Service System." The union envisaged such tactics as blocking buses carrying pre-inductees to testing centers, disrupting induction proceedings, picketing local draft boards, breaking up draft-exemption testing sessions, harassing recruiters at the MSU student union, and distributing We Won't Go pledges. Chapters would form at Lansing high schools and in the ghetto as well as on the university campus. The organization would be community-wide but limited in membership because of the risky nature of the work. Its goal was ambitious: to stop the war by building a strong antidraft union. They announced its formation by publishing a We Won't Go statement signed by forty-two draft-eligible men and twenty female supporters.

In the succeeding months We Won't Go statements and antidraft unions mushroomed from coast to coast, some of them instigated by SDS, some arising independently. The second University of Chicago statement appeared on February 3, 1967, with seventy-five signatures (up from thirty-two), including six who would go on to form CADRE, the Chicago Resistance group, in the spring. A first University of Wisconsin statement appeared in February with forty-seven signatures, a second two months later with 115. In late February the Queens College *Activist* printed a statement signed by twenty-six men which approached the limit of brevity: "We, the undersigned, draft-age male students at Queens College, will not serve in the armed forces of the United States—for varying reasons and regardless of personal consequences." The only expression more succinct than this was now being chanted at demonstrations everywhere: "HELL NO! WE WON'T GO!"

Many antidraft unions accompanied their We Won't Go statements with a picket line at an induction center, especially if one of their number was refusing. Gary Benenson of Chicago wrote to

Marty Jezer of *WIN* magazine, a New York pacifist journal, about

> a demonstration we helped to organize when Stan Smith went to the induction center to refuse induction. 75 people, plus newspapers, radio, and network TV showed up at the induction center at 6 AM. According to Stan, the demonstration was a real source of strength to him when he went inside. But the induction center was shaken too; Stan heard an officer get on the phone and ask for 100 MP's, fearing the demonstrators would storm the building(!). He was shuttled from room to room, talking to people everywhere, finally they announced that he had failed the physical and was 1–Y, and let him go.

Mark Harris of Antioch wrote about similar activity on a regional basis.

> Last night [February 26] we formed an anti-draft union here at Antioch. Our statement reads, "We, the undersigned, men of draft age, are opposed to conscription, we will refuse to be inducted into the armed forces and we support the right of all young men to refuse induction." Last week, a similar preliminary statement was signed by eighty men. We believe that the union will take on significance as our members become involved. Our first test will come on my induction date, March eighth. We plan to picket the induction center along with other anti-draft unions being formed in the area.

More than fifty supporters from antidraft unions at Antioch, Earlham, and the University of Cincinnati turned out March 8 in Mark's support.

As of March, Marty Jezer and Jeff Segal (at the Chicago SDS office) between them knew of We Won't Go groups or antidraft unions at twenty-six colleges and universities. At least half a dozen more were formed in April. And after the great peace marches of April 15, in which perhaps half a million joined in New York City and San Francisco, the pace intensified. Early in May a second We Won't Go statement was published at Cornell, signed by 176 draft-eligible men and 103 "not eligible for the draft who support and encourage the above." The Boston Draft Resist-

ance Group announced that a Boston area We Won't Go statement had been signed by 170 persons from seven universities. On
May 10 more than 250 students at twenty-five medical schools
across the nation announced their refusal to serve in the armed
forces. On May 21 a third Cornell statement brought the totals of
signers and supporters to 391 and 170. In a letter of May 23 an organizer for the W. E. B. Du Bois Clubs, a Marxist group, claimed
that they alone had organized nine colleges and high schools into
antidraft unions in New York City. A letter of June 6 to *WIN*
magazine brought word of a We Won't Go pledge circulating in
England by the "Stop It" Committee, a group of Americans living
in London. In midsummer 1967 Marty Jezer estimated that about
sixty We Won't Go groups had been organized with as many as
two thousand young men pledged not to fight in Vietnam. Ron
Young of the Fellowship of Reconciliation put the figure lower, at
about forty, with membership in individual groups ranging from
twenty to over two hundred in some places.

It was the We Won't Go group at Morehouse College, Atlanta,
whose stand appears to have prompted alumnus Martin Luther
King finally to come out flatly against the war. On April 4, 1967,
at Riverside Church in New York City, Dr. King delivered an address which came to be known as his "Declaration of Independence from the War in Vietnam."

> As we counsel young men concerning military service we must
> clarify for them our nation's role in Vietnam and challenge them with the
> alternative of conscientious objection. I am pleased to say that this is the
> path now being chosen by more than seventy students at my own Alma
> Mater, Morehouse College, and I recommend it to all who find the
> American course in Vietnam a dishonourable and unjust one. Moreover,
> I would encourage all ministers of draft age to give up their ministerial
> exemptions and seek status as conscientious objectors. Every man of hu-
> mane convictions must decide on the protest that best suits his convic-
> tions, but we must all protest.

Despite all this activity, the antiwar movement had still not
quite become a collective resistance. On the one hand, a determination to refuse service in Vietnam had become widespread on

college campuses, and was expressed in many We Won't Go statements. On the other, only a few people like David Miller and David Mitchell had gone beyond verbal commitment and actually refused induction or burned draft cards, and these isolated deeds could understandably be dismissed as ineffective moral witness. A means had yet to be found that would tie together in one political process the hundreds of signers of We Won't Go statements and the bold tactics of the draft card burners.

Notes to Chapter Four

Annual Report of the Director of Selective Service for the Fiscal Year 1967 . . . , 31, gives monthly induction totals from July 1966 to June 1967. See also "Resist-Draft Cases Soar," *National Guardian,* August 20, 1966, and "Wider Resistance to Draft," *National Guardian,* November 12, 1966.

For CNVA we have drawn on David Reed, "From Harvard to Prison to Peace," reprinted with very minor changes in James Finn, ed., *Protest: Pacifism and Politics* (New York: Random House, 1967), 257–268; memorandum from A. J. Muste to CNVA Executive Committee, August 23, 1966, enclosing Martin Jezer's "Proposal For CNVA Draft Refusers Project" and "Tentative Draft Of Draft Refusal Statement"; Dave Miller, Jim Wilson, Dave Reed, Paul Mann, John Cooke, Chuck Matthei, "Call to Eastern Conference on Noncooperation with Conscription," October 28–30, also mimeographed "Notes of Conference on Non-Cooperation" and handwritten notes by Alice Lynd; "Dear General Hershey: Please Remove My Name," *WIN,* November 23, 1966; "Hold Three-Day Conference on Noncooperation with Conscription," together with "Statement of Noncooperation with Military Conscription," *Peacemaker,* November 5, 1966; and Martin Jezer to Staughton Lynd (August 30, 1969).

The May 2nd statement was printed in the *National Guardian,* April 25, 1964 and in the *New York Herald Tribune,* May 28, 1964, with 149 signatures. See also "87 Youths Sign an Ad Declaring They Wouldn't Fight in Vietnam," *New York Times,* April 26, 1964. The description of the New York Anti-Draft Union is based on three mimeographed leaflets and on Leonard Liggio to Staughton Lynd (July 17 and 25, 1966).

The description of the gatherings in New Haven in July 1966 is based on personal observation by Staughton Lynd, and on the hectographed We Won't Go pledge produced at the first meeting and a hectographed "Report" on the second meeting. The Des Moines meeting was characterized in conversations between Gary Benenson, John Wilhelm, Paul Booth, Florence Howe, Paul Lauter, and Staughton Lynd, and on Tom Bell to Staughton Lynd (May 1, 1969), a letter much used throughout this section.

Other sources for the early We Won't Go movement include letters to Staughton Lynd from participants in the New Haven meetings; David M. Gracie to Staughton Lynd (April 29, 1969); *New York Times,* December 23 and 29, 1966; *Detroit News,* January 13, 1967; David Wheeler in the *Fifth Estate,* February 1–15, 1967; program, "Conference on the Draft," December 28, 1966. Also University of Chicago We Won't Go statement, November 1966; "We Won't Go Meeting Ready to Go Sunday," *Chicago Maroon,* December 2, 1966; flier announcing "A Public Confer on Draft Resistance" for December 4, 1966 and mimeographed proceedings, containing major speeches; Florence Howe, "We Won't Go Conference," *New Left Notes,* December 9, 1966; and the second University of Chicago We Won't Go statement, *Chicago Maroon,* February 3, 1967.

David Harris, student body president of Stanford University, was one of the signers of the statement reported in "Student Leaders Warn Presidents of Doubts on War," *New York Times,* December 30, 1966. SDS endorsement of draft resistance is chronicled in Earl Silbar to "Dear Friend of the Movement" (December 9, 1966) (containing the text of the National Council resolution on the draft of September 1966) and to Staughton Lynd (January 10, 1967); Earl Silbar, "Our Man on the Draft," *New Left Notes,* November 18, 1966; text of the National Council resolution on the draft of December 1966; Greg Calvert, "From Protest to Resistance," *New Left Notes,* January 13, 1967; description of the Berkeley National Council meeting, *National Guardian,* January 7, 1967; and conversation between Greg Calvert and Staughton Lynd (March 24, 1969).

Among sources for the growth of antidraft unions and We Won't Go groups after January 1967 are statements from Queens College, Wooster College, and the students of twenty-five medical schools, reprinted in Alice Lynd, ed., *We Won't Go* (Boston: Beacon Press, 1968), 204–205. The Michigan State antidraft union is described in *MSU State News,*

January 13, 1967 and April 12, 1967; *Paper,* January 16 and February 6, 1967; leaflet, "You and the Anti-Draft Union," n.d. See also NYU *Heights Daily News,* May 5, 10 and 17, 1967; *New Left Notes,* March 27 and May 8, 1967; *New Haven Register,* May 22, 1967; Ron Young, "Building Resistance to the Draft," *Fellowship,* July 1967; and *WIN,* especially April 7 and June 30, 1967. Unpublished sources include mimeographed form letter from Dan Swinney, Draft Resistance Clearing House (April or May, 1967); Gary Benenson to Martin Jezer (n.d.); Mark Harris to Martin Jezer (February 27, 1967); Dan Werner to Martin Jezer (May 17, 1967); and David Holstrom to Martin Jezer (June 6, 1967); also Martin Jezer to Alice Lynd (March 14 and 26, 1967); and Matty Berkelheimer to Lennie Heller (May 23, 1967).

Dr. King's speech is quoted in Lillian Schlissel, ed., *Conscience in America* (New York: E. P. Dutton, 1968), 435.

CHAPTER FIVE

Sheep's Meadow

The We Won't Go group at Cornell University was the only one in the country to move directly into mass civil disobedience. Two of its key organizers were Tom Bell and Bruce Dancis.

Tom had been active in the Cornell SDS chapter from its founding in the fall of 1965. He helped distribute the counterexam throughout western New York and joined the sit-in in the Cornell president's office. That summer he went to Des Moines, and when he came back he set to work organizing an antidraft group. His own description of the unusual way he proceeded is the best available account:

> My experience as an organizer had been very limited—working mostly with SDS [Students for a Democratic Society] chapters and with demonstrations. For me, the natural thing to do in organizing draft resistance would have been to go to an SDS meeting and propose that the chapter adopt a "we won't go" position; or to make a general announcement that all those interested in draft resistance should come to room X at 8 o'clock to discuss formation of a new group. I rejected these approaches for several reasons.
>
> It would have been impossible to reach a consensus on draft resistance within SDS at Cornell. After weeks of heated discussion we likely would have had less understanding of what we wanted to do than before. In the end, a group of us from SDS would have started a resistance union, but with much delay and considerable bad feeling. The group formed in this

way would have been ten or more to start, which I consider to be too large to get the initial solid understanding which has been so important to the development of our group. We would have had to fall back on the "normal" reliance on a single leader to formulate most of our decisions.

The announcement to form a new organization would have brought an unwieldy number of people together (at Cornell, probably about forty). The sheer numbers would make impossible the necessary personal discussion and individual understanding. Within that number, compounding the problem, would be people of a whole variety of positions about draft resistance. Some would proclaim that resistance was martyrdom, therefore apolitical. The same or others would say that we must go into the army and organize from within (a position I do not reject in principle, but which never seems to go anywhere because its proponents never volunteer, and because they are usually unacceptable to the army anyway). One or two hecklers might be present. Certainly, someone would have the position that we should forget all the talk about "union" and organize a massive draft card burning for some time in the next week. Once such a meeting was called, no subsequent meeting would be free of the endless differences. To attempt to reconcile these differences, making action possible, would be a complete waste of time.

The method of organizing actually used in Ithaca is very simple and direct. I had never done it before and had only discussed it briefly with people who have done community organizing. I feel that it could be used by anyone with a fair degree of patience.

Committed to the idea of draft resistance, I began to talk independently to three people who I felt would share my opinions. We discussed the meeting I had attended and the ideas current at that point. There was considerable difference of opinion among the four of us—especially about how to go about organizing draft resistance. We got outside help at this early point, in the form of an experienced community organizer. He talked with us a great deal, raising crucial questions. We were able at this period to begin to agree on a method of organizing and to clarify some of our other points of difference. Our experience was that this outside help was very important.

We continued to meet in sessions of three or four until we came to a pretty solid understanding. We had talked about our personal draft positions, our willingness and reservations about following a course of resistance, the possibilities we saw for resistance organizing, and the next step we would take. There was argument for each of the methods of organizing mentioned above, but we finally agreed that each of us would talk to one or two other people, discuss the idea with them and then all meet together in a week. In this way, all four of us were now organizers, and with considerable success. We managed to reach people, even at this early point, who had not been politically active in Ithaca before, but who were involved personally in the draft question. These people were interested in the type of resistance community which we were trying to build.

With the expanded group—now seven—we had roughly the same discussions as before. This time it did not take so long to reach a solid understanding. The new people, by chance I believe, were *more* turned on to the particular method of organizing. We decided to make the same move as before; each person would talk to someone new, give him an understanding of what we were about, get him to talk with some of the other people already involved, and bring him to a meeting in two weeks. We also decided to discuss the draft among ourselves, outside of a specific meeting, thus getting to know each other better and developing personal communication.

Understanding the risk of prosecution under subversive control acts, seven of us had agreed that under no circumstances would we go into the U.S. military; that we would encourage others to stay out of the military; and that we were all willing to take our stand publicly upon a collective decision on the right time and means. . . . Everybody in the group had essentially taken on the job of being an organizer of the group. Our organizing had relied on long hours of soul-searching discussion and a healthy rejection of the press or already organized groups. The building of the draft resistance community had in no way challenged existing groups nor did it pretend to make decisions for anyone but those people participating in the resistance community.

Bruce Dancis moved the group one step forward when he decided to tear up his draft card. Like Tom, Bruce had been an active member of SDS, and at the time of his decision he was Cornell SDS president. To the usual "pragmatic" approach of SDS Bruce brought a perspective of nonviolence. His father had been a CO during World War II and the summer before he went to college Bruce met and was much impressed by David McReynolds of the War Resisters League.

From the day he registered with Selective Service, Bruce was at odds with the system. His registration coincided with a protest against the "rank," and he joined other students sitting-in in the president's office. He was convinced, even as early as his freshman year, that he did not want a 2–S deferment, but he was not yet sure what status would be acceptable to him. He informed his draft board that he wanted a 1–O classification, but that he might not do alternative service if it were granted. By the next fall Bruce had decided to reject the CO status altogether. He perceived then what has since become a commonplace, that the manpower allocation system powered by the threat of the draft reinforces the class and caste system of America.

> I began to see that CO had the same things wrong with it that 2–S had. I saw that a guy from the streets of Harlem, who couldn't get a 2–S deferment since he wasn't in college, couldn't get a CO since it is such a difficult form to fill out. I also couldn't see myself having to explain to a bunch of old men why I should be exempted from killing people. . . . In December 1966 I finally decided that I must sever my ties with Selective Service. On December 14, outside a meeting of the Cornell faculty which was discussing the university's policy towards Selective Service, I read a statement to my local board before a crowd of 300 people and then ripped up my draft card.

The Cornell antidraft group agonized over Bruce's action. Tom tells how their first response was to "go public" by making a We Won't Go statement and linking it to Bruce's action.

> Some tried to dissuade Bruce from his action while others simply accepted his decision. We met to decide how we might support Bruce. We found it all too obvious that the only meaningful support from us would be to destroy our draft cards with him. Not being willing to take that action at the time, we were discouraged, and could only give publicity-type support. Bruce went ahead with his decision. The effect on the group at first was disturbing. While it did raise the level of seriousness, as only an action can, we found no way to be *together* in the action. The

group published an ad on the same day as Bruce's action saying, "WE WON'T GO. The undersigned men of draft age will not serve in the U.S. military and encourage others to do the same." This ad was effective in its own right. We were together in it. But it was an action taken independently of Bruce's action.

Then on March 2 five men—Jan Flora, Burton Weiss, Robert Nelson, Michael Rotkin, and Timothy Larkin—took the step which Peter Irons had proposed six years before. They called on other young men to pledge to burn their draft cards April 15 if at least five hundred people acted at the same time. Their call was eloquent:

> The armies of the United States have, through conscription, already oppressed or destroyed the lives and consciences of millions of Americans and Vietnamese. We have argued and demonstrated to stop this destruction. We have not succeeded. Murderers do not respond to reason. Powerful resistance is now demanded: radical, illegal, unpleasant, sustained.
>
> In Vietnam the war machine is directed against young and old, soldiers and civilians, without distinction. In our own country, the war machine is directed specifically against the young, against blacks more than against whites, but ultimately against all.
>
> Body and soul, we are oppressed in common. Body and soul, we must resist in common. The undersigned believe that we should *begin* this mass resistance by publicly destroying our draft cards at the Spring Mobilization.

(The Spring Mobilization was the name given to the two huge marches being planned for April 15 in New York City and San Francisco by a coalition of antiwar groups. Its honorary chairman, A. J. Muste, had died in February while working on it.) The statement continued:

> The climate of anti-war opinion is changing. In the last few months student governments, church groups, and other organizations have publicly expressed understanding and sympathy with the position of individuals who refuse to fight in Vietnam, who resist the draft. We are

ready to put ourselves on the line for this position, and we expect that these people will come through with their support.

We are fully aware that our action makes us liable to penalties of up to five years in prison and $10,000 in fines. We believe, however, that the more people who take part in this action the more difficult it will be for the government to prosecute.

Even after the call had been issued, Tom Bell struggled with the question of whether the decision had been right. He was one of the first to face the *inner* consequences of the big bang approach. At the Des Moines conference critics had talked about the strategic limitations, but Tom anticipated the very real problem Resistance groups would meet a few months later: draft cards returned by the hundreds, but only a handful of the returners sure enough of themselves to hold to their commitment. In the middle of March he wrote:

> I still have some pretty serious reservations about our action—especially as I see it at work. . . . What disturbs me is that almost 50 Cornellians have pledged to burn their draft cards and I am afraid for many of them the decision comes from the emotionalism of the moment. The sessions in the [student] union are very much like revival services (even including some of the rhetoric at times). We have speeches, a collection for the anti-war office and on the spot conversions—signing pledges, plus a lot of personal witness. I am going to try to get all the people who have signed pledges together for some collective thinking about what we are doing and I hope that we can get some things cleared up. There is a real agony for me in the dilemma presented by seeing this great opportunity for political organizing and action vs. the likelihood that a lot of people are going to be hurt (including myself) by the action being taken. I'm even more afraid when I think of the impersonal situation of sending out the calls. Don't really know why I am unloading all of this except that I feel caught—I don't like national actions but I do want to change America. I like a personal, deep communication type of politics but perhaps this is not really political. I don't want to manipulate anyone but I feel that it is essential for my own struggle and for the development of all of us as human beings that people change.

Two weeks later he wrote again.

> I've begun to feel better about the draft card burning, as a political act at least, but it looks like it will not come off. We have only about 90 pledges so far and the Spring Mobilization (Almighty Executive Board) has apparently refused to let us take the action as part of the April 15 action anyway.

A compromise was eventually reached with the Spring Mobilization. The Mobilization would not sponsor the card burning, but it would take place just before the march at its departure point, Sheep's Meadow in Central Park. The remaining question was whether, in the absence of five hundred pledges, the mass burning would come off at all. On April 14, the evening before the march, the number pledged was still only about 120. The Cornell initiators and others gathered in the New York Free University loft on Fourteenth Street to consider their position.

"I can remember very little of the meeting," Tom wrote afterward,

> Except that it was totally unsatisfactory. We had time to discuss only practicalities which I considered to be much less important than talking about our lives and developing some basis for real solidarity both during and after the card burning.

For Martin Jezer, who had pledged to burn his card, the "practicality" of the decision to go ahead with the action was itself deeply moving.

> We . . . decided that 50 would be the minimum number of burners to make it an important political act. There was a tense moment when Bruce Dancis asked, "How many will burn their cards if 50 do it at the same time?" Hands shot up around the room. The count was 57.

Marty hardly slept that night. His feelings reminded him of the night before graduation from college. "Burning a draft card, I thought, would be a more meaningful graduation."

The next morning, to everyone's surprise, between 150 and 200 burned their cards. The original group of sixty, which had gathered on a large knoll in a corner of the meadow, was surrounded by a chain of supporters to keep hecklers and reporters at a respectful distance. But they could not keep out a hundred other young men who came forward spontaneously from the crowd to add their flaming cards to the tin can being passed around. A number of girls burned half their husband's or boy friend's cards, and a sprinkling of older men, including several veterans, mingled with the group.

For the participants the advent of Gary Rader was particularly dramatic. One recalls:

> The draft card burning began amidst much confusion. People like Grace Paley, Karl Bissinger, WRL people, Veterans and Reservists for Peace (Walter Bursten, Keith Lampe and Bob Ockene) had organized a circle around the burners to keep the crowd back but there was a press of reporters and onlookers and it was never clear just who was there to burn a card and who was there to watch. In the middle of this appears this very rugged, blond-haired youth in a Green Beret uniform. Gary really looked military in that uniform. He was much heavier than he is today and, of course, much more rigid-looking. I didn't know why he was there but my first reaction was uh-oh, here's some super-patriot going to cause trouble. So imagine my (and I suppose everyone else's) surprise when Gary pulled out his card and set it afire. It was a cathartic moment; because with Gary on our side we knew the burning was going to come off OK and be important, as it was.

Paul Goodman remarked that the draft card burning gave point to the huge march which followed without obscuring it.

> The burners neither got lost in the shuffle nor did they hog the publicity. What came through the static was the clear message that the [Mobilization] Committee itself had finally come to: that open civil disobedience, as an act of political power, was not yet an *official* part of the proceedings, but it was *not* unthinkable.

Paul's son Manny, a Cornell student, was one of the burners.
For Tom Bell, Bruce Dancis, and the Cornell We Won't Go group it was a moment of triumph. Martin Jezer remembers that

the Cornell contingent [to the march], numbering in the thousands, was led by its "We Won't Go" organization and draft card burners under a large banner, "WE WON'T GO" emblazoned in the school colors. Locked arm in arm they were literally dancing down the street, joyful, defiant, irresistible. "Hell, No, We Won't Go," their words vibrated between the sterile buildings on Madison Avenue and echoed up and down the canyonlike side streets.

It was, in fact, resistance. They had called for it—"powerful resistance . . . : radical, illegal, unpleasant, sustained"—and they were bringing it about. Tom remembers how they clung to the word.

When we wrote the call we used the phrase "resist the draft" as a key phrase. The phrase must have been in the air at the time for us to pick it up but it was not a well established position (terminology).

After they finished a draft of the call a prominent adult supporter

was furious about the term "resist." I got on the phone as someone who defended the use of the word and he denounced me as a Trotskyist. . . . We sort of said "well fuck him" and decided to use the word anyway.

Notes to Chapter Five

Sources for the history of the Cornell We Won't Go group include Tom Bell's account printed in *New Left Notes,* March 27, 1967, and reprinted in Alice Lynd, ed., *We Won't Go,* Bruce Dancis to Alice Lynd (April 26, 1967); Tom Bell to Staughton Lynd (March 18, 1967), and to Alice Lynd (March 25, 1967); minutes of the working committee of the Spring Mobilization to End the War in Vietnam, March 30, 1967; Martin Jezer's account of April 14–15, published in *WIN,* April 30, 1967, and partially reprinted in Alice Lynd, ed., *We Won't Go* (Boston: Beacon

Press, 1968); *New York Times,* April 16, 1967; Paul Goodman, " 'We Won't Go,' " *New York Review of Books,* May 18, 1967; mimeographed letter to "Dear Friends" from Bruce Dancis and Tom Bell (April 21, 1967).

CHAPTER SIX

David Harris
and the Palo Alto Commune

In this chapter and the next two we tell what might be called the cosmogonic myth of the Resistance, the sacred history of the Resistance tribe. We dwell on David Harris and his friends at Stanford and the Palo Alto commune, not only because they were the originators of "the Resistance" (with Lennie Heller and Steve Hamilton from Berkeley) but because of the things they did before and during their organizing. Their exploits reflect many of the philosophical and cultural (or "countercultural") movements of the last twenty years; it is as if they felt compelled to rehearse everything that went into the world view of their generation before they were ready to make a contribution of their own. Into the antidraft movement they injected a way of thinking and working that derives neither from religious pacifism nor from revolutionary political theory—nor even from the pragmatic style of the New Left—but from a unique California blend of cowboys, Nietzsche, drugs, Jung, motorcycles, and Gandhi.

David and half a dozen fellow undergraduates at Stanford were the nucleus of the Resistance. He and Dennis Sweeney were two of the four who issued the call for October 16. Paul Rupert became a key Resistance organizer in Chicago. Joel Kugelmass and Ira Arlook joined the New England Resistance and worked in it for over a year. Jeff Shurtleff, among other things, joined Joan Baez Harris in the summer of 1969 on a tour of the country as the Struggle Mountain Resistance Band.

But if anyone deserves the title of Founder of the Resistance it is David Harris. He was not, strictly speaking, the first to propose its name or its first target date of October 16—they were due to Lennie Heller and Steve Hamilton—and the idea of a mass draft card turn-in was an old one, going back at least to Peter Irons in 1961. Nor have Resistance members outside David's group in Palo Alto always (or even often) agreed with his deeply nonviolent philosophy. But he has had an effect more pervasive than that of any other individual on the style of Resistance work and on the quality of Resistance thinking—on the range, audacity, and vitality of the ideas, if not on the ideas themselves. He has been criticized for doing too much public speaking and not enough "shit work," but he has thrown himself with boundless energy into all the tasks he has assumed. He has probably given more "Resistance raps" than any six other organizers. And of the original four who called themselves "the Resistance" in March 1967 only David has followed through in his commitment to noncooperation and antidraft organizing. As of this writing he is in solitary confinement in the Federal Prison of La Tuna, Arizona.

ROOTS OF RESISTANCE

In the spring of 1966, to everyone's surprise, David was elected president of the Stanford student body. He had been involved in politics before. He had worked briefly in Mississippi, with the Vietnam Day Committee that staged a mammoth teach-in in May of 1965, and with Delano grape strikers in the fall of 1965. (David grew up in the San Joaquin Valley, and picked and packed grapes every summer as a teen-ager.) But he was not a very likely candidate. Three years later, David, Dennis Sweeney, and other friends reminisced about the election and the commune and the early Resistance; most of the quotations that follow are from a tape of their conversation.

The unlikely candidate had not wanted to run, and when he was prevailed upon, he had no campaign apparatus.

We had a bunch of buttons. We were going to run a strike [on another issue], and we had a bunch of buttons printed up for the strike, which never happened, because we won without the strike. We had one which said "Hind Swaraj." We figured nobody would understand that, so we translated it: "Home Rule." The other one was "Community not Colonialism." So we threw all the surplus buttons into the campaign.

I had all these supporters who wanted to write a platform. I was too busy during the day the platform was being written, and got in a traffic jam and never made it back for the platform-writing, so about twelve people got together and threw together a platform which included everything from legalized marijuana. . . . Everybody just put down everything they wanted, which was generally agreeable to me.

I was the ideological dark horse. There were seven candidates. I was the guy who was right but hopelessly impractical. There was that position: "He says a lot of very good and interesting things but he looks a little strange." I had a moustache, and long hair, and wore work shirts and levis, and looked a trifle wild. Stanford students had a general fear of that. At the same time they liked what I said.

Much of later Resistance organizing style was evident in the rap-and-theater manner of David's electioneering. "All the other candidates had the traditional huge campaign organizations." One of them, the pre-election favorite, even had Paul Rupert as campaign manager, who a year and a half later became a crack organizer for the Resistance. "They had sixty, seventy people working for them. They would speak maybe four, five times a day. I would speak no more than twice a day," usually in long rap sessions in freshman dormitories. Debating his leading rival on the plaza, however, David came on with what he called a "huge brashness." He compared students to niggers and to southern sharecroppers, alike powerless and exploited.

For some reason Stanford students dug it. I'm really not sure what the process was. Perhaps the drama of it all. I mean, we did it with the big theatrical sense. We drove around conspicuously in a Volkswagen bus at late hours of the night. We were fuzzy, and very mysterious, rumored to do things like take drugs (before anybody was taking drugs). There was a certain amount of awe when we went out on that campus.

A band played on the plaza all day before the election.

Toward the end of the campaign, alarmed by indications that he might actually be elected, David talked more and more about the war. He also called fraternities "the biggest pile of crap in the university" at a meeting of the inter-fraternity council. But he won, by the largest majority in Stanford's history.

The beginning of the summer following his election he, Jeffrey Shurtleff, and two others rented a house in East Palo Alto which became "the commune." Dennis Sweeney, Ira Arlook, and their wives lived in another house nearby. "The houses made communication, and we began doing things like dropping acid together." At some point that summer "the houses" began to talk seriously about the draft. Until then most of the group had considered themselves conscientious objectors. Jeff was classified 1-O. David had filled out a Form 150 which had not been acted on. The Stanford sit-in against "the rank" fueled the discussion. David signed a We Won't Go pledge. "And then suddenly," as Dennis Sweeney recalled,

> about the time McNamara made that speech in Montreal, talking about the army being one of the primary forces for education of poor people and black people, it became obvious that it was pointless to say you "won't go" if you weren't being asked to.

There was great interest, therefore, when Mendy Samstein came through the Bay Area. Dennis and Mendy had worked together in Mississippi SNCC. When whites were no longer allowed by SNCC to do primary organizing, Mendy felt the need to translate their quality of work to the north and create, in Dennis' phrase, "a white SNCC." Dennis agreed that the kind of risk-taking that characterized SNCC was conspicuously absent in the northern movement, and he responded to Mendy's call for draft resistance. It seemed like the best issue on which to pull together serious white radicals for longtime work, "a net," as Dennis put it, "to pull through the campuses of the country and collect the people you really wanted to work with." Dennis, David, and others from the commune talked for a long time with Mendy.

But the time was not yet ripe for creating a draft-resistance

SNCC. Dennis, for one, remembered that he had not wanted to launch into noncooperation unless large numbers of people were ready to take the action without being pushed. He traveled with Mendy to Oregon and Washington, and found few people whose thinking had gone beyond applying for 1–O status.

> When you'd go out on strange campuses people weren't there, ready for the idea, like they were six months later. It was incredible, just that small amount of time, the difference that it made. It wasn't the kind of thing that you could feel good about persuading people to do, like selling. It was something that you just had to go and toss out and people were there, ready to say the same things back.

At those original meetings of the commune in the summer of 1966 there began to develop, David thought, "a synthesis of the style developed in the South, and what may have been my generation's contribution to the synthesis, centering around a vision of self." Part of that vision derived from existentialism.

> I remember Jeffrey and I went through a big Nietzsche thing: Nietzsche's talk about the *Übermensch,* the idea that man could build himself into anything he could see, talking about the base of power being the self, consciousness. I remember going through a very heavy existential thing, reading lots of Kierkegaard, lots of Sartre, lots of existential novels. At the time I ran for Stanford student body president I was taking a seminar in German existential literature.

His professor later congratulated him on the existential "authenticity" of his campaign.

A more fundamental part of the style was riding motorcycles.

> We were all into a motorcycle thing. Jeffrey had a big triumph 650. At the beginning of the summer I bought an old Broyle-Enfield 750. . . . It is the most existential position possible. I still use it in my rap. I have a conception of what you do in emergencies that's gained from motorcycles. There is no defense on a motorcycle. The brake is meaningless if you're in trouble. If you go for the brake the back end of your motorcycle swings right around and you're flat on the pavement. I remember hit-

ting corners, and hitting gravel, and the bike starting to go out from under you. The only defense you have at that point is to open up your accelerator and hope that your bike develops enough torque to pull you through.

We were riding life like a motorcycle, on top of it, opening it up as far as it would open. Nowadays there are all of these laws, you have to wear helmets, jackets. We never would wear any of that. The only way to ride a motorcycle was in your T shirt, with a pair of big dark glasses.

One bond between resistance and biking was that "part of riding a motorcycle is being an outlaw." The biker, roaring past startled motorists, blew people's minds somewhat in the manner of the later resistance organizer. "We would do things that people never thought of doing," David recalled. "You had this vision of opening up consciousness, and you were doing that every day to people, or trying to." "The spirit," in Jeff Shurtleff's words, "had a throttle."

There were also vulnerability and death. "We all had friends killed on motorcycles," David said.

We all knew that we could be killed. We all had gone through experiences on motorcycles when we knew we came close to dying. When you lay a motorcycle down it's very serious: if you're going at forty-five miles an hour, and you don't have a helmet, if your head hits the pavement you're a dead man. . . . The experience you have if you almost drop a bike is that you pull off, you start driving slower. You don't push the bike any more because it goes right up your spine, there's a real chill. I used to do things like get on my motorcycle and ride as hard as I could ride, taking every corner as fast as I could go, until I almost dropped it, and then I'd back off.

Part of it was seeing how far you could push yourself. Part of it was that heroic image of the man who always goes beyond his limits. It's an endurance thing. . . . I lived for virtually a year on three hours of sleep, cramming everything you could into your life, pushing yourself all the way to all the limits that you knew, and trying to push those limits back. Like on the bikes, trying to get so you could ride faster and faster, and be less and less scared.

After teasing death for a while you came to feel immune to it.

"Somehow," David went on, "you feel that nothing can touch you. It was where we began believing, and I really still believe, that you can't be stopped. We didn't think anything could stop us. And I still don't think anything can stop us." What mountain climbers call exposure—"that open and free sensation where there was nothing between you and the world," in David's words—was experienced by the bikers as a kind of power, a triumphant openness to anything which life might bring.

Motorcycling even contributed to the developing sense that wherever they were moving, they were moving together. "Riding a bike wasn't just a situation of being a loner," according to David.

> Lots of times you rode your bike alone, but bikes rode in packs too. . . . The most fun was getting five or six of these big bikes together, and come roaring into some town blasting your pipes and playing Hell's Angels, making sure there were no Hell's Angels around.

Much of life in the late summer of 1966 consisted of turning the day's events into the having and sharing of adventures.

> In that close relationship which we began to assume during that summer every movement into the outside world was seen as an adventure. Nobody went anywhere alone. If we were going to go somewhere someone would say, "Why don't we go to the beach?" And then someone else would say, "Why don't we drop some acid first?" And we'd all drop acid. And then we'd pile into the old Oldsmobile and stop at Dennis' house. And we'd hang around Dennis' house for an hour, every one laughing and preparing for the adventure and then we'd head out over the mountain to the beach.

Somehow, out of existentialism, motorcycles, the California countryside, and a deep opposition to the draft, came the "synthesis" David spoke of. It became a new style of nonviolence, very different from that preached and practiced by Quakers and members of pacifist groups. Looking back on his development three years later, after six months in prison, David summed up the elements of his own version of nonviolence.

My introduction to nonviolence was anything but in the Quaker meeting context. (I have, in my life, gone to one Quaker meeting and recall wanting to smoke for the entire time.) I like the Quaker style as practiced by a few of the more radical Quakers on the west coast (the only ones I have any lasting acquaintance with), but it isn't my own. It has always seemed a very rigorous personalism to me, like sexual abstinence or meditation.

The curious thing about my own attachment to nonviolence is that it came in the same period when I was reading Nietzsche, riding motorcycles, and visiting women late at night by the back door. It came in a time when (maybe as always) I was gobbling up experience. The nonviolence came as a function of a vision of adventurous, hell-bent, wild-west manhood. (After my election as Stanford student body president, the *Stanford Daily* described me as "swashbuckling.") What brought me to it, and keeps me pursuing it, was the idea of "truth" itself as a force. I see truth as rugged, solid, and big chunks, which was the way I want to live. To me it appears that a man must be twice as strong to do truth and what else would the young reader of Nietzsche want.

Nonviolence also became central to my life at a time of intense comradeship. I became overtly and full-speed nonviolent just as the commune was taking shape.

I remember being surprised at meeting others involved in "nonviolence." Most were old CNVA people who tended to be isolated, very moralistic, very puritanical and confined, which is why I could never handle the label "pacifist." It connotes a style that generally repulses me. There is nothing of the earth about it and I couldn't feel free in it. I saw (and see) nonviolence as a freedom and not a restriction to a given mode. Once again, I feel that in the idea of truth. What could be bigger and more expansive as a way of doing than truth? Or more manly?

. . . For me to adopt "pacifism" (meaning a whole style) would have meant giving up my neo-juvenile delinquent past, my days as a football player, and in many ways my love of people, not to mention my childhood fantasies. (I think my decision for nonviolence was to be a Gary Cooper who didn't *need* guns.) I think of all of these things as strengths, and out of them brewed up the style that makes sense to me. Out of them I've found a truth that is stronger without weapons than with. (In the gang I ran with in junior high school, carrying a weapon was considered "chicken shit.")

I had to find a way to reconcile my nonviolence with my long-held childhood dream of being a cowboy. What I came up with is as far from "pacifist" circles as it is from the Panthers. . . .

I . . . am for salty, rugged (Marlon Brando in *On the Waterfront*), virile nonviolence. (What is gentleness without strength?) I agree with Gandhi that the only true nonviolence is, in itself, an evidence of strength and is only a tool of the strong. (The *strong,* not those in the advantageous position.)

David led the Stanford delegation to the National Student Association's annual conference in August. The scene was a replay of the election campaign the previous spring.

We took a portable tape recorder with all the tapes we had made of our records. We took a lot of dope. At that time I had a full beard and hair down to my shoulders. Big wide leather belt, and moccasins with holes rubbed in the bottom of them. You can imagine how that hit NSA. We pulled in at seven o'clock in the morning, red-eyed from having driven all the way cross-country, and from having had a couple of more visions on the way across. We got a room in the place where everybody was staying and set up our tape recorder, playing it full blast, sort of to announce our presence. We didn't know anybody there and didn't know at all what they were into. We would stumble into the cafeteria and sit down at a table in the corner, and pretty soon half the people in the cafeteria would come over around our table, sort of watching us.

The conference was the first place David talked about noncooperation publicly.

We soon collected a sort of alliance of people from Pennsylvania, New York, California. One of the things was on the draft. We presented a resolution calling for complete noncooperation. I gave a speech and waited around to be arrested. We came within two votes of getting it passed. We lost 193 to 191.

By the end of the summer the inner life of the commune had become less frenetic, more religious. David began to read through Jung. "And I remember having, at the end or close to the end of

the summer, a vision, a physical sensation, about nonviolence."
Sitting in the back yard of the commune with his friend Jeff,
among five-foot weeds, an overgrown geranium, assorted cats,
and a huge fallen tree, there came an experience "of being stoned
. . . but much more than that: . . . seeing God."

Another such experience brought him to his decision not to cooperate with the draft.

> I was in the city staying in the apartment of a girl who was gone
> for the weekend, and I was sitting and watching the sun go down over
> San Francisco, and then sort of out of nowhere, in my mind, whatever
> the voice your mind talks to you with, saying, "You're going to refuse to
> cooperate with the draft."

If he had any doubts about the primeval authority of that voice,
which Jung had taught him to respect, they vanished when he
called his friend Jeff to tell him what he had decided. Jeff said he
had just made the same decision. David mailed his draft cards
back to his local board. A little later, Dennis announced that he
too would refuse to cooperate.

The next steps were unclear. David knew that, because he was
Stanford student body president, whatever he did as an individual
would be publicized and to that extent be "political." Dennis' situation was like that of most other resisters: only by acting with
others could his personal act of noncooperation take on political
significance.

> A lot of us knew inside that that's where we were going to be,
> but we didn't know exactly when we would be there. I was sure I was
> going to do it but I was sure I wasn't going to do it by myself, because I
> believed that to have an impact, to have some kind of political effect, it
> had to be a number of people doing it together.

Dennis felt in the fall that he did not yet have his own head together enough to give other people the strength they needed to
act. So he spent a few months working in Oregon, reading, sitting
by the fire, walking on the beach, doing a lot of thinking, and
talking it out with a friend.

Thinking back on his own experience that winter, and contrasting it with the experience of those who went to the Des Moines conference in August, it seemed to David that they were separated by different processes of thought. He and his friends were much less political, not mainly concerned with "objective social conditions." They were attached to noncooperation "as a means of expression of the lives we were trying to do. We were into the idea that your life was your art."

Meanwhile the commune, by now grown to about a dozen people, became more cohesive in its attitude toward the draft. By December 1966 everyone in the house was a noncooperator. "For us," David said, "resistance began when that community began." One of the things the commune did was investigate the experience of prison. They had talked that summer with Paul Seaver, and now they sought out others like Roy Kepler. Both Paul and Roy had been noncooperators and had served prison terms. Roy and Paul's father Benjamin, also a noncooperator, had formed a Committee for Draft Resistance the previous April. Talking with each other about their fears, the commune members shared them and so diminished them. After oscillating between feeling horror at prison and playfully making light of it they came to what they felt to be a realistic view.

In January David was called to Fresno for a pre-induction physical. He was the first in the commune to whom "anything had happened." Two weeks after the physical a 1–Y classification card arrived in the mail. After another two weeks he returned the card, having found the "energy" to do so after seeing slides of the destruction in North Vietnam taken by Felix Greene.

Also in February David resigned as student body president. "Looking back on it, I realize I had to stop doing that before I could get into organizing resistance." But the decision was also prompted by a belief that it would stimulate Stanford students to act for themselves rather than acting, vicariously, through a representative. Reading Jung's autobiography, *Memories, Dreams, Reflections,* one evening, David put the book down, wrote a letter of resignation, and took it over to the campus newspaper.

Early in March Lennie Heller and Steve Hamilton came from Berkeley to meet with David and Dennis. For the first time,

David and Dennis encountered people from another place who wanted to do the same thing they did, and that made it possible to envision resistance as an organized political process. Previously David had kept aloof from political organizers: at the NSA conference he had debated with Allard Lowenstein, interpreting the experience as a final break with the liberalism Lowenstein represented; during the winter he had discussed Bay Area draft activity with Mario Savio and Bettina Aptheker from Berkeley, but rejected this opening to the Left when Mario made it clear that he favored staying out of the army by any means necessary. Lennie and Steve, however, in Dennis' words,

> were two cats who were talking exactly about the idea we had had the previous summer, and not only were they talking about it, but they had some literature which they'd already printed up, and it had this name: it was The Resistance. They wanted to know when would be the first day. The feeling I had that day was, yeah, now is the time.

As David recalls that moment:

> They came about eight o'clock in the morning and we sat around and talked. The talk was life-sharing. We all wanted to get a feeling of what kind of people the other people were. We smoked a lot of dope and everybody was rapping about their hopes and dreams, and what they did every day, and what kind of music they liked; and we played some of our music and they talked about some of their music. It was almost like a cultural exchange, a meeting of two gangs. Hamilton was very quiet. He sat behind Lennie; Lennie did all the talking; Lennie was the front man. I remember digging Lennie. We all dug each other and we said, "Well, we're going to do it."

If anyone was David's match for prolific and provocative oratory it was Lennie. In the summer of Resistance organizing, David talked his way up and down the west coast, but Lennie talked his way across the country to Boston.

At that first meeting David, Dennis, Lennie, and Steve set October 16 as the day they would ask others to join them in a mass turn-in of draft cards. The four felt that a distant date would give people time to make a considered decision. They decided also to call for the return of cards rather than their burning because to burn a card was to destroy the evidence of one's act.

At the April 15 National Mobilization march in San Francisco David was one of the speakers. He remembers that it was Eldridge Cleaver's first public speech, and that he (David) was the only speaker not in suit and tie. David announced the existence of the Resistance and the target date of October 16, 1967. A leaflet was passed out:

WE REFUSE—OCTOBER 16

The Resistance is a group of men who are bound together by one single and clear commitment: on October 16 we will hand in our draft cards and refuse any further cooperation with the Selective Service System. By doing so we will actively challenge the government's right to draft American men for its criminal war against the people of Vietnam. We of the Resistance feel that we can no longer passively acquiesce to the Selective Service System by accepting its deferments. The American military system depends upon students, those opposed to war, and those with anti-Vietnam war politics wrangling for the respective deferments. Those opposed to the war are dealt with quietly, individually and on the government's terms. If they do not get the deferments, they must individually find some extra-legal alternative. A popular last resort is Canada, and those who go to Canada must be politically silent in order to stay there. Legal draft alternatives are kept within reach of elite groups—good students, those who are able to express objection to all war on religious grounds, and those with the money to hire good lawyers. For the majority of American guys the only alternatives are jail or the army. While those who are most opposed to the war have been silenced, the system that provides the personnel for war crimes continues to function smoothly.

Many who wish to avoid the draft will, of course, choose to accept deferments; many, however, wish to do more than avoid the draft. Resistance means that if the government is to continue its crimes against humanity, it must first deal with our opposition. We do not seek jail, but we do this because as individuals we know of no justifiable alternative and we believe that in time many other American men will also choose to resist the crimes done in their names.

After schools closed for the summer, David and Dennis traveled to Los Angeles, San Jose, Portland, Seattle, and other west-coast communities. They attended the sentencing of resister Malcolm Dundas in Los Angeles. They went to the northwest and met Ken Swanson and Bill Vandercook. (A ninety-year-old Wobbly stood up at one of their meetings and said that in seventy years of politics he had learned one thing: "Don't ever send the members of your organization to jail.") They would find someone prepared to "do it" and then spend time with him.

I remember hours at Ken Swanson's playing guitars, and auto-harps, and talking, and making merry with each other, and trying to create a relationship before you left. Part of the process was creating a sense of intimacy between us which, whether we articulated it or not, we felt was the basis of our organization. I don't think we consciously understood it. Part of it was reinforcement of ourselves, and part of it was instinctively feeling that that closeness had to be there for the thing to function.

Notes to Chapter Six

This account of the Palo Alto Commune and the origin of the Resistance is drawn from three conversations: Paul Rupert and Staughton Lynd (January 1, 1969); Dennis Sweeney and Staughton Lynd (March 12, 1969); and David Harris, Joan Baez Harris, Dennis Sweeney, Connie Fields, Alice Lynd, Bob Freeston, Kerry Berland, and Staughton Lynd (March 12–13, 1969). It is supplemented by memories of meetings with Lennie Heller, David Harris, and Dennis Sweeney by Michael Ferber. Letter from David Harris to Staughton Lynd (December 20, 1969).

CHAPTER SEVEN

CADRE

No one who was part of the anti-war movement then will forget the months from April to October 1967. The war was escalating steadily. President Johnson seemed inured to all criticism and immune to all challenges. Draft calls were high, and it was widely believed that under the new draft law students would be called up in substantial numbers. At the same time the movement was growing. The demonstrations in New York City and San Francisco on April 15 had been larger than anyone expected. The card burning in Sheep's Meadow had brought protest to a new and more serious level, to resistance. Talk of massive civil disobedience was heard even from previously reluctant liberals. Martin Luther King had joined the antiwar movement and had agreed to co-sponsor Vietnam Summer, a national coordinating committee which promised help and money even to radical antidraft groups. The battle lines were drawn, people were joining up in droves, the cause was clear and just, and the target was an unyielding and unattractive man who had come increasingly to embody all responsibility for the war.

To the exhilaration and fever spreading through the movement a desperate note was added in April and May. From several sources that sounded reliable came the report that Johnson was planning to declare war against North Vietnam and drastically escalate the fighting—invade across the DMZ, bomb the dikes, destroy Haiphong, or use nuclear weapons. The rumor made sense in view of the military stalemate and the rising impatience of the American public. Reliable or not, it was bruited broadly across the country, and many in the movement believed it or were shaken by the possibility that it was true. The June War in the Middle East, it was claimed, altered U.S. plans for a declaration, but as the summer went on the disquiet resumed.

Sheep's Meadow in April 1967 and the draft refusal of heavyweight boxing champion Muhammad Ali (Cassius Clay) two weeks later raised the possibility of a genuine resistance movement in a black and white coalition large enough to shake the country's commitment to the war. That possibility was posed gravely by spokesmen for the liberal establishment, not just by radical visionaries. Tom Wicker, in a *New York Times* column called "Muhammad Ali and Dissent," asked what would happen

> if all young men of draft age took the same position?
> What, indeed, would happen if only, say, 100,000 young men flatly refused to serve in the armed forces, regardless of their legal position, regardless of the consequences?
> A hundred thousand Muhammad Alis, of course, could be jailed. But if the Johnson Administration had to prosecute 100,000 Americans in order to maintain its authority, its real power to pursue the Vietnamese war or any other policy would be crippled if not destroyed. It would then be faced not with dissent but with civil disobedience on a scale amounting to revolt.

Wicker went on to say that "given the difficulties of organization and the personal and social dangers to all involved," such a movement "is unlikely to develop at all."

Three days later, however, Wicker's senior colleague James Reston revealed that the Administration was worried about college students refusing induction on the scale Wicker envisioned. Student deferments would continue, Reston stated, because it was feared "high in the Administration" that

> abolition of all or most college deferments might lead to massive defiance among undergraduates. The estimate here is that if college students were called like any other nineteen-year-olds, as many as 25 per cent of them might refuse to serve.

One of the Sheep's Meadow card burners commented two years later: "This was [the] first establishment acknowledgement of our existence. It cheered us all up."

And as the establishment began to pay attention, the group calling itself the Resistance, at first only a handful of men, a few thousand leaflets, a single tactic, and a visionary style, was already laying plans for the most serious and most audacious antidraft demonstration in this generation.

This chapter and the next are about two antidraft groups that joined the Resistance. One of them, CADRE, was already functioning when it got word of the new plan, while the other, New England Resistance, was created in response to it. They were different in other ways, working with different styles of organizing and speaking, and in cities with different atmospheres and possibilities. That is one reason we choose to discuss them—not because they are "typical" of the thirty or forty groups that joined the Resistance, if any groups could be. Another reason is that we each knew one of them well. Staughton Lynd was a friend, observer, and occasional participant in CADRE, and Michael Ferber was an organizer and full-time activist in New England Resistance.

Gary Rader, the Green Beret who burned his draft card at Sheep's Meadow in New York, was not only the most famous of the original CADRE activists, but probably the most zealous and energetic. As the "chief nag" of the Chicago group, his story is a good place to begin.

Gary was a student at Northwestern in the summer of 1965 when his draft board classified him 1–A. That fall he joined a Special Forces Reserve unit and began part-time training. But in the spring he read Green Beret Donald Duncan's article in *Ramparts* magazine condemning the U.S. Special Forces in Vietnam and grew disillusioned with the war and his probable role in it.

> Then, in the fall of 1966, I went on active duty. I was sent to Ft. Bragg, North Carolina, for the first ten weeks. Ft. Bragg happens to be the home of the Regular Army Special Forces. While I was there I spoke to a great number of Green Berets who were Vietnam returnees. Many of them quite candidly reinforced what Duncan had said. When I pressed them as to why they still supported the war, I usually got one of two responses.

The first was that the correctness of the war was not their business, that they were simply soldiers obeying orders from civilians who are supposed to decide such things. What a horrible idea, especially to be held by those who do the killing! But I fear it may be widespread. The other response was the "well, the peasants and the common men have been deluded by communism, don't really know what's good for them, aren't ready for democracy and must be trained" argument. I felt that this piece of thinking was an unbelievable act of arrogance on their part: first to assume that the American governmental system was right for the Vietnamese, irrelevant of cultural and political differences; second to presume to tell the Vietnamese peasant that we know better what is good for him than does he.

However, some of the Green Berets not only reinforced what Duncan had said, but openly said that they felt the war was wrong. A few said that they would refuse to be shipped back to Vietnam. I was even informed of a rebellion by several men in a combat platoon, who one day all refused to fight any longer against the VC. Strangely, no news of this was ever released to the American public.

Back at Northwestern in January 1967, now in the Reserve, Gary became as troubled over his military training as he was over the war where it might be put to use.

Let me give you an example of this abasement and loss of all dignity. In my reserve unit, during sessions of long, punishing, physical training for the recruits, if a person's body finally gives out, he is sometimes forced to go up in front of his fellow recruits, lie on his back, wave his arms and legs in the air while yelling, "I am a dying cockroach, I am a dying cockroach." His fellow recruits meanwhile laugh and berate him. Does this sound like part of a harmless fraternity hell week? It's not. It's part of a systematic campaign to destroy one's self-respect and self-confidence, to make you into a mindless, vicious automaton. What kind of institution can produce these things?

Gary, who had never been in a fight,

who had walked away from fights time after time as a child, was enormously aggressive, pugnacious, belligerent, and ready to fight at any time. I had learned how to maim or kill a person with my hands and feet in a few seconds, and I was damned proud of it. Suddenly, one day I realized what had happened to me, and was disgusted. I am not as of this moment a pacifist, but the Army, having given me a full appreciation of violence, has turned me towards non-violence better than any other experience in my life.

So here sits Gary Rader, in his reserve unit in February and March, watching the new recruits undergoing this treatment, feeling so deeply for them that he is sometimes drawn to tears, feeling so disgusted at the Army that he sometimes has a psychosomatic reaction and is sick to his stomach. He is unable to correct or lessen any of the horrors. Increasingly, he can no longer stand the thought of this happening to himself or to any of his fellow human beings. He especially cannot stand the idea of anyone being drafted and forced to undergo such a process.

For Gary, intellectually opposed to the war and viscerally outraged at the degradation of military training, the final straw came at a Reserve meeting in April. The commandant announced that henceforth if any reservist came to a meeting wearing long hair, he would be forced to wear a pair of diapers as well.

I realized now is the time. On the morning of April 15th, wearing my uniform covered with a black ski jacket to avoid getting busted, I got in contact with a leader of the Cornell contingent. Around 11:30 I appeared out of the crowd, removed my jacket, placed my beret on my head at the correct angle, and burned my draft card.

Two days later I wrote a letter of resignation to my company commander, informing him that I was quitting the Army and that I would no longer attend any meetings of the reserve unit.

Gary was not the only one from Chicago at Sheep's Meadow; others were John Dolan, Dennis Riordan, Don Tylke, Erwin Feldman, and Jeremy Mott. When they returned home they got in touch with each other through an attorney to talk about mutual defense and support when they were arrested and prosecuted. They felt they had little time. But when several weeks went by and nothing happened they began planning a permanent antidraft group. By this time Dennis' roommate Rick Boardman had joined the group, and before long Kerry Berland, Jeff Falk, and five or six others were also involved.

Jeremy and Rick were both Quakers and had secured 1–O status with little trouble. Jeremy was already working at his alternative service job when the war "moved me from one form of radical disaffiliation to another." In June he wrote the Illinois Deputy Director of SSS:

> Our draft seems to me to be a fantastic game, dividing and classifying people into arbitrary groups for our war machine. It is a dreadful game, because the losers become slaves, murderers, or dead men. Even though I am winning this game, since I am being allowed to stay out of the military, I refuse to play any longer.

Rick was in the process of finding a job acceptable to his board when he too felt he could no longer play the game. He wrote to his board the same spring:

> When my claim as a conscientious objector was recognized I was pleased and began to think that perhaps we had a very "reasonable" system of conscription after all. I found myself thinking that it's a very good system of conscription that "allows" a man to try to help his fellows to live constructively instead of destructively. I had failed to stop to question by what authority it came to be that a man should have to justify this creative inclination to his draft board. I had failed to realize that my deferment as a CO was a convenient way by which my resistance to conscription and the military (and the resistance of thousands like me) was effectively silenced. I had failed to acknowledge that my claim as a conscientious objector was only begrudgingly given to me because my "credentials" were good, because I was articulate, because my education had made it easy for me to produce a convincing defense of my desire to live peaceably and lovingly: in short, because I fell within a certain small, carefully defined group to whom the government felt it was both wise and safe to give deferments: wise, because otherwise this small group might raise some embarrassing questions about the legitimacy of conscription and militarism, and safe because the group is small enough so as to have little influence on the populace at large.

Kerry Berland and Jeff Falk had both joined the sit-in against "the rank" at the University of Chicago, had boycotted the SSS exam, and had refused to send their class ranks to their local boards. Each was dismayed that most of the students who sat-in also took the test. The following fall, when the We Won't Go group formed on campus (which Jeff helped start), they were again disappointed, this time by the many students who signed the pledge and yet balked at noncooperation. Both felt the need to do more, but both were in doubt, personally and strategically, which way to turn. In the summer of 1966, Jeff recalled, "a white guy who used to work with SNCC in the South visited the U of C and talked to a friend of mine," about a mass card turn-in. But "it was not something I would do unless there was a large number of people involved, unless he could get commitments." Kerry also hesitated. Both filled out CO forms. But in the spring, they each joined CADRE, and eventually returned their cards.

Bob Freeston was deeply impressed by the We Won't Go conference in Chicago, December 1966.

> Two speakers there particularly affected me: David Mitchell, who talked very quietly and was not a very good speaker, talked about the German people during World War II; and Jim Bevel, whose fiery oratory hit me at the gut level. And then I came home and knew I was pushed over the cliff and at that point it was a clear break and I decided to refuse induction.

But it was hard to know how to express that decision. Bob fiddled around, as he put it, talked with friends at Madison and Ann Arbor, went to the April 15 march but "didn't want to destroy my draft card because it was a classic thing that would turn people off, and it did." In May he was called for a physical, and at that time he decided to refuse cooperation. His letter to his local board drew a parallel between the Vietnam war and "another long 'difficult' guerrilla war":

> While in VISTA I worked for a year in a Pima Indian Village. In that year I learned a different perspective on American history. Many

American Indians have a deep distrust of White America. It comes from better than 300 years of contact with the white man. During all that time there have been varying programs to get rid of the Indian. Today we call for his assimilation into white society. By this we mean we want him to disappear. This is a more humane form of the policies of extermination we once had. There was great propaganda and sloganry surrounding stealing of Indian lands and shipping tribes off to barren reservations. Defensive actions and isolated attacks by Indians were used in the newspaper propaganda of the day to justify the massacres that the U.S. Army carried out. The army also conducted the forced marches, starvation and the deliberate introduction of smallpox—a good Indian was a dead Indian.

CADRE became distinguished among Resistance groups for its mastery of the chief genre of Resistance literature, the Epistle to the Draft Board.

The expanded group (not yet called CADRE) was just getting its bearings, setting up a counseling program, circulating a We Won't Go statement, and giving speeches on noncooperation, when Lennie Heller showed up in May. As Bob Freeston recalled,

I was at a Student Mobe [Student Mobilization] conference here in Chicago and at the conference people came in from the West Coast who turned out to be Resistance people. It was sort of a crucial meeting. The draft session was just loaded with people and it went round and round in circles about organizing the new working class and organizing colleges and organizing this and organizing that. Lennie Heller got up—he was one of the guys that originally started Resistance out at Berkeley—and so he gave a speech about how this discussion that had been going on for hours was a lot of bullshit and people should talk about what they were going to do. The discussion went right back again and he just got up and left the meeting. And about a dozen people drifted out of the meeting: Lenny Brody from New York, Fred Rosen from New York, guys who started WDRU [Wisconsin Draft Resistance Union], Gary Rader and myself, people who started Resistance groups in their own cities. And the discussion we had was very much different in character from the discussion we left. We talked about specific programs and the kinds of things we wanted to set up, action kind of stuff, and they were non-doctrinaire people.

David Greenberg's reaction to the Resistance idea was less positive. About a week after the Student Mobilization conference a meeting was arranged between Lennie, Dickie Harris (another Bay Area Resistance organizer, a black), and some Chicago people. David felt that most of those who heard them were unimpressed, and did not welcome the idea of returning draft cards.

> Partly I think this was a reaction to their personalities: male chauvinist in the extreme, talking about noncooperation as a way of proving one's masculinity, just as the Army talks about making a man out of you. But there was a feeling among some that it was better to burn cards than to return them, because it was silly to give the government evidence that could be used against you. With only a few exceptions, most of the draft acts that CADRE people engaged in during its first summer were burnings not turn-ins.

Lennie, to be sure, presented the Resistance rationale with swagger, with a combination of earthy humor (he changed his first name in honor of Lennie Bruce) and reckless *machismo*. He managed to alienate quite a few as he crusaded across the country, but he also fired the imagination of a handful who were seeking something new, and who went on to organize Resistance groups. Perhaps because the "west coast style" clashed with the more serious, intellectual temperament of the midwest resisters, only one person from the Chicago group decided to devote himself to October 16.

After several private gatherings the group held a public meeting in a coffee house run by John Dolan called "The Other Side." SDS sent a delegation. A minor disagreement over the wording of a fund-raising letter led to a major debate over nonviolence. One or two from the antidraft group sided with the SDSers against nonviolence, but they were outvoted, or out-talked, and they left the meeting. (Among those who walked out was Jeff Segal, who had spoken at the December We Won't Go conference and had already refused induction.)

But CADRE wished to include SDS members who were not pacifists, so it adopted tactical nonviolence and imposed no ideology. It sought escalated confrontations, militant disruptions of the draft, and tight discipline. "We speak of squads, escalation, campaigns," Gary Rader wrote in *Liberation* that summer. "The terminology is no accident—it fits our attitude. We are no longer interested in merely protesting the war; we are out to stop it." The name CADRE was finally chosen for the group of which Gary Rader was already drill sergeant. Gary, who dreamed up the name, considered it a brilliant acronym (Chicago Area Draft Resisters) except for the last letter which stumped him for weeks. Then at two or three A.M. one night Rick Boardman was awakened by a delirious ex-Green Beret who shouted over the phone, "I've got it! The second letter of 'Resisters' is 'E'!"

In the summer CADRE was busy, though not with plans for October 16. CADRE people picketed the induction center when the buses full of inductees arrived, leafleted draft boards, joined other peace groups in their demonstrations (sometimes burning a draft card), and gave speeches on campuses, street corners, and coffee house stages. They were frequently arrested. They also made overtures to the black community, helped arrange a black antidraft conference, and raised money for SNCC.

CADRE's attempt to reach the black and white working-class youths who were not in college and for whom resistance most naturally meant, not noncooperation, but induction refusal or draft evasion, was in step with the thinking of the larger movement. In June 1967 Congress made the 2–S deferment mandatory for college students. For two years college students had been wondering whether they would be drafted and in ever-larger numbers preparing to resist if called. Now it seemed clear that undergraduate students at least would not have to go. For those thus deferred to say "we won't go" now lost all meaning. Accordingly, many draft organizers concluded that they should turn their attention to the nonstudents actually being drafted.

Even before passage of the new draft law more emphasis on off-campus work was urged by many voices. The Draft Resistance Clearing House, established by several Resistance groups at a meeting in New York City the day after the mass burning on Sheep's Meadow, stated in its first newsletter:

At this time most draft resistance activities are located on the campus. When summer comes and most students leave the campuses, the

Movement will be extremely vulnerable and scattered. We feel that it is necessary to relocate draft resistance activities to the urban areas where students will probably be located, and where organizing can really begin.

Writing in the *National Guardian,* a black antidraft organizer commented: "Community organizing has been a conspicuous weakness of the antidraft movement. Members of antidraft groups tend to be antiwar college students." He added that many antidraft groups were reaching out to the community with the help of money from Vietnam Summer, the left-liberal effort to promote antiwar sentiment in new constituencies.

In midsummer draft resistance groups from all over the United States met for a weekend conference in Madison. The knottiest element in a much-tangled discussion was the conflict between campus-oriented and community-oriented organizers. One summary described the dispute this way:

> At the meeting were a number of organizers who had been working in black and white working class neighborhoods. They expressed the feeling that draft resistance, put in terms of a call to individual conscience, was of no appeal to the groups they worked among. Not that these groups were without conscience; the main point was that the Resistance, defined as giving up one's deferment and refusing induction, made no sense to them. In the ghetto and the poor white neighborhoods, opposing the draft meant beating it; get out however you can. "Anyone who gives up his student deferment is nuts." The meeting was split into two groups: the campus organizers favored the Resistance, the handing in of draft cards to force the government into a moral confrontation; the community organizers favored using opposition to the draft as an issue to reach those people away from the campus who actually were threatened by the draft.

From this point of view CADRE's decision to affiliate with the Resistance and to become midwestern coordinator for October 16 represented both a narrowing of programmatic focus and a reversion to a primarily student constituency. At first only Paul O'Brien was deeply interested in October 16. "After the call went out," Dianna Anderson remembered, "people started saying, 'I don't think we should spend very much time on it,' and Paul said, 'I'm going to spend all my time on it.' " With the help of a few others he put together a demonstration where two dozen cards were turned in and several got arrested. CADRE was impressed.

After October 16, making card turn-ins the heart of CADRE's work was no longer seriously questioned. A participant in the October 16 demonstration at the Chicago Federal Building said: "One thing that really surprised me was that almost as soon as I got there someone handed me a December 4 button, and I said, 'What's this?' 'Well, that's our next turn-in.' It had already been decided." David Greenberg commented: "From 150 in April to 1200 in October [the national total] seemed like a qualitative leap and gave the feeling that there was unlimited potential growth."

Notes to Chapter Seven

This account of CADRE is drawn primarily from a tape-recorded conversation (arranged by Staughton Lynd) with Rick Boardman, Kerry Berland, Bob Freeston, Dianna Anderson, Sheilah Dorcy, Jeff Falk, Michael Presser, John Welch, Carol Berland, and others, on February 16, 1969; and from letters to Staughton Lynd from David Greenberg (December 4, 1969; December 31, 1969), Dan Stern (January 16, 1970), and John Dolan (January 21, 1970). The tape of the February 16 conversation was transcribed by Bert Gall.

Rick Boardman's "Letter to Local Board #114" appeared in *Hear Ye* (Acton, Massachusetts, June 1967) and was reprinted by AFSC as a leaflet. It is also in Hugo Bedau, ed., *Civil Disobedience: Theory and Practice* (New York: Pegasus, 1969), 178–186.

The importance of the off-campus constituency was stressed in Robert L. Allen, "Draft Resisters Split on Strategy," *National Guardian,* June 24, 1967 and by Robert Pearlman, "Two Worlds of Draft Resistance," *Paper Tiger* (Cambridge, Massachusetts), spring 1968.

An account by Muhammad Ali of his reasons for refusing the draft is included in Alice Lynd, ed., *We Won't Go* (Boston: Beacon Press, 1968), 226–234.

 CHAPTER EIGHT

New England Resistance (by Michael Ferber)

Lennie Heller, who had agreed to organize all of the United States east of California, showed up in Boston in the late spring of 1967. The Boston Draft Resistance Group (BDRG) was then about a month old, had published its We Won't Go statement, opened a counseling office in Cambridge, and had begun to leaflet and picket the army base. Particularly the We Won't Go statement, but the other efforts as well, left the BDRG with the feeling they had already accomplished something new and difficult and were too busy following through and developing the acts and plans already initiated to give much attention to new ideas. But a meeting was arranged at Harvard, and a handful came to hear Lennie speak. Tom Shapiro, a law student who worked with draft resisters for the next two years, remembered the feeling of dismay that BDRG people felt when Lennie denigrated We Won't Go statements:

> There was something in the way he curled his lip and thickened his voice when he pronounced the words "We Won't Go" that turned people off. Here they had just published their statement and were looking around to see if they would all be thrown in jail for it, and this guy from Berkeley arrives to tell them they hadn't done anything and that the thing now was to turn in draft cards.

Lennie got little response. Months later, when he returned to Boston to find a large and thriving Resistance, he confessed he had been (and remained) baffled by the "Harvard style" that so contrasted with his own, which Norman Mailer well described in *Armies of the Night* as "cocky" and "knowledgeable." It was probably less style than differences in program, however, that ruled out a Resistance committee in Boston that spring, though some who heard Lennie at least felt challenged in their own commitment by "the latest blast from Berkeley," and one of them, Bob Talmanson, who had already refused induction, kept the Resistance idea alive through the summer.

Tally, as we all called him, was given a corner of the BDRG office but very little else in the way of support. Not an aggressive organizer or effective speaker, he made slight impression, and by the end of the summer he had little to show but a small list of names of interested people and tentative pledges for October 16.

Two Boston students, Bill Dowling and Alex Jack, drifted independently toward the Resistance by the end of the summer, hesitating initially because the prospects for October 16 looked poor, but ready to turn in their own cards. Bill, a graduate student in English at Harvard, became the "sparkplug" of the New England Resistance (or "chief nag" in the Chicago dialect) through his extraordinary capacity to work for anything he invested his commitment in. To borrow Axelrod's famous characterization of Lenin, Bill was a man "who for twenty-four hours of the day is taken up with the Resistance, who has no other thoughts but thoughts of the Resistance, and who even in his sleep dreams of nothing but the Resistance." Like Lenin, he would become consumed with the smallest details of postage and paste, as well as with grandiose schemes for future Resistance exploits. And like Lenin, he exerted a command over all decisions of the group that gathered around him that September, a situation that might have become disastrous but for the unanimity of purpose the group quickly developed. Unlike Lenin, however, Bill mixed madness with his method. He was touched with a spirit of reckless confidence, with visions of the effect his small band of draft-defiant supermen could have on the government and the armed forces. Such a forceful and magnetic spirit was important in the early days of the Resistance, when uncertainty and loneliness were greatest. The charisma of Bill Dowling, Lennie Heller, Gary Rader, and David

Harris in part accounts for the dramatic rise of Resistance groups after only a few months of organizing. But it also in part accounts for the equally dramatic lapses and collapses Resistance groups underwent when either the "strong men" left or the others rebelled. It also promoted a numerical instability, as many who may have thought too lightly on the act they entered into were led too much by a temporary fascination or faith in the group or its "leaders." As for Bill, without him there would have been no Resistance in Boston October 16, but with him, afterward, the slower democratic processes that began to develop in the now much larger community created tensions that made him leave it. He was a lone wolf, who could lead, but not join, his pack.

Alex Jack was a student at Boston University School of Theology. He was deeply experienced in the movement, both in the South, where he had narrowly escaped murder at the hands of white bigots, and at Oberlin College, where he had organized antidraft work while editing the college paper. In fact he had tried to organize a turn-in for the fall of 1966, but Oberlin was no more responsive to him then than it was to Peter Irons in 1961. His editorship led to a six-month assignment in 1967 to South Vietnam for the student press, where he flew with fighter pilots on strafing missions and made contacts with the university peace movement. He had also spent a year in India, and on his way home he stopped in Japan long enough to help arrange a Zengakuren demonstration against Ambassador Reischauer. Though already a legend, he was modest and quiet in behavior, almost inscrutable in his oriental calm. His personality was the opposite of Bill Dowling's, but he shared his passionate industriousness.

I made the third. I had known Bill for several months as a fellow Harvard graduate in English, and Alex and I had recently met through his well-known father Homer, whom I knew from his work in the Unitarian Universalist Association. Around the middle of September the three of us found ourselves picketing the Boston army base with BDRG and PLP members in support of four men who were up for induction. I introduced Bill and Alex, who discovered their mutual interest in October 16. Bill and I had already talked about noncooperation, but through the summer I had held aloof, waiting to see how my CO claim would turn out.

By September, however, I had grown increasingly angry over my draft hassles and the worsening news from Vietnam, so when Bill and Alex began talking about October 16, I offered to help. Within a few days I resolved to turn in my own card. I was 1–A, my CO claim rejected with an appeal pending, Bill was 2–S, Alex 4–D. As we talked in the car (driven by my roommate Donald Bobo, who to his own surprise joined us October 16) on the way home from the demonstration, we hatched ideas and our spirits soared.

We soon had a committee of seven or eight. Three were Bill's friends from Dartmouth, Ric Bogel, then a graduate in English at Yale (like Bill, concentrating on the eighteenth century, a fact which always seemed strange), Neil Robertson, and Steve Pailet,* both then working. All three were excellent jazz musicians, Ric on trombone, Neil on drums, Steve on bass. Another was Jim Harney, then in his final year of seminary for the Catholic priesthood. Better known later for his involvement in the Milwaukee 14 draft file burning, his decision to turn in his card was probably more serious than his decision to raid a draft board, for in the first he risked not only prison but rejection of his candidacy for the priesthood. Throughout the early months of the New England Resistance (NER) Jim was a stalwart and enthusiastic believer. The committee met or conferred by phone every day. Tasks were divided up. Alex was in charge of gathering support from seminarians, clergymen, and religious groups. I did most of the public speaking, not because I was in any sense the leader but because I was the best public speaker (I had the low-key "Harvard style"). And so on. Tally was not really part of the original group. Bill was frustrated working with him, and Tally's relaxed anarchistic outlook was offended by Bill's high-powered organizational drive. Matters were more or less taken out of Tally's hands, though he remained on friendly terms with the developing group. He became one of the first two to take "symbolic sanctuary" the following May.

In late September Alex suggested we hold the turn-in in a

---

* In the summer of 1969 Steve was murdered while driving his cab in Roxbury to make money for back Resistance debts.

church. We had come to expect five or six fantastic new ideas
from Alex each day, but this one turned us on much more than
the others. What better way to underscore the moral gravity of the
act we were embarking on than to hold it in a place of worship? It
was a little like confirmation or baptism: a rite of passage into
manhood, from slavery and "channeling" to the promised land of
peace and freedom. True, most potential resisters were not religious, but then neither was I in the usual sense, and I found the
idea compelling. And there were many seminarians who were
ready to join us. But what church? "Fat chance we'll find one,"
we agreed. But Alex did—his own, the Arlington Street Church.

The Arlington Street Church grew out of a congregation started
by William Ellery Channing, the "founder" of modern American
Unitarianism, a century and a half ago. Channing had been a
moderate radical, not only in his unorthodox theological views
but also in his social views, which embraced women's rights and
abolitionism. The Arlington Street Church since Channing's day
has intermittently maintained his progressive spirit, especially
during the last decade, under the leadership of Rev. Jack Mendelsohn. During the year preceding the Resistance service, for example, the church had endured a rain of rocks and eggs for spon-
soring a peace rally and a storm of protest for allowing a sermon
by Allen Ginsberg, who solemnly suggested that Bostonians
ought to dance nude in the Common. When the Resistance asked
Mendelsohn for the main sanctuary for a service of mass civil disobedience, Mendelsohn said, "Certainly. Do you want me to take
part?" He did.

For the main speech Alex suggested William Sloane Coffin,
chaplain of Yale University, who had organized a clergy group
against the war and had been advocating the revival of the old
practice of "sanctuary" for conscientious resisters and deserters.
Ric Bogel asked him to preach and receive cards from resisters,
and he agreed, a little jealous that it should be the Unitarians who
came through first, not the Presbyterians. "Unitarians are a little
thin in theology," he said, "but pretty thick in ethics." Alex's
uncle, Rev. George H. Williams, Hollis Professor of Divinity at
Harvard, agreed to speak and even issue the call for the cards.
After the service a divinity student who had turned in his card

claimed he felt more moved by this scholarly church historian, not known for radicalism, than by the more brilliant activist Coffin. Father Robert Cunnane offered to represent the Catholics. He later joined Jim Harney, whose card he received October 16, in the draft raid in Milwaukee. We were never able to find a Rabbi, though one offered and then reneged. At Father Cunnane's request, we invited Hilary Putnam, professor of philosophy at Harvard, to represent the atheists. I was chosen to represent the Resistance itself, and Alex was to read a Vietnamese prayer.

Meanwhile the small band was busy organizing. Proof that individuals make history only when history is ready to be made seemed to grow daily, as only half a dozen of us easily galvanized a dozen organizations and five thousand people into action for October 16. When the BDRG saw several people seriously committed to noncooperation, and heard a plan involving churches, famous people, press conferences, and the like, they offered their support, which came tangibly in the shape of marshals for the march before the service and—this a surprise—several more draft cards. I gave a couple dozen speeches or raps, mainly at universities, and everywhere found an enthusiastic response; everywhere but Harvard SDS, anyway, which after I appealed at three meetings for help finally expressed solidarity by formally endorsing us. We put their name on the Order of Service. Several religious groups responded to Alex's prodding and issued calls to their membership to take part in the march, rally, and ceremony. A faculty group of several hundred placed a large ad in the *Boston Globe* supporting the Resistance. The Boston University *News* endorsed us. We grew hot.

Just why we caught hold is an interesting question. Of course we were operating in the rarefied and volatile atmosphere of universities, not the ghetto or white working-class districts. Several of the original organizers, moreover, had extensive organizational connections, so the task was often a matter of inducing existent groups to shift their focus rather than building up a whole structure from scratch. Still, the network the Resistance built up was substantial, and it formed the basis for all large-scale city-wide demonstrations for the next year, with the exception of the official Martin Luther King memorial sponsored by the mayor and the cardinal (and which was smaller than the one organized by the Resistance a few days earlier). And though it was largely to students and suburban whites that the Resistance was so attractive, the attraction was deep and widespread among them. It was probably due in part to the same factors that led resisters to turn in their cards in the first place. The war was worsening and no "political" hope was in sight: neither Kennedy nor McCarthy had made a move, and while there had been a huge march in New York City the opinion polls were still noncommittal. The spirit of resistance was spreading, but slowly, and something was needed to spark it, make it peak and reach focus. Within the movement there was dismay over the exhaustion of new ideas and dread that violence would come to seem the only viable strategy. Factionalism was on the rise. The only other hopeful prospect was the Pentagon demonstration, but until a few weeks before it took place there was no confidence that it would be nonviolent. The Resistance presented itself: new, confident, and brave, respectable yet audacious, nonviolent (or at least unviolent), and full of energy. It dropped like a crystal into a supersaturated atmosphere. For a year or so, in Boston, we were the center of attention.

Thirty thousand leaflets got passed out, mostly on campuses, written in the low-key style that came to be characteristic of the early Resistance. There was a torn draft card, an American eagle without a head, a paragraph about what would happen on October 16, a pledge form, and this quote from Albert Camus' *Neither Victims nor Executioners*:

> Whether these men will rise or not I do not know. It is probable that most of them are even now thinking things over, and that is good. But one thing is sure: their efforts will be effective only to the degree they have the courage to give up, for the present, some of their dreams, so as to grasp the more firmly the essential point on which our very lives depend. Once there, it will perhaps turn out to be necessary, before they are done, to raise their voices.

The rally on Boston Common Monday was larger than anything Boston had seen yet: about five thousand people. We were elated. Howard Zinn, Noam Chomsky, Nick Egleson (former national SDS president), and Ray Mungo (of Liberation News Service) all spoke, after which the crowd marched to the church.

Inside there was a hushed, tense atmosphere. People felt a sense of purpose and power, of awe perhaps, and most important, of solidarity. Would a true community grow out of today's events, durable and resilient enough for a long struggle? The scene was set for a momentary and climactic act: would it be the final act or the first of many? In the service we passed out bread to symbolize our community, but would there be bread tomorrow and next week and all the days to come while FBI agents lurked, draft boards processed induction orders, and one by one we refused induction? Church services and bread cannot sustain a community without shared ideas and common work, and where would these come from? We could not imagine then how vital these questions would become for us, as the community we inaugurated in the service would lapse and surge in the months ahead, reaching a great peak and finally dwindling to nothing over a year and a half later. That day, in the church, we felt together.

The sermons that Coffin and I gave became the basis for our inclusion in the Spock conspiracy case three months later. But probably the most moving speech that day was by Jim Harney, who found in the lives of two German Catholics the courage that might cost him his priesthood:

> These last few weeks, I have been doing some reading about those men of faith who spent their last days and years in jail during World War II. Their witness has affected my life enormously. Father Alfred Delp, for example, a German priest who died in a concentration camp, wrote:
>
> The most pious prayer can become a blasphemy if he who offers it tolerates or helps to further conditions which are fatal to mankind, which render him unacceptable to God, or weaken his spiritual, moral, or religious sense.
>
> The German peasant, Franz Jägerstätter, who died in solitary protest, wrote:
>
> For what purpose did God endow all men with reason, and free will, if, in spite of this, we are obliged to render blind obedience, or if, as so many also say, the individual is not qualified to judge whether this war

started by Germany is just or unjust? What purpose is served by the ability to distinguish between good and evil?

For me, these words from the past have great meaning: my faith is put on the line, and above all, my life is directed to the cross-roads of the living. They are hard words to live, for they point to the very crucibles of life and death. Now I must take a stand on behalf of the living.

When Rev. Williams gave the call for the draft cards, no one knew what would happen. Maybe fifty, or seventy-five? A trickle of men started down the aisle to the row of men or to the candle. The aisle soon filled, the line grew longer, the doors were opened to let in those from outside who wanted to join. The organ played, flash bulbs popped, and TV cameras hummed away. It must have been twenty minutes before it was over. More than sixty burned their cards at the candle, and over two hundred handed them in. The New England Resistance was born.

One of the best speeches in the rally before the service had been Nick Egleson's. He spoke of the anguish we feel in the movement, anguish that is born of powerlessness and uncertainty:

> We are . . . revolutionaries without a revolution. We have no base of power to give us an alternative to moral acts, no route on which an end to this war can be a milestone, no evidence to give us hope that there will be a role for the agents of change we feel ourselves to be.

He then spoke of the temptations that beset those who are anguished:

> The first temptation, one which now affects the draft resistance movement, is to measure actions in the movement by a code of individual conduct. Some refuse to enter the army because no moral man could engage in combat in Vietnam; some dissociate themselves from the Selective Service System because association with the machinery of slaughter is unconscionable; others assume the jeopardy of draft refusal even if they are not subject to the draft because no moral man can let others suffer injustice alone.

> In this country such an individual code easily becomes the primary or only standard for political conduct. This country's individualist ethic

points in this direction; the religious frame of reference into which much political dissent has been pushed by repression and political intolerance leads in this direction; and the absence of widespread political experience closes off the possibility of other, political, standards. . . .

Equipped only with a standard of individual conduct and a calculus of right and courage we lose sight not only of the many kinds of change needed but also of the motivation for change. So equipped, we easily confine our organizing to the campus. People there are not immediately threatened by the draft. One and only one main force can move them to assume a jeopardy in order to protest it: a standard of individual conduct. We feel we must organize the campus.

But all the while the men of Charlestown and South Boston and Riverside, of Roxbury and Dorchester and of the working-class parts of cities all over the country are threatened by the draft and are more gently coerced by the security of enlistment. . . .

Our solution must be to begin to organize those most threatened by the US armed forces. How many people gave out information about the October 16 rally in Boston in poor and working-class neighborhoods? Who put up posters speaking the language of those communities? Who tried to counter, thereby, the image the press promotes of us as hippies, cowards, and peace finks? Who suggested in those places that we—not the US Army—speak to people's immediate and long-range interests?

The first temptation Nick described was a real one to the Resistance, and I tried to bring home his point in a different way in the speech I gave during the service, though I could not accept his tacit near-equations of "moral" with symbolic, personal, middle-class self-sacrifice and "political" with practical, mass, working-class self-interest. I am not sure my religious terms would have been adequate for all the parts of Nick's argument, but they seemed to meet the problem uppermost in my mind then, the conflict between private "virtue" and public engagement:

We are brought to a third difference among us. Earlier today Nick Egleson spoke out against the kind of resistance whose primary motivation is moralistic and personal rather than political. He is saying that we must make ourselves relevant to the social and political condition of the world and must not just take a moral posture for our own soul's sake, even though that too is a risk.

To some extent this argument depends on terminology rather than fact. Today we have heard our situation described in religious terms, moral terms, political terms, legal terms, and psychological terms. Very few of us are at home in all these different modes of speech, and each of us habitually uses only one of them to talk and think in. But what is happening today should make it clear that these different modes of speech all overlap one another and they often all say the same essential things. Albert Camus, who struggled in a more serious Resistance than ours, believed that politics is an extension of morality, that the truly moral man is engaged in politics as a natural outcome of his beliefs.

To return to Nick's concern, the real difference is not between the moral man and the political man, but between the man whose moral thinking leads him to political action and the man whose moral thinking leads him no farther than to his own "sinlessness." It is the difference between the man who is willing to go dirty himself in the outside world and the man who wishes to stay "clean" and "pure."

Now this kind of "sinlessness" and "purity" is arrogant pride, and I think we must say No to it. The martyr who offers himself meekly as a lamb to the altar is a fool unless he has fully taken into account the consequences of his sacrifice not only to himself but to the rest of the world. We cannot honor him for his stigmata or his purple hearts unless he has helped the rest of us while he got them.

Reading these speeches again after two years I see in them the germ of the antagonism between the Resistance (or part of it) and SDS, but I also see the germ of a conciliatory dialogue. That the dialogue got little further is a permanent loss to the movement.

Notes to Chapter Eight

Jim Harney's speech has been circulated in mimeographed form, but as far as we know has not been published elsewhere. He wrote the preface to the new edition of Gordon Zahn's biography of Jägerstätter, *In Solitary Witness* (Boston: Beacon, 1968). Nick Egleson's speech was printed with small changes in *Paper Tiger* (Cambridge, Massachusetts)

November 1967. Michael Ferber's sermon, "A Time to Say No," was carried in several religious journals; in Jessica Mitford, *The Trial of Dr. Spock* (New York: Knopf, 1969; Vintage, 1970); and in Massimo Teodori, ed., *The New Left* (Indianapolis: Bobbs-Merrill, 1970).

CHAPTER NINE

The Call to Resist

"Adult" and feminine supporters of the draft resistance movement, unable to imitate the example of the resisters, have turned to a variety of tactics, of which the first has usually been a public statement of solidarity. Words alone, no doubt, have little impact beyond what they portend of future deeds, but statements in support of draft resistance gain some potency from the fact that, under the law, these words themselves may be considered deeds. If the words can be construed as having the intent of moving others to resist the draft, their author or speaker can be indicted for violating the same draft law that makes criminals out of resisters. Section 12 of the draft law reads, in part:

> Any person who . . . knowingly counsels, aids, or abets another to refuse . . . registration or service in the armed forces . . . shall, upon conviction in any District Court of the United States . . . be punished by imprisonment for not more than five years or a fine of not more than $10,000, or by both.

In the fall of 1964, A. J. Muste and other pacifists initiated the first statement in support of draft resistance during the Vietnam war, the "Declaration of Conscience Against the War in Vietnam." Several New York pacifist groups circulated it, and by August 1965, when it was delivered to the White House, it had garnered over four thousand signatures, including those of draft-resistance veterans Bayard Rustin and A. Phillip Randolph. Of its five resolutions, two had to do with military service:

> We encourage those who can conscientiously do so to refuse to serve in the armed forces and to ask for discharge if they are already in.
>
> Those of us who are subject to the draft ourselves declare our own intention to refuse to serve.

A note at the bottom warned signers of possible prosecution under section 12 of the draft law. There had in fact been much discussion of the wording of the "counseling" sentence. Paul Goodman, one of the signers, recalls insisting that the word "urge" in the original version be changed to "encourage," not because "urge" might be illegal, but on the moral grounds that older men (and women) had no right to coerce, entice, or in any way mislead younger men into an act that almost certainly means a long prison term. The clause "who can conscientiously do so" was included to make it doubly clear that no manipulation was intended; rather that, *after* an individual has decided in his conscience that he can no longer cooperate with the military, then the older supporters will encourage him to act according to his convictions. (It came out in the Spock conspiracy trial almost four years later that, in the opinion of the prosecutor and the judge, such encouragement, even of one who is "inwardly fixed" to disobey the law anyway, is just as illegal as outright incitement.)

The drafters of the Declaration were quite consciously imitating the French *"Manifeste des 121"* of the summer of 1960. That statement, called "Declaration Concerning the Right of Insubordination in the Algerian War," came to the support of the growing Young Resistance movement of draft refusal and desertion and had a substantial impact on public opinion and government policy. The Young Resistance movement was not as well known to its later American counterpart as its adult supporters were to theirs, although when Staughton Lynd read an account of the French struggle to the Chicago We Won't Go conference (December 1966) it made a deep impression. Only 121 people signed the French Declaration initially, but they were well-known intellectuals (in a country that respects intellectuals far more than

America does), not professional pacifists, and the country was already torn over the protracted and brutal colonial war so near to home. It is interesting to note, however, that the *Manifeste* stopped short even of encouragement:

> The undersigned . . . believing that they themselves, in their place and according to their means, ought to intervene, not to counsel men who have decided personally in the face of serious problems, but to demand of those who judge them that they mistake not the words and values of these young men, declare:
> —We respect and consider justifiable the refusal to bear arms against the people of Algeria.

Among the concerns of the group that met in New Haven in July 1966 was the mustering of support from those beyond the reach of the draft. The group asked Staughton Lynd to help organize such support, and he agreed. One of the signers of the first declaration, he had already felt the need for a new statement, stronger, more detailed in its argument, and better publicized.

He wrote his first draft August 14 while visiting Carl Oglesby, who had just finished his term as SDS national president. It included an explicit reference to the French manifesto, and had a broad list of acts of resistance the signer is asked to encourage: sending medical aid to the NLF and DRV, obstructing troop movements and munitions movements, refusing induction, refusing orders to fight in Vietnam, and refusing to pay income taxes. Carl felt they should claim earlier precedents, and American precedents, for acts of civil disobedience that were bound to offend or frighten even many of those who sincerely opposed the war. He listed Thoreau's tax refusal against the Mexican War, the abolitionists' defiance of the Fugitive Slave Law, and the imprisonment of Debs, Randolph, and others for opposing World War I. He included the French precedent, of course, as well as the most dangerous and noble precedent of modern times, the German resistance against the Nazis. The final statement, now twice as long as Staughton's original, included the same list of acts to "support and encourage." They both signed and began to circulate it. Their cover letter mentioned their hope to publish it in the fall with several hundred signatures.

Signature collecting went slowly, however, and the goal of fall publication was not reached. Neither Carl nor Staughton had the time needed to push the statement, and by the end of the year perhaps only fifty or so had signed. The closest it came to the public eye that fall was in the October 1966 *Liberation,* where Staughton, in a long editorial, elaborated and defended the six kinds of direct action promoted by the statement. On the points about refusal of induction and refusal to fight in Vietnam, he wrote " 'We Won't Go' remains the single best slogan around which to build opposition to the war, superior to 'Bring the Troops Home' because it asks people to change their lives." He thus touched on the two poles of the movement, the public and collective vs. the personal and existential, or, as some would have it, the political vs. the moral. These poles would widen in the years to come, on the one hand creating a precarious balance within each Resistance group (and perhaps within each resister) and on the other leaving a split in the movement as a whole. The editorial concluded with a request for signatures and a list of the thirty signers so far.

By March of 1967 the Inter-University Committee (IUC), the coordinating group for Vietnam teach-ins, had taken over circulation of the Lynd-Oglesby statement. The Committee planned to release it to the press on the eve of the April 15 marches in New York and San Francisco, but failed to gather enough signatures in time: as late as April 11 another appeal went out. Then at the April 15 rally James Bevel, one of its co-chairmen, impulsively announced a May 17 march in Washington. The Mobilization Committee canceled the May march at its next meeting, but while the idea was alive it gave another impetus to the IUC and its signature collecting.

By this time another statement came to the attention of the IUC, Robert Zevin's long declaration urging young men to refuse to fight in Vietnam. Bob, a professor of economics at Columbia, had garnered a few signatures from colleagues, and was pushing for organizational support to collect more signatures in time for the May march. At a meeting in late April Staughton deferred to

Bob, and on May 3 the IUC sent out the new statement with an appeal for signatures. But within a few days this statement too was dropped in favor of another, one initiated by Art Waskow and Marc Raskin in Washington.

In the Bay Area, meanwhile, a Committee for Draft Resistance, organized by Roy Kepler and others, issued a Declaration of Conscience supporting draft resistance which received wide circulation in the west over the next year. It was strongly worded, more strongly than any of the east-coast statements:

> We, the undersigned, are compelled by the fundamental immorality and increasing brutality of our nation's course in Vietnam to now commit our lives to changing that course. We hereby urge and support open resistance to the draft and the military establishment which shapes and carries out this disastrous policy. . . .
>
> To all young men who are outraged by our nation's deeds in Vietnam and who find it unthinkable and impossible to participate, we counsel, aid and abet their nonviolent refusal to cooperate with the military draft.

More than eight hundred signed this call by the spring of 1967. Among them was author Mitchell Goodman, whose eagerness to do more than sign declarations would make him one of the prime movers of the antidraft demonstration in Washington that October, and one of the four indicted with Dr. Spock for conspiracy to encourage draft resistance.

Throughout the country that spring a thousand statements bloomed: declarations, manifestoes, calls for support, confessions of "complicity," and appendices to We Won't Go statements. These last, the appendices, had recently become detached and were circulating independently. One from Berkeley read:

> We believe our war in Vietnam is immoral, unjust, unconscionable.
>
> Most of us, like the majority of our countrymen, are not among those called on to offer life and limb in Vietnam. No sacrifices demanded of us can equal the loss of a single life, Vietnamese or American. With all Americans, we share a responsibility for those of our youth who have been ordered off to war.

We believe that every young man has the obligation to choose for himself whether he will train to kill and perhaps be killed in this war. This decision of conscience cannot be made for him by any external authority, including the American government. We therefore urge young men to consider whether they are willing to be executioners and victims. We pledge our support to all who decide they must refuse to serve.

Each supporter was asked to sign several different statements, none of which was completely satisfactory. Everyone was confused, not least the resisters who were the intended beneficiaries of all the verbiage: there seemed to be as many drafts as draftees. Gary Rader of CADRE understated the confusion in a letter to a New York coordinating committee: "We wish all the groups could kind of get together and work together, if possible." Eventually, most of them did.

From the welter of declarations one emerged pre-eminent in scope, publicity, and political impact. Art Waskow and Marc Raskin, colleagues at the Institute for Policy Studies in Washington, D.C., had seen many of the statements then circulating, but felt that yet another was needed. After long discussions Art typed the first version of "A Call to Confrontation with Illegitimate Authority." It was different in several respects from its predecessors. Except for acts of noncooperation with the draft (refusal to serve, emigration) no specific acts were endorsed. Instead the statement developed a moral and legal argument against the war and a justification of general resistance to it. Art cited the lack of a declaration of war from Congress, the United Nations Charter, and the Nuremberg verdict as criteria to prove the illegality of the war; and the right of religious liberty as an argument that conscientious objection to a particular war is constitutional. The emphasis of the statement was on draft refusal, but it added briefly that "the same logic applies to men already in the Armed Forces who refuse to assist in the American War in Vietnam." A vow of support followed the argumentative part, and then a paragraph about the legal consequences of support:

We firmly believe that our statement is the sort of speech that under the First Amendment must be free, and that the actions we will undertake are as legal as is the draft resistance of the young men themselves. But we recognize that the courts may find otherwise, and that if so we might all be liable to prosecution and to jail terms of five years. In any case, we feel we cannot shrink from fulfilling our responsibilities as intellectuals to resist the war machine with our full weight: our responsibility to the youth whom we teach, to the country whose free citizens we are, and to the ancient traditions of religion and philosophy whose guardians we happen to be in this generation.

They sent their statement to Bob Zevin, who had already been circulating his own, longer and more detailed in its description of the political and legal situation in Vietnam, and which stressed resistance within the armed forces as much as draft resistance. He deferred to the Waskow-Raskin statement, but sent it back to them expanded to twice the original length and re-paragraphed in a more logical way. He even expanded the title to "A Call to Confrontation and Resistance to Illegitimate Authority." Waskow and Raskin then made a few additional minor revisions, reduced the title to "A Call to Resist Illegitimate Authority," and began mailing it out to other movement people for signatures, help in circulation, and suggestions. One suggestion, later adopted, was to strike the sentence about the possible outcome of prosecutions, on the grounds that there was little point in second-guessing the Justice Department and the courts. (Early versions continued to circulate, however, and one fell into the hands of the Justice Department, which used it in the Spock trial to harry Marc and Mitch Goodman. The sentence was suspicious enough, but its absence in the final version was considered even more suspicious.)

The response came quickly and steadily. By early July 1967 about a hundred had signed it, and by the end of the month the goal of 121 had been exceeded. Many prominent men and women signed, including some who would not have done so only a few months before. Several wrote to praise the statement, or to criticize it. Allen Ginsberg wrote (in a letter that now hangs proudly in the office of Resist in Cambridge): "I can't recommend the humorless prose. You'd be better off telling people to goof off or fuck off from the draft than all this gobbledygook which takes too long to read. But I'll sign anyway." Hans Morgenthau made a principled objection: "I do not think that people who are not of draft age ought to tie up the Vietnam War with the draft. What people of draft age wish to do is a matter of their own conscience." Norman O. Brown wrote darkly: "I can't go along with your proposed action or declaration. I wish my last book had made it clearer why I can't." And Dr. Spock added this to his signature:

> I also sign this call because I believe that Pres. Johnson's prosecution of this illegal war is not only not helping but is damaging the U.S. —by alienating its allies, outraging the people of the world, slowing efforts to solve this country's domestic problems. Furthermore it threatens to involve this country in a pointless and suicidal war with China and the U.S.S.R.

"A Call to Resist Illegitimate Authority," with 158 signatures, was published in the *New York Review of Books* and the *New Republic* in late September. A year later over two thousand had signed it.

A number of supporters wanted to do something more concrete, more serious, and therefore more risky than signing statements. In New York a group formed around Grace Paley, Karl Bissinger, Paul Goodman, and others to support the Cornell card burners. They made declarations, called press conferences, held rallies, raised money, and stood with the burners in Sheep's Meadow. Their group, called Support-in-Action, became the New York affiliate of Resist, the national committee that sponsored the "Call to Resist Illegitimate Authority" and the Washington demonstration in October.

When it became known that the Resistance would turn in draft cards in October, Mitchell Goodman, Denise Levertov, and Henry Braun, all three writers and teachers, issued a call for support. Impressed by the planned participation of their west-coast colleagues in the Oakland Stop the Draft Week, and dissatisfied with the planned Pentagon demonstration, they searched for "something more decisive—an act of opposition more pointed, more penetrating, led by the core of America's middle-class community: the clergy, the people of the professions, the teachers, the artists and writers." They came up with "an act of direct creative resistance to the war": a visit to the Justice Department by notable public figures to deliver the draft cards collected around the country by the Resistance. The participants would then be incurring risks comparable to those of the resisters—for "counseling, aiding, and abetting," or, though it occurred to hardly anyone, for conspiracy. During the summer they linked up with the New York Support-in-Action group, the group circulating the Call to Resist, and clergymen like William Sloane Coffin, Jr. On October 16 many of them took part in Resistance turn-in ceremonies and on October 20 they all went to Washington.

The events of October 20 have passed into history as the pivot of the conspiracy indictment against Dr. Benjamin Spock, Rev. William Sloane Coffin, Jr., Mitchell Goodman, Marcus Raskin, and Michael Ferber, and we will not recount the story that has been told so often and so well. (See the note at the end of this chapter.) The trial, however inconclusive legally (some of the defendants regret their decision to have a technically complicated trial), served as a focus for older activists for a number of months. The "overt acts" named in the indictment were repeated by thousands of clergymen and professors around the country. New calls to support draft resisters circulated everywhere; one limited to North Carolina, for example, gathered five hundred signatures from nineteen colleges and universities. Over twenty-eight thousand signed a statement confessing "guilt" equal to that of the defendants. Rev. Martin Luther King, a few days before he was assassinated, made plans to bring suit against the government for "chilling" his rights of speech and assembly. Indeed, if the government hoped to cool off the antidraft movement by indicting its best-known members, their hope failed. The Spock trial, a herald of increased government repression, was also a symbol of the increasing seriousness of resistance "supporters." Many stopped being supporters only to become resisters themselves.

Notes to Chapter Nine

The Declaration of Conscience is in Staughton Lynd, ed., *Nonviolence in America: A Documentary History* (Indianapolis: Bobbs-Merrill, 1966),

376–378; and in Hugo Bedau, ed., *Civil Disobedience: Theory and Practice* (New York: Pegasus, 1969), 160–161. On "encourage," Paul Goodman to Ferber (April 1969). "Le droit de l'insoumission" appeared in *Cahiers Libres* 14 (Paris: Maspero, 1960) and in *Evergreen Review,* November–December 1960; mentioned in *Civil Disobedience: Theory and Practice* 124; for additional information on the Young Resistance see Martin Verlet, "A Protest of the Young," *Liberation,* January 1967.

Most of the material on the Lynd-Oglesby statement is drawn from the files of Staughton Lynd. Letters to Lynd from Oglesby (n.d.) [August? 1966]; Chomsky (May 10, 1970); Zevin (May 31). Gary Rader to Norma Becker and Keith Lampe (n.d. [June ? 1967]).

The first drafts of the "Call to Resist Illegitimate Authority" and the comments of the original signers are in the files of Art Waskow and Marc Raskin. It was printed in *New York Review of Books,* October 12, 1967, and *New Republic,* October 7, 1967. Further correspondence about the Call may be found in the files of Resist, 763 Massachusetts Avenue, #4, Cambridge, Mass. 02139. Goodman-Levertov-Braun call in files of Lynd, Ferber, Resist, and elsewhere.

On the Spock trial much has been written. See especially Noam Chomsky, Paul Lauter, and Florence Howe, "Reflections on a Political Trial," *New York Review of Books,* August 22, 1968; Michael Ferber, "On Being Indicted," *New York Review of Books,* April 25, 1968; Daniel Lang, "The Trial of Dr. Spock," *New Yorker,* September 7, 1968; Denise Levertov, "The Intellectuals and the War Machine," *North American Review,* January 1968; David Lyle, "Dr. Spock Misbehaves," *Esquire,* February 1969; Jessica Mitford, *The Trial of Dr. Spock* (New York: Knopf, 1969; Vintage, 1970). The first two articles have been reprinted in *Trials of the Resistance* (New York: New York Review, 1970).

CHAPTER TEN

The Resistance, the Pentagon and Stop The Draft Week

THE MEANINGS OF RESISTANCE: SUMMER 1967

From its outset the Resistance met criticism from other sections of the movement. Most of it was leveled at the consequences of willful, illegal confrontation: the seeming disparity between an almost certain tangible loss (through imprisonment) and a very uncertain symbolic or educational gain.

Tom Gardner, chairman of the Southern Student Organizing Committee (SSOC), wrote in February 1967 that sentiment in the South was

> toward evasion. I guess that feeling might be offset slightly by, for instance, the growth of anti-draft unions in the North, such as the one at the Univ. of Chicago. On the other hand, as politically effective as the WE WON'T GO statements may be, the larger percentage will still tend toward one form or another of evasion as their own confrontation gets closer. The nature of resistance seems most often to reflect the resister's view of appealing to the morals and good sense of the American people. Many non-cooperators place great importance on the effect they feel they will have on the Judge, their Board, court spectators, and associates. Others feel . . . that "suffering is no longer redemptive in this society."

SNCC, which had launched the slogan "We won't go," nevertheless opposed public confrontations like those planned by the

Resistance. "Revolutionaries who now see themselves as 'fighting against' rather than 'appealing to' don't intend to 'let the enemy put them away,'" Tom went on.

The typical SNCC statement is, "I intend to keep working with SNCC, I'm not going to be drafted, I'm not going to jail, and I'm not leaving the country." As difficult as this may sound, an amazing number of the SNCC staff have stayed out on every thing imaginable, including pending court cases (most common), physical exemptions, bad security risks, series of appeals, homosexuality.

When SNCC organizers were cornered by the system and forced to defend themselves in court, they tried to raise political issues. SNCC program secretary Cleveland Sellers refused induction on May 1, 1967, after filing suit in which he charged that of 1,691 draft board members in South Carolina, Georgia, Alabama, Mississippi, and Louisiana only six were black. By June 1967 SNCC had seventeen staff members under indictment for refusing induction.

SDS, too, sought ways to resist the draft effectively without losing its organizers to exile or jail. Greg Calvert and Bill Hartzog, SDS national draft coordinator in early 1967, had endless conversations in the SDS national office about how to make resistance more than ineffective martyrdom. One suggestion, to take a public stand in the early stages of court proceedings but to go underground before conviction and sentencing, was acted out by Bill. (Several subsequent issues of *New Left Notes* appeared with a mysterious box which said, "Hartzog Lives!") Carl Davidson, SDS inter-organizational secretary, urged resistance activity at induction centers where the flow of manpower to the war could be physically, not just symbolically, obstructed.

Ambiguities abounded in the complex and protracted debate between SDS and the Resistance. Resisters perceived their naysaying as an affirmation of manhood, but Carl Davidson asserted that the resister who permitted himself to be imprisoned made other people "feel weak." Resisters believed that in defying the government they were going beyond middle-class politics, with its "prayers to an unjust king," but Steve Hamilton, one of the four founders of the Resistance, broke with it on the ground that it was

an attempt to "stir one more wave of middle-class liberal sentiment against the war." Resisters felt that they were challenging
young men to take a step which would have consequences for the
whole of their lives, but organizers for the Jobs Or Income Now
(JOIN) community union in Chicago argued that the draft was a
"strategically weak" single issue.

During the organizing for the first national card turn-in relations between SDS and the Resistance were uneasy. David Harris
remembers almost uniform condemnation of the Resistance by
SDS chapters on the west coast. Michael Ferber recalls that when
he approached the Harvard SDS chapter for support for October
16 he received only perfunctory endorsement. Lennie Heller's experience was that students not affiliated with SDS responded
much more warmly than SDS chapters. Nevertheless, there was a
widespread admiration for the Resistance which local and national SDS groups reflected in their public pronouncements. The
SDS-oriented Portland Draft Resisters Union, for instance, reported to *New Left Notes* in early June 1967:

> Most of our energy now is going into working towards the Oc-
> tober 16th action. We sent 3 members down to a planning conference
> May 14th in Berkeley. We'll have at least one person traveling all sum-
> mer in Oregon and Washington, and probably two in the fall, working
> primarily on October 16 and draft resistance, but generally on SDS.
> We're really anxious for the October 16th thing to happen, and we hope
> for 75 to 150 non-cooperators in Oregon.

Similarly the Stanford Anti-Draft Union indicated that it was "in
loose cooperation" with David Harris, who, it said, had "broadened the perspective of all draft-age men at Stanford."

"October 16" Resistance buttons were common at the SDS national convention in June. The convention passed a resolution
which affirmed "that a sense of urgency must be developed that
will move people to resist the draft," urged "tactics such as civil
disobedience and disruption of the Selective Service System," and
carefully noted that "SDS does not urge going to jail as a means
of resisting the draft, but supports all those whose actions result in
imprisonment." SDS had always been wary of narrowing its focus

to any one issue or tactic. If it eventually seized the draft issue, it seized others as well, and used all of them (at least in theory) as tools for multi-issue community or campus organizing. It is a measure of its esteem for the Resistance, then, that national SDS organizations urged support for it, while maintaining contempt for massive demonstrations against the war. At the June convention SDS criticized the call for a march at the Pentagon:

> The National Convention of SDS regrets the decision of the National Mobilization Committee to call for a March on Washington in October. We feel that these large demonstrations—which are just public expressions of belief—can have no significant effect on American policy in Vietnam. Further, they delude many participants into thinking that the "democratic" process in America functions in a meaningful way. The U.S. government has the power to simply ignore demonstrators who threaten its interests. Nor do we accept the contention that such large demonstrations are the best tool for organizing. Other methods include organizing around local demonstrations, referendums, or draft resistance.

On the eve of the antiwar actions of October 16–21, the SDS National Council passed the following resolution on the Resistance:

> The SDS N.C. encourages all chapters to seek out and support all men participating in the Oct. 16 refusal to cooperate with the SSS and should aid them in further resistance to—that is, relevant obstruction and disruption of—the American war machine wherever vulnerable. SDS encourages and will help all members of "the Resistance" to defy all state authority, overt and covert, over the control of their lives.

A second paragraph of the resolution indicated the point at which friction between SDS and the Resistance would develop—on the question of broad-based "political" work versus single-issue "moral" play-acting—but still expressed its criticism fraternally and constructively:

> SDS recognizes the validity of all direct challenges to illegitimate authority, but seeing the insufficiency and misdirection of symbolic-

confrontation-oriented movements, urges members of "the Resistance" to involve themselves in local community organizing projects aiming to build a powerful insurgent white base inside the United States.

Apart from such statements of support there was in the period April–October 1967 considerable ideological kinship between SDS and the Resistance. After all, SDS had just endorsed draft resistance, coined the slogan "From Protest to Resistance," and put out the buttons "Resist" and "Not with My Life You Don't." It was difficult not to regard the Resistance as an expression, indeed at that point as *the* expression, of this spirit.

Moreover, national SDS officers Greg Calvert and Carl Davidson had developed a language for talking about resistance which was remarkably similar to the rhetoric of David Harris or Dennis Sweeney. What both the SDS and Resistance leaders tried to do was to understand personal liberation and political effectiveness not as opposites, things to be chosen between, but as aspects of a single process. "Our lives and our politics," Dennis declared, "are really inseparable." Speaking to the National Student Association convention in August 1968, Michael Ferber and David Harris reiterated this view. "We take a lot of grief," Michael said, "from other groups and people who do not understand that, finally, 'personal' and 'political' are the same thing, or that one is an extension of the other." David put it this way: "The assumption I want to begin with is that the tool that you and I have is not a new set of words; it's not a new slogan, a new candidate, a new set of officers. The tool that you and I have is the tool of a life." In 1967 this assumption also was made by many persons in SDS.

The classic exposition of the resistance process was Greg Calvert's speech to an SDS conference at Princeton in February. At this conference a former editor of the *Daily Worker* told the assembled New Leftists that the blue-collar worker wanted not things of the spirit but bread. Greg, himself the son of a blue-collar worker, stayed up all night furiously writing a response.

>   All authentically revolutionary movements are struggles for human freedom.
>   Contrary to what was suggested here last evening, revolutionary mass

movements are not built out of a drive for the acquisition of more material goods. That is a perversion and vulgarization of revolutionary
thought and a misreading of history. Revolutionary movements are freedom struggles born out of the perception of the contradictions between
human potentiality and oppressive actuality.

Whereas the liberal acts on behalf of others, driven by a sense of
guilt, the radical understands that he himself is unfree and oppressed and so joins in "a struggle for collective liberation of all
unfree, oppressed men."

Even closer to the spirit of the Resistance was Greg's vignette
of "the Guatemalan guerrilla approach":

> It is said that when the Guatemalan guerrillas enter a new vil-
> lage, they do not talk about the "anti-imperialist struggle" nor do they
> give lessons on dialectical materialism—neither do they distribute copies
> of the "Communist Manifesto" or of Chairman Mao's "On Contradic-
> tion." What they do is gather together the people of the village and then,
> one by one, the guerrillas rise and talk to the villagers about their own
> lives: about how they see themselves and how they came to be who they
> are, about their deepest longings and the things they've striven for and
> hoped for, about the way in which their deepest longings were frustrated
> by the society in which they lived.
>
> Then the guerrillas encourage the villagers to talk about their lives.
> And then a marvelous thing begins to happen. People who thought that
> their deepest problems and frustrations were their individual problems
> discover that their problems and longings are all the same.

This was the way Tom Bell proceeded when he built the resistance group at Cornell, and it was the procedure of the Resistance
when it offered, as an initial pamphlet in the Bay Area, six individual statements by resisters. In the spring of 1967 it was also the
style of SDS speakers who told their college audiences (in the
words of the Michigan State student newspaper, reporting such a
meeting) "how they themselves got into the movement." Speaking
of his own experience with the "Guatemalan approach," Carl Davidson told the *National Guardian*:

You'd be astonished at the reception . . . when people realize that they aren't alone, that the failures and problems they ascribed to themselves stem in large part from the society in which they live and the images of themselves they accepted from society.

In 1967 both Resistance and SDS leaders saw their task as breaking down these socially conditioned self-images, in the same way that SNCC had redefined the black self-image through Black Power. Greg commented:

A resistance movement, based on the slogan, "Not with my life, you don't," is basic to helping people break out of their own prisons. People are capable of doing extraordinary things when they are in resistance. They can walk out on their studies and take on new lives, if necessary. They do not walk to gas chambers. In the process of resistance, in struggling against the powerlessness that capitalism imposes on the individual, there is a rediscovery of the self in the midst of a dehumanized society.

During the first half of 1967 these ideas of SDS leaders crystallized into a theory. A critical step in the process was Peter Henig's discovery of the Selective Service System memorandum on "Channeling." Distributed to local draft boards in 1965, "Channeling" became known to the movement when Henig quoted it extensively in *New Left Notes,* January 20, 1967. This celebrated document proved from the mouth of the enemy that the draft functioned not so much to procure manpower for the military as to allocate human resources throughout the society. A few paragraphs will suggest the tone of the whole:

The line dividing the primary function of armed forces manpower procurement from the process of channeling manpower into civilian support is often finely drawn. The process of channeling by not taking men from certain activities who are otherwise liable for service, or by giving deferment to qualified men in certain occupations, is actual procurement by inducement of manpower for civilian activities which are manifestly in the national interest.

While the best known purpose of Selective Service is to procure manpower for the armed forces, a variety of related processes take place outside of delivery of manpower to the active armed forces. Many of these may be put under the heading of "channeling manpower." Many young men would not have pursued a higher education if there had not been a program of student deferment. Many young scientists, engineers, tool and die makers, and other possessors of scarce skills would not remain in their jobs in the defense effort if it were not for a program of occupational deferments. Even though the salary of a teacher has historically been meager, many young men remain in that job, seeking the reward of a deferment.

The memorandum went on to speak of "the club of induction" (not a group, but a stick) and of the Selective Service System as "pressurized guidance." It explicitly stated that the draft performed in a veiled or indirect fashion the task more forthrightly implemented in totalitarian states.

> The psychology of granting wide choice under pressure to take action is the American or indirect way of achieving what is done by direction in foreign countries where choice is not permitted. Here, choice is limited but not denied, and it is fundamental that an individual generally applies himself better to do something he has decided to do rather than something he has been told to do.

A New York Resistance leaflet later commented, "the Selective Service memo 'On Manpower Channeling' is truly the biography of our generation."

As resistance to the draft was leading young radicals into other forms of resistance, so the concept of channeling merged with developing insights into other institutions. Herbert Marcuse's essay "On Repressive Tolerance" argued that the governing class could readily permit, even encourage, a modicum of dissent which led people to believe that the system was free and democratic. Marcuse and others argued that in a neocapitalist, postscarcity industrial economy exploitation might take the form of inducing a person to consume (while at the same time he believed his choices to be free) as well as depriving him of the fruits of his labor. In a pamphlet entitled "Consumption: Domestic Imperialism," developed "in discussions with the Wisconsin Draft Resistance

Union," David Gilbert insisted that "the *channeling* into commodity form of basic human needs has reached a qualitatively new phase" (italics added).

What was most important in this constellation of ideas was that the middle-class white student was considered a legitimate revolutionary protagonist rather than a mere auxiliary to other classes or races. The "Channeling" memorandum made it clear that the deferred student was oppressed by the system along with the inducted soldier. Perhaps, as the French writer André Gorz believed, the student was a kind of preworker, and the white-collar employees which students were trained to become constituted a "new working class," growing in size and power, joining (or even replacing) the industrial proletariat as the potentially revolutionary class.

In the summer of 1967 nearly everyone in the movement could identify with the term "resistance" and affirm that he was moving from protest or dissent "to resistance." Deep ambiguity lurked in the concept, however, as persons drawn toward the example of Che Guevara and the theories of Regis Debray used the term along with persons who, however revolutionary in aspiration, were nonetheless stubbornly nonviolent. These multiple meanings are suggested in a little essay by former SNCC worker Julius Lester which appeared in the *National Guardian* August 19, 1967, reprinted from the August 4 issue of *Vietnam Summer News*. It was entitled "To resist is to . . ."

> To protest is to speak out against. To let it be known that you do not like a certain action of another.
>
> To protest is an act of intellectual commitment. It is to say, "Sir, I protest" when you are slapped in the face . . .
>
> To protest is to play a game. You go to a demonstration, listen to speeches, wave signs, and go home to see if you got on television. . . .
>
> To resist is to say No! without qualification or explanation.
>
> To resist is not only to say I Won't Go. It is to say I'll make sure nobody else goes, either.
>
> To resist is to pit Life as you define it against Life as they define it and to do all that is necessary to see that their definition is destroyed in all of its parts.

To resist is to not go to jail when sentenced, but only when caught and surrounded and there is no other choice but death.

To resist is to make the President afraid to leave the White House because he will be spat upon wherever he goes to tell his lies, because his limousine will find the street filled with tacks and thousands of people who will surge around it, smashing the windows and rocking the car until it is turned on its side.

Have we forgotten? The man is a murderer. . . .

To protest is to dislike the inhumanity of another.

To resist is to stop inhumanity and affirm your own humanity.

One does not protest murder.

One apprehends the murderer and deals with him accordingly.

Julius Lester's gloss of "resistance" coexisted tensely with that of David Harris and Michael Ferber. After the week of October 16–21, when these differences were acted out on the steps of the Pentagon and in the streets of Oakland, SDS and the Resistance began to diverge sharply.

THE PENTAGON

Quite accidentally the dates chosen by the Resistance for the first national draft card turn-in and by the National Mobilization Committee for a fall march on Washington turned out to be five days apart, a Monday (October 16) and a Saturday (October 21). Once this coincidence was recognized organizers expanded their initial plans. West-coast resisters projected a "Stop The Draft Week" in Oakland which would begin on the sixteenth and continue through the twenty-first. Resist, the adult support group for the Resistance, decided that the draft cards turned in on the sixteenth should be presented to the Department of Justice in Washington on the twentieth, the eve of the march.

SDS reevaluated its initial opposition to the march on Washington when, shortly before October 21, the government refused to grant permits for the demonstration. The call for the march spoke of "confronting the warmakers" at the Pentagon. When the government announced that it was deputizing marshals and flying in paratroopers so that the Pentagon could be protected, it sud-

denly seemed that the confrontation might be more than symbolic. The prospect caused the SDS National Council to change
its mind about the march and urge the organization's members to
participate. What finally happened both in Oakland during Stop
The Draft Week and at the Pentagon on October 21–22 was for
the most part massive improvisation from below, unplanned by
leaders. For example, no one seems to have intended that the
Pentagon would be the largest mass draft card burning in the history of protest against the Vietnam war. It happened quite spontaneously as students and soldiers, facing each other in long lines
on the Pentagon steps, began to settle down for a night in one another's company.

"Suddenly, as the daylight died," Paul Lauter and Florence
Howe later recalled,

> two or three tiny flames burst from different places in the
> crowd. There was only red in the west, and the earth was black, when
> dozens of draft cards began to burn, held aloft, amid increasing cheers
> and applause. One by one, the lights flickered, burned, then went out.
> The burnings travelled to the other side of the Mall, beyond the soldiers
> that split our large group from a small one on the right, and eventually
> down to the grassy plains below. The sight silenced even the cheering.

Mike Goldfield of SDS remembered that the burning of "several
hundred" draft cards took place after "a man with a Veterans for
Peace hat" burned his discharge papers. Tom Bell tried to count
the burning cards on the steps of the Pentagon and gave up. He
had been standing on the platform, bullhorn in hand, trying to
count for the crowd, when he suddenly remembered how fearful
of repression the early organizers of draft resistance had been. But
now, "there we were standing on the upper parking lot of the Pentagon, with the generals in clear view, smoking pot and burning
draft cards, victorious, audacious, no sense of fear."

During the night miniature versions of that scene were repeated.

> A muted voice said, "Christ, it's getting cold," and a louder
> voice called out, "Burn a draft card! Keep warm!" This was greeted by

laughter and some cheers, and immediately several voices chanted it, "Burn a draft card! Keep warm!" A few moments later a much louder cheer went up. Three youths, in different parts of the group, were holding aloft their flaming cards. Soon there were a dozen such fires. A friend beside me, an instructor at Columbia, pointed to one of the youths and laughed. "Last April he used to come to our meetings and talk against the protest. Now look at him." The youth was staring at the flames of his card and looking richly pleased with himself.

The next day Paul Johnson of *WIN* magazine encountered at the Washington Greyhound station a Bennington girl and her Ivy League escort for whom the night at the Pentagon had been their first demonstration. " 'She burned my draft card up there,' he told us proudly."

Paul Rupert, active in the Resistance both on the west coast and in Chicago, was one who burned his draft card at the Pentagon. There had been something about the October 16 turn-in in Chicago that had made him not want to turn his own card in, according to Paul. At the Pentagon the moment seemed right. After returning from the Pentagon demonstration, Paul wrote to his draft board, explaining why he had given up his divinity student's deferment.

Last week-end I joined with my young brothers and sisters at the Pentagon to express our opposition to the war in Vietnam and to the draft which feeds that war. Young, naive and scared, we sat singing at the feet of young, naive and scared brothers who were in uniform. We spoke with them and offered them food and coffee, but they could neither speak nor move. For four hours we sat before these troops while federal marshals clubbed and arrested us one-by-one.

The most intense memory for many demonstrators at the Pentagon was that of communication with the troops, as thousands of demonstrators called out to the soldiers facing them, "Join us!," and (according to movement legend) two or three servicemen attempted to lay down their guns.

"It is difficult to write about what happened that night and not sound corny," Martin Jezer wrote.

You had to have been there and felt the vibrations to understand how real it was. We began pleading with the soldiers to "Join us,"
singing "Soldiers are our friends, we shall overcome" and chanting "We
love you." Corny words, silly slogans, cliches that have long lost their
meaning. But we were communicating with the soldiers, putting them
through changes. And they, with their silent faces, were communicating
with us, putting us through changes. For us it was a shock of recognition
that despite their arms, their uniforms, and their orders to attack us, the
soldiers were very much our brothers.

The demonstrators, to be sure, acted partly in self-protection.
Susan Kent recalls: "We talked with the soldiers in front of us,
looking at them pleadingly: 'You don't want to hurt us, will you
do that, will you have to, please don't hurt us, arrest us, but don't
hurt us, we mean no harm to you. . . .' " But the impulse of that
weekend was much more than self-protection.

George Dennison wrote a compassionate description of the encounter with the troops.

While daylight lasted, I looked as closely as I could at the soldiers in front of us. Many were Negro: almost all were young. They were
not violent faces, but those of boys from small towns and city slums,
many with an unfinished, hangdog look of profound uncertainty in the
conduct of life. Their cheeks and jaws were wooden with embarrassment.
Their eyes flitted here and there, some with hungry surprise, others with
a kind of wide-eyed fearfulness, drinking in the age-mate faces of those
before them.

After dark the number of demonstrators was reduced to four or
five hundred. "We kept hearing news," Dennison continues:

". . . a soldier just passed out cigarettes to three demonstrators
down in the Mall and said, 'Keep up the good work.' " This was greeted
by cheers, which suddenly—as if at a signal, but none had been given—
turned into a prolonged and urgent chant of "Join us! Join us!" In the
brief silence that followed, the strained, high-pitched voice of a girl could
be heard, "We are brothers and sisters!" And again, absolutely spontaneously, a great chant, "We love you! We love you! We love you!" It is

impossible to convey the sound of this chant to those who did not hear it. By sound I mean its real meaning. It was not a tactical maneuver. The time for such things had long since passed. Nor were these words addressed to the troops, as such, and certainly not to individual personalities. Our sense of ourselves as a community—the community that could be, the one we felt *had* to be (and a deeply American one, at that) was acute. And there before us—one would say in panic might—was the vast engine that is in fact destroying the modern world.

About the middle of the night the lines of armed men began to move slowly forward in an attempt to clear the Pentagon steps. It was the MPs and marshals deputized for the occasion, not the soldiers, who were most brutal. As the students slowly retreated,

Gary Rader addressed the troops, standing a few feet from their front line and speaking into a bullhorn. The officer in charge tried to drown him out and for a few minutes we heard an overlay that sounded like this:

My name is Gary Rader. I'm twenty-three years Company B hold your line. Nobody comes, nobody goes I want to tell you what led me up to that Company hold your line what led me up to that decision nobody comes nobody goes we will be heard.

And Rader was heard, for the officer realized that he was shaming his men by plugging their ears in public. He must have guessed, too, what detestation they felt for him. He fell silent and Rader continued speaking, carrying the teach-in to the troops themselves. It was a beautiful occasion and a rare one, for the troops had no choice but to listen—and some at least had long since been softened by the youthful voices, the beards, the lack of beards, the long hair, the short hair, the silky legs, the courage and the communal generosity of the Traitors, Reds and drug addicts assembled before them. Rader spoke in a forthright way, without condescension or moral superiority, telling of his own enlightenment, the history of Vietnam and the lies our government has addressed to its people.

A little later Greg Calvert addressed himself over the bullhorn to the leaders of the government: "The troops you employ belong to us and not to you. They don't belong to the generals. They belong

to a new hope for America that those generals never could participate in."

STOP THE DRAFT WEEK

Whereas the Pentagon action drew together near-Marxists like
Calvert and pacifists like Dave Dellinger, chairman of the National Mobilization Committee, the effect of Stop the Draft Week
in Oakland was to split pacifists and Marxists apart.

There were a few precedents for the effort to physically obstruct
the operation of an induction center. In the summer of 1965 the
Berkeley Vietnam Day Committee (VDC) had made some attempt to block troop trains, and in the fall of 1965 the VDC tried
repeatedly to march to the Oakland induction center to communicate with those about to be drafted. Also on October 15, 1965,
three dozen students at the University of Michigan sat-in at the
Ann Arbor draft board and were arrested for trespassing. On
May 23, 1967 a bus carrying men bound for induction in Ames,
Iowa was blocked for seventy-five minutes by demonstrators who
locked chains around its wheels and stood in its path. And on
June 29, 1967 twenty people sat-in at the Oakland induction center itself.

Steve Hamilton of the Resistance wrote to Norma Becker of the
National Mobilization Committee on July 7:

> We have just been discussing a plan here that people are pretty
> well sold on and many of us from the Resistance and other groups will
> probably be starting to implement immediately. There was a sit-in at the
> Oakland Induction Center recently with only twenty people participating
> that drew a great amount of support and news coverage—and surpris-
> ingly sympathetic coverage. Many people are considering some kind of
> direct action on Oct. 21st. How about declaring National Draft Resist-
> ance Week, Oct. 16–21 and closing down many of the major induction
> centers across the country for the entire week? I know that it could be
> done at the Oakland Center which serves Northern Calif., Oregon and
> half of Nevada. As mild as the demonstration on June 29th was, they
> didn't resist arrest, and as small a number as there was they still gummed
> up the works for quite a while. You only need 15 people at a time to

block the doors and with several hundred people ready to take their places they would have to tell the guys who showed up for induction to go home by the middle of the day.

For the first time we would be doing something that borders on more than symbolic protest.

Originally conceived as an action supporting the draft card turn-in on October 16, the project soon drifted out of the control of the Resistance and took on independent life of its own. As David Harris remembers:

It began as a question of what we could do with our support people to give them a sense of engaging in action also. Dennis, and Hamilton, and I discussed it at one point and said we ought to call a meeting. There was a disagreement as to how the meeting should be called. Hamilton wanted to invite all the groups and have them get together and decide what they wanted to do. My reaction was to say we ought to develop a specific idea for an action first, and use the meeting to present that action. We never resolved that discussion. Dennis and I went on a trip to the Northwest, and when we got back Hamilton happened to mention that he had called the meeting.

The planning committee for Stop The Draft Week (STDW) became the scene of vehement disagreements between pacifists and nonpacifists, resisters and SDS. The pacifists included the War Resisters League, the Institute for the Study of Nonviolence, and other groups, as well as members of the Resistance. Dennis Sweeney recalls that the majority in STDW criticized the Resistance because "we didn't have an approach to working-class kids." The literature of STDW emphasized the hope of "involving young people who are facing conscription: black people, high school students, the unemployed and young working people"; the action was "seen as a way to speak to those young people who have not, before now, seen the peace movement as theirs."

The dominant group in STDW perceived nonviolence as an obstacle in reaching working-class youth. "The gentle, almost timid tone of peace demonstrations has left many young people, black and white, feeling they have no place" in the peace movement, one presentation asserted. Another added:

> Most draftees come from lower and working-class white communities. Rejecting non-violence was seen as necessary to reach them and to forge cooperation with black militants. (Those are the POLITICAL reasons for dropping non-violence; the real reason was that the organizers were angry and fed up with getting themselves arrested and attacked and accomplishing nothing more than ineffective moral protest.)

Dennis remembers David Harris standing up and observing that the people meeting were all middle-class white people, and "talking about the freeways, and the cars, and the swimming pools, and the drive-in theaters, that ocean of shit that we live in, as being ours and something we had to confront ourselves and change, and not something you could turn your back on."

Stuart McRae, another early member of the Resistance, saw the planning process for Stop The Draft Week in this way:

> Much of the planning and organizing for STDW was spent in strife over the issue of non-violence. The argument polarized into a debate between the traditional pacifists who envisioned the usual kind of sit-in (which they conducted on Monday) and radicals, mainly SDS people, vicariously intoxicated by the summer riots, who spoke at first clearly, but with increasing vagueness of violent confrontation with the power structure, i.e. cops. This debate, perpetuated in great heat, put people off, broke the demonstration into two groups and made the bulk of organizing time a sorrowful waste. Many, including myself, felt left out somewhere in between the rigidity and near righteousness of the old-line pacifists and the irresponsibility and shrillness of the STDW organizers.

The resolution of these conflicts was to divide the week between the contending groups, with the pacifists taking Monday and (as it turned out) Wednesday and Thursday, while the militants were responsible for Tuesday and (in the upshot) Friday.

On Monday October 16, three hundred draft cards were turned in by the Resistance at the Federal Building in San Francisco and about 120 people from pacifist groups were arrested nonviolently sitting-in at the Oakland induction center. On Tuesday three thousand demonstrators massed at the induction center resisted a furious police attack for half an hour, with over twenty injuries and 25 arrests. Tuesday night there was confusion about what to do next. Terry Cannon states: "The STDW Steering Committee was split over whether to continue the blockade the next 3 days. The San Jose, Stanford, and San Francisco representatives voted to continue; most of the Berkeley group voted to stop. It was decided to have only peaceful pickets the next two days." As David Harris remembers that evening:

I intended to just rest for a few days after the 16th but it didn't work out that way. I did stay home on Tuesday but the reports of the holocaust made me both sad and angry. (I remembered telling them that precisely what happened would happen.) Then a girl from the War Resisters League called me and asked if I would come to the evening rally and talk about non-violence. I decided to go and expected another dose of crap about being a "counter-revolutionary" and "bourgeois fascist." When I got there the rally had been going on for an hour and a half at the open mike and the primary question of debate was whether to go and march on the Chancellor's office the next day or on city hall in protest of police brutality. So I stepped in and said I thought every one ought to go back to the induction center and sit in. After debate, the group (3000 people) decided to go back and I was put in the position of having to help organize the next day's action. The STDW steering committee was a shambles and couldn't reach any decisions or marshall any resources. The results of their rhetoric seemed to have left them overwhelmed. So I was in front of the induction center with a bullhorn the next morning. A total of 97 sat in and I was arrested off the sidewalk for disturbing the peace. I spent the next ten days in Santa Rita.

On Friday, October 20, ten thousand demonstrators surrounded the induction center, many wearing helmets and shields. The police advanced as they had on Tuesday but this time the demonstrators, using preplanned "mobile tactics," melted away before them. Acting in small groups the demonstrators reassembled at street intersections outside the police lines, where they built barricades and for a considerable time prevented buses from

reaching the induction center. The élan of that day is well described by Jeff Segal, at the time SDS national draft coordinator
(replacing Bill Hartzog) and subsequently one of the seven men
indicted for the Oakland events.

> People were mad about Tuesday and the brutality they saw and
> were determined to make the power structure pay for what it did. They
> went into the streets and built barricades from whatever they could find
> handy—benches, large potted trees, parking meters, garbage cans, and
> cars and trucks (these were placed in the middle of the streets and the air
> let out of the tires.) People would run up behind buses and rip the igni-
> tion wires out or would climb into trucks and steal the keys. They ran
> into the streets and let their imaginations and new-found sense of power
> run wild.
>
> Typically a group would march into an intersection and form a moving
> circle in the area of the crosswalks. People would then come out and start
> to paint things on the streets and sidewalks. The paint was really the orig-
> inal catalyst that loosened the people up and led to the many other great,
> beautiful things. Once this loosening process had taken place, small
> groups of demonstrators would break out of the circle and begin to move
> all kinds of objects into the streets.

"People involved in those activities had the feeling of power," Jeff
concluded. Something had been shown, a reporter for the *New
York Review of Books* wrote months later, "about the possibility of
collective action, and of collective resistance."

At Oakland and at the Pentagon people experienced power, but
the experiences were different, and after the week of confrontations debate raged throughout the movement about what it all
meant. "This week," a demonstrator wrote from Oakland, "the
first crack appeared in the egg that will hatch white revolution in
America." Pacifists feared that something altogether different had
been hatched: delusions of grandeur, *machismo* posturing, even
fascism. For the most part pacifists and street fighters condemned
each other's actions, but to a few persons the question seemed
more complex. Frank Bardacke of the Oakland Seven wrote:

> Although most of the Left admired the passion and eloquence
> of the Resistance leaders they disapproved of burning and turning in

draft cards as an anti-draft tactic. They claimed that the Resistance was moving back to a position of apolitical moral witness and they demanded to know what was the political purpose of spending five years in jail.

Never has the Left so thoroughly missed the point. The Resistance made Stop The Draft Week possible. Young men burning their draft cards on Sproul Hall steps changed the political mood of the campus. This example and that of hundreds who turned in their draft cards gave the rest of us courage.

The conclusions drawn by most of the movement from the events at Oakland and at the Pentagon were summarized in a leaflet put out in New York in December 1967. Announcing a sit-in at the Whitehall Street induction center, the leaflet stated that the lesson of the Pentagon was that soldiers were not enemies but potential allies:

> We went to the Pentagon to confront the warmakers only to discover that the young soldiers were our brothers. Two defected, many more showed solidarity with our cause. . . . Our power comes from our ability to blow their minds, win them over to our side. We're not their enemy, they're not ours.

And the lesson of the Oakland induction center was to avoid static confrontations:

> Using mobile tactics, the people in Oakland closed down the induction center and surrounding area for over three hours. Then the National Guard was called. So the people split. They held a victory march back to Berkeley; the Guard had nothing to do. Good guerrilla tactics! Take a stand only when superiority in numbers and tactical position are yours.

Each of these "lessons" raised questions about the strategy of the Resistance. The Resistance emphasized keeping young men out of the army. The teach-in with the troops during the long hours of confrontation at the Pentagon on October 21–22 suggested that it was at least equally important to find ways to reach the persons who, despite the best efforts of the Resistance, were drafted anyway.

The Resistance employed a version of the traditional pacifist tactic whereby individuals publicly broke a law and permitted the government to jail them for it. The heady experience of over-turning cars, effectually (if temporarily) blocking access to the Oakland induction center, but still avoiding arrest, led to very different strategic ideas. To make matters more complicated, the lessons of the Pentagon and of Oakland were in some tension with each other. The Pentagon, after the first few hours, was a static confrontation in which seated demonstrators faced out-wardly impassive soldiers, marshals and MPs. The thrust of the weekend experience was a confirmation of nonviolence, in that it held out the hope of winning over one's armed opponents. Oak-land, on the other hand, besides creating a new model of mobile tactics, also turned participants toward a street-fighting style in which they abused and (at least in fantasy) destroyed the armed opponents whom they episodically encountered. Some of the staunchest advocates of the Resistance were deeply moved and impressed by Oakland. Lennie Heller, speaking in Washington on October 20 after flying in from the west coast, his eyes still smart-ing from the tear gas, was obviously more excited by the mobile tactics planned in Oakland than by the draft card turn-in he had done so much to organize.

Both the Resistance turn-in and the Oakland demonstration, finally, led to conspiracy indictments of the leaders. The sedate trial of the Spock defendants, which led to conviction by the jury and a technical reversal a year later, and the provocative defense of the Oakland Seven, which led to outright acquittal by the jury, hardly helped unify the movement, even over such traditionally rock-bottom concerns as protection against repression.

Two years later, with Resistance and SDS groups going to pieces in most parts of the country, it was easy to look back on those days in October with longing. Steve Suffet wrote in *WIN* magazine:

> We almost made it once. I don't think people in the movement appreciate how close we came last time around, back on that cold Octo-

ber evening two years ago. The Resistance had just begun, and Oakland Week had just happened, and there we were on the steps of the Pentagon. And when a solitary soldier dropped his gun into the darkness and crossed the line to our side—and then another, and another yet—the critical mass was almost reached. In another moment ten thousand soldiers would throw away their weapons and the next morning the news would reach Vietnam. Entire battalions would make their way to a jubilant Saigon and the war would be over. Jet bombers and helicopters and artillery would be left abandoned throughout Southeast Asia. And you know something? We almost did it. You see, the big difference isn't between one desertion and a million, but between zero and one.

In his nostalgia Steve seems to draw the wrong conclusion, for the gap between three deserters and a million is greater than he admits. One glorious day brought three men to break, temporarily, their military discipline. The lesson to draw from *that* fact is: come back the next day, and the next. The intoxicating mood was not enough to overcome the new divisiveness and the familiar · laziness of the movement, but what happened that day still stands as a reminder that the movement does have the potential, given enough patience to match its energy, to reverse this country's seemingly remorseless course of death and destruction.

Notes to Chapter Ten

Tom Gardner is quoted from letters to Alice Lynd (February 21 and June 22, 1967).

Sources for early SDS attitudes include a conversation between Bill Hartzog and Staughton Lynd (May 29, 1969); Carl Davidson, "Praxis Makes Perfect," *New Left Notes,* March 27, 1967; Steve Hamilton, "October 16 . . . A Moral Witness?," *New Left Notes,* October 2, 1967; Michael James and others, "Take a Step into America," *The Movement,* December 1967. Also *New Left Notes,* June 5, June 12, July 10, October 23, 1967; conversation between Greg Calvert and Staughton Lynd (March 24, 1969); Greg Calvert, "In White America: Radical Consciousness and Social Change," *National Guardian,* March 25, 1967; Peace and Liberation Commune, East Palo Alto, "Six Statements for Peace in America," mimeographed, n.d.; "Anti-Draft Leaders Bring 'Gospel' to SDS," [Michigan] *State News,* April 24, 1967; Jack A. Smith, "Report on SDS: Students Now Stressing 'Resistance,' " *National Guardian,* April 17, 1967.

Greg Calvert's Guatemalan guerrilla story presents an interesting problem in movement mythology. Greg thinks he heard it from Carl Davidson. George Abbott White writes (to Staughton Lynd, November 24, 1969): "Oglesby mentions it in *Containment,* and in an earlier paper, but he got it from Mike Locker, who got it around 1965 working with Peter Henig." This account would make Henig both the source of that seminal anecdote and the discoverer of the channeling memorandum.

On the Pentagon: Florence Howe and Paul Lauter, "Besieging the Pentagon," unpublished mss.; Mike Goldfield, "The Washington Siege of '67," *New Left Notes,* October 30, 1967; Tom Bell to Staughton Lynd (May 1, 1969); George Dennison, "Talking with the Troops," *Liberation,* November 1967; Paul E. Rupert to Local Board No. 1, Hyannis, Massachusetts (n.d.) reprinted in *Resist* #1 (Palo Alto); Martin Jezer, Paul Johnson, and Susan Kemp in *WIN,* October 30 and November 15, 1967.

On Oakland: Steve Hamilton to Norma Becker (July 7, 1967); conversation between David Harris, Dennis Sweeney, and Staughton Lynd (March 12, 1969); STDW, *An Open Letter to All People Fighting the Draft,* n.d.; *The Movement,* October 1967 and November 1967; Tom W. Smith, "Oakland Police Brutality Plants Seeds of White Revolution," *Rag,* October 23, 1967; Emma Rothschild, "Notes from a Political Trial," *New York Review of Books,* July 10, 1969, reprinted in *Trials of the Resistance* (New York: *New York Review,* 1970); Robert Meriwether and Roy Kepler, "The Meaning of Oakland," *WIN,* November 30, 1967; Stuart McRae, "Oakland Week," *Resist,* December 1967; David Harris to Staughton Lynd (August 22, 1969); Frank Bardacke, "Stop-the-Draft Week," *STEPS No. 2,* quoted by Mitchell Goodman, "Year of the Flea," *WIN,* April 1, 1969.

The "lessons" of the Pentagon and Oakland are in the leaflet *Hang Loose, Be Beautiful, Hang Cool,* n.d., New York City.

Steve Suffet's nostalgic paragraph occurs in Martin Jezer and Steve Suffet, "From Dissent to Resistance to Dissent to . . . ," *WIN,* December 15, 1969.

CHAPTER ELEVEN

Life in the Resistance

After the confrontations of October 16–21 resisters settled down to the long haul. National organization existed only in the form of a network of communication which produced a national resistance newsletter, planned three annual national conferences, and decided on the days for further draft card turn-ins. Apart from these common dates, each of the local groups was essentially on its own.

Resistance groups, in the words of an early leaflet, were "action committees" made up of people who had turned in or burned their draft cards. How to follow that act was not obvious, either to individual or group. One answer was to appeal to others to do likewise, but such work was not wholly satisfying, and someone who turned in his card on October 16 could not indefinitely postpone making a decision about the future, or about how he was going to live his life, simply by organizing for the next turn-in. Early resisters assumed that the government would resolve the question for them by rapid and massive prosecutions, but in fact the reaction of the authorities was slow and inconsistent. In the pause that followed October 16, then, a serious problem confronted most Resistance groups: beyond the single tactic of draft card turn-ins they had no political program, no plan of day-to-day work (comparable, say, to voter registration in the South) which could help individuals and groups keep themselves together.

149

For many people the problem was never completely settled. Even when groups made committees and developed programs to maintain and spread day-to-day resistance, the feeling of uncertainty remained. The members of a group could never be sure that a project begun one week would continue through the next, since the group was, almost by definition, a committee without a permanent staff. In its first year of existence, for example, CADRE lost a half-dozen members to prison. The situation was made more difficult by the groups' awareness that they could not fill the jails after all, and that going to prison was an event in the lives only of the resister and his few friends.

The sense of uncertainty, and at times of waste, left its mark on the style of Resistance work and organization. It was in part responsible for the informal structure of most groups and the great amount of individual freedom retained by the members. When a problem arose that affected the group as a whole, it would be considered at the business meetings held once or twice a week, and a decision reached (almost always) through consensus. Most decisions, however, were made privately, as members worked out the details of day-to-day activity. In some groups, like the Twin Cities Draft Information Center (TCDIC), a "work ethic" was established, which demanded long hours, solid execution, and a precise division of labor. Other groups were more fluid. CADRE encouraged its members to "do their own thing," and projects were usually initiated by people who were interested in certain areas and came to CADRE seeking support. In both groups individual autonomy was the rule, though members were expected to discuss their work with other people. As Sandy Wilkinson of TCDIC explained,

> the idea of consulting other people before a final decision was made served not so much to spread out decision-making, although it did that to a certain extent, but more importantly, it kept everybody else aware of what a person working on some other project had in sight.

It was natural for Resistance groups to spread out the decision-making process, since membership was always so uncertain, and those most experienced in leadership were the most likely candidates for prison.

The diffusion of authority also reflected a spirit of comradeship which was inevitable among people who had taken risks together. Because they faced the same dangers, resisters tended to feel a personal responsibility toward one another. As much as possible they encouraged spontaneous, informal talk, and attempted to make their daily work part of an ongoing discussion. They expected to be isolated in prison; they did not want to belong to a group which also isolated them through impersonal, bureaucratic techniques.

The kind of work done by Resistance groups often required an informal and flexible approach. Activities varied, depending on the nature of the group and the character of the city in which it was located. In Minneapolis–St. Paul, where there had been relatively little antidraft work, TCDIC set up the first program to train draft counselors. Because the city lacked radical roots, TCDIC worked to establish a base of "adult" support for the Resistance, and organized a series of turn-ins of which one was oriented toward people over draft age. At the same time a high-school program was begun, which eventuated in a vigorous student union, addressing itself to arbitrary authority in the schools as well as to the draft. The Philadelphia Resistance confronted a different set of problems. While TCDIC was forced to start from scratch, Philadelphia already had a long history of dissent, and was the home of myriad antiwar organizations. The founding members of the Philadelphia group had been active previously in such projects as Vietnam Summer, and brought from them an interest in community work. Though they too provided counseling services and arranged turn-ins, they attempted to reach beyond the usual middle-class constituency of the Resistance. But they also tended more toward acts of civil disobedience than other groups, and consequently spent more time in jails.

Whether they struggled toward respectability or away from it, Resistance groups across the country continued to experiment with many different programs. They marched, picketed, leafleted, sat-in, debated, rallied. They talked to church groups, housewives, high-school dropouts, draft boards, and servicemen. They wrote volumes of statements and letters. Their offices were turned into counseling centers, legal defense bureaus, fund-raising centers, and coffee houses. But in spite of the wide range of activities, Resistance groups shared a certain style, not only in their informal and autonomous structure, but in their attitude toward the life and work of the movement.

RESISTANCE STYLE

A week before Christmas, 1968, twenty members of the Philadelphia Resistance went to the police headquarters to sing carols. After half an hour of traditional songs, the carolers ended with "The Twelve Days of Christmas":

On the twelfth day of Christmas my true love sent to me
12 mayors proclaiming
11 jailers jailing
10 bondsmen bailing
 9 sirens wailing
 8 tanks a-rolling
 7 dogs all growling
 6 rolls of barbed wire
 5 cans of mace
 4 billy clubs
 3 cattle prods
 2 tear-gas bombs and
 a Smith and Wesson from the armory.

Then one of them, dressed as Santa Claus, "offered the police boxes of cookies, as our gift to the police and prisoners. Lt. George Fencl, in the true spirit of the holidays, refused to accept them, saying that police cannot accept gifts." The disappointed celebrants released to the press a statement making clear that, "while we have had confrontations with the police, we do not regard the men of the police force as our enemies, nor do we feel that they are the initiators of the policies of repression which we object to."

This little scene, typical of the Philadelphia Resistance, illuminates several aspects of the Resistance in most parts of the country. By and large, Resistance groups have hesitated to brand anyone as the enemy, at least not such obviously oppressed agents of the system as 'the police or IRS men. They have preferred the shout made famous at the Pentagon, "join us," to the cry of "pig!" Not that they expected the police to "join" the Resistance, but for a movement that claims all men are brothers to brand some as enemies, they felt, is not only inconsistent but will only guarantee that they remain enemies. It may be naive to expect the police to be neutralized, or confused, by Christmas carols, but it is not naive to plan for the day when the movement will embrace its present enemies, and there is no point making the task harder than it already is.

Somehow, of course, the police must be dealt with, and humor, where possible, has often seemed the best recourse. If there was a touch of mockery and arrogance in the Christmas caroling it was incidental to the main point, but in the now-legendary encounter of Alex Jack with the FBI in Boston it *was* the main point. Immediately after October 16 nearly everyone in New England who had turned in his card was visited by the FBI. Not everyone was prepared, and a few were frightened. The Resistance office and several lawyers worked overtime apprising people of their rights, calming parents, and keeping a record of the interviews. Things were tense. But when Alex Jack was visited by his two agents, he so adroitly reversed roles that everyone who heard about it relaxed.

He borrowed the office of the Boston University *News* for the occasion, staffed it with Resistance people (cleverly disguised as students), and took over the central office himself. When the agents presented themselves, he ushered them into the inner office, put his feet on the desk, and said, "Thank you for coming. I just have a few questions." He handed them each three sheets of paper, all carefully mimeographed. The first was a questionnaire with spaces to check yes or no. After filling in their name, address, phone, and alias, the agents were to answer such questions as these:

> Do you believe that Justice Department employees, including FBI agents, should be given "essential" job deferments while peace and

civil rights workers are denied? YES _____ NO _____. If your answer is NO, do you plan to relinquish your present status and apply for
conscientious objection? YES _____ NO _____.

Do you believe that the Justice Department was derelict in its duty to
uphold the law when in Washington, D.C. on Oct. 20, 1967 the Attorney
General's Office refused to accept 994 draft cards as evidence of that
many crimes being committed against the Selective Service System?
YES _____ NO _____. If your answer is yes, do you plan to investigate the Attorney General and his assistants for aiding and abetting draft
resistance? YES _____ NO _____.

Do you feel that it is the patriotic and legal duty of the Bureau to investigate President Johnson, Secretary Rusk, Secretary McNamara, the
Joint Chiefs of Staff, the CIA, and General Hershey for war crimes,
crimes against humanity, treason, and other misdemeanors against the
American people, the Vietnamese people, and the peace and security of
the world on the basis of the US Constitution, the American and Vietnamese Declarations of Independence, the UN Charter, the 1954 Geneva
Agreements, and the Nuremberg Statutes? YES _____ NO _____.

The second sheet was nearly identical to the form the FBI
carries for their victims, a waiver stating the signer has been informed of his rights under the Fifth Amendment.

The last sheet was entitled "FBI for the Resistance Support
Pledge" and offered five courses of action to check off, including
"I will join other FBI agents for the Resistance and turn in or
burn my draft card in Boston on November 16th when 500 New
England students and 500 faculty and clergy join the second wave
of non-cooperation" and "I wish to organize in my local community and my place of employment."

When they knew they had been had, they left in a huff. They
were followed by a band of Resistance "agents" who looked them
up and down, scribbled noisily in pads, and said "Ah yes" and
"Very interesting" until they drove away.

For most of its first year the New England Resistance had an
uncannily friendly relationship with the police. The Resistance,
for its part, was interested in confrontations not with the police
but with the draft boards, army brass, and courts. The police in
turn seemed to worry only about violence and traffic control, and
found the Resistance cooperative enough, though probably they

also sensed a fair amount of community support (the *Boston Globe,* for instance) behind it. A number of policemen admitted they did not like the war, and "wouldn't want my son drafted to fight in it."

The peak of cordial relations came late on April Fool's Eve, 1968, about three hours after President Johnson's television abdication. Over two thousand young people had gathered near Boston University and began a victory parade down Commonwealth Avenue toward the Public Garden and the Common. With honking cars, drums and trumpets, singing, dancing, shouts of "the wicked old witch is dead," the crowd rolled down the malled avenue—to the apparent delight of the police. The officers obligingly stopped traffic for the parade, smiled and flashed V-signs, and yelled "Down with Johnson" (whether they were for McCarthy, like most Massachusetts Democrats, or for Wallace, like most policemen, was not clear). Everybody was having fun.

It got tense only when the crowd neared the State House overlooking the Common, and threatened to storm it out of sheer joy. Police looked nervous, clasped clubs, radioed for reinforcements. At that point Bill Hunt and Michael Ferber from the Resistance arrived with bull horns to give a rap on war resistance and plug for the turn-in on April 3. When the police captain recognized them he turned to an officer and said, "Ah, thank God the anarchists are here! Now everything is under control."

The Philadelphia Christmas carolers were also giving expression to a conviction, common to Resistance groups (as well as to some SDS groups and the Yippies) that revolution should be fun. Of course "fun" suggests trivial playing at revolution, shrinking from responsibility and risk, but it can also mean a celebratory and joyous involvement in the struggle. The issue, as some Resistance groups have seen it, is this: are we to forego all the playful, artistic, sexual, and spiritual aspects of life—the kinds of things that will flourish in the liberated society we want—during the struggle to bring about that society? If so then we risk becoming unfit to bring it about or live in it if we do. Or are not the forces of creativity and festivity vital parts of the struggle itself? The issue is important. One of the most oppressive features of highly organized modern societies is the dearth of authentic creative work and joy. It is one of the tasks of revolution-minded groups not only to prepare a place in the future where these things can occur but to make them happen in the times and spaces available in the present. A slogan of the May 1968 insurrection in France reads, "Une révolution qui demande que l'on se sacrifice pour elle est une révolution à la papa" ("A revolution that asks you to sacrifice yourself for it is one of daddy's revolutions")—it mirrors the society it aims to replace. Resisters were ready to go to prison, but not to sell their souls.

Probably without being conscious of general ideas like these, Resistance groups continued to exemplify them by enjoying themselves as they worked. The Philadelphia Resistance showed their healthy sense of whimsy in other demonstrations besides the caroling. A few weeks before Christmas the Resistance guerrilla theater group staged a bloody battle in the toy department of a large store.

           December 3 was chosen as the date for no particular reason. Gimbels was chosen as the department store since they are among the most aggressive in the advertising of war toys. . . .

In preparation for the event toy guns were solicited from sympathetic parents who had erred in the past. Packets of fake blood that could be palmed and exploded when slapped against a combatant's face were made. Plans were kept secret, or so it was thought.

D-day arrived and eight resisters marched off to war, down Walnut St., trying to look inconspicuous with weapons and army coats concealed in shopping bags.

The troops arrived at the front, Gimbels' toyland, and imagine their surprise when they discovered the place occupied by good old Lt. George Fencl and company. Not desirous of becoming involved in a real war (rumor has it that their guns are real) the Resistance troops retreated after a very short period of negotiation.

Determined to have a war despite the opposition, Resistance members searched for a new battleground.

This time E. J. Korvettes in Cedarbrook Mall was chosen and after a short ride the troops arrived ready for action.

After reaching the gun counter of the toy department, the war was begun. Shoppers were at first startled and confused but one middle-aged woman offered an explanation to everyone around her by stating with assurance that "it's just an advertisement."

When things started to get "bloody" people realized that it was not an advertisement although they also realized that it was not a real shoot-out. Their bewilderment was cleared up when they were handed an anti-war leaflet by a resister circulating through the crowd.

In honor of the sentencing of the Spock trial defendants in July 1968 the Philadelphia Resistance put white gags around a dozen statues of American revolutionaries.

Meanwhile Palo Alto started a "cleanliness and Godliness Skiffle Band" that played for Resistance events. Ray Mungo dressed up like a drum major to refuse induction at the Boston Army Base, and then invited his six hundred supporters to breakfast at the Arlington Street Church. Ray Frenchman wore evening clothes, with top hat and cane, to his induction refusal in Providence, Rhode Island. By expressing the high-spirited life of the Resistance these escapades and styles attracted sympathy and support (not to mention publicity). Conversely, they have served to expose the clumsiness, pomposity, and impersonality of an oppressive system. Though not too much thought has gone into this, the aggressive or mocking side of these demonstrations seems to have great potential. What aggressive humor can accomplish on a large scale might be inferred from the May events in France, where the puckish Cohn-Bendit and his army of Groucho Marxists and mad sloganeers drew vastly more public sympathy than the more powerful but grim Communist Party.

For resisters to have enjoyed their work so much they had to enjoy each other. Most groups tried to find ways to bring the membership together for occasions separate from organizational work and decisions, such as picnics, parties, and sporting events. The New England Resistance and the Boston Draft Resistance Group played two football games ("Peace Creeps" versus "Commie Dupes"), and the Philadelphia Resistance football team played a whole season of games against such opponents as the Trots, the radio station of the University of Pennsylvania, and the Young Americans for Freedom. A typical, at one time almost universal, Resistance institution was the Monday-night dinner.

Somehow nearly every sizable group in the country independently settled on Monday nights as the best time to eat overcooked spaghetti, hear news, rap about Resistance projects, and horse around. Policy decisions, such as they were, usually waited for the steering committee meetings, to which everyone was always invited.

Meetings, as we have said, were conducted informally, and usually by consensus rather than balloting. Some of the early Resistance organizers, who set the style of their groups, gained their movement experience with SNCC, which reached most of its decisions by consensus. In SNCC the decisions were so vital to individual and group safety that only a unanimity bred of common experience and careful discussion made any sense at all. Many projects had a chance of success only if everyone worked devotedly; for a project to receive only 62 percent of the vote suggested less than adequate commitment, and even those who voted in favor would be reluctant to risk their lives carrying it out. Other Resistance organizers came from northern student organizations like early SDS, CNVA, or Quaker youth groups, where consensus was the rule. Some organizers, of one or both backgrounds, encountered the new style in SDS that began to prevail around 1966: long ideological wrangling, slogan chanting, intricate parliamentary maneuvers, and voting, instead of reports of experiences, informal and open-ended discussions, and decisions by consensus. SDS meetings became celebrations of two little red books, Mao's maxims and Robert's rules. Resistance organizers were determined that the groups they worked in did not fall victim to the same style.

At times Resistance meetings resembled group-therapy sessions. Resisters, or those on the verge of resisting, stayed up all night talking, "getting their heads out," probing themselves and each other in a very personal way. At other times meetings had specific problems or "business." These often were tedious and long, like any business meeting, and the spirit of candor and fellow feeling often weakened. The informal style also failed to prevent those with strong personalities and well-articulated ideas from dominating the discussions. At one point New England Resistance meetings were reduced to long dialogues between the two most articulate members, and when they quarreled Resistance work came to a near standstill. More formal parliamentary procedure might have dampened their ardor, but it could not have invigorated the group as a whole. Ultimately only the honesty, open-mindedness, and deference of the members can make a meeting worth the effort, and no procedure can compensate for them if they are absent. The informal style of the Resistance at least allowed the innate energy and generosity of the membership its maximum play. In most cases it worked well.

Perhaps another reason for the relatively tolerant style within the Resistance lay in the stiff initiation rite of the membership. As David Osher of the New York Resistance put it:

> It's as though every member of the group had met his existential test. At meetings, no one is called cop-out, and individuals can oppose militant stands without being denounced as chickens. A tolerance exists, a sense of brotherhood, a lack of the radical status-seeking all too often found among most of the other New Left groups. This confidence becomes increasingly important as political actions start to be defined as tests of guts. One does not go out into the streets or get busted solely to test one's manhood. That, and I am afraid we are heading there, is middle-class politics.

One aspect of middle-class politics that the Resistance did not escape was male chauvinism. Some Resistance groups tended toward a tacit acceptance of male superiority that was based on little more than pride or insecurity. Quite a number of women worked with resisters, but most of them were not at the center of decision-making, action, and attention. When an exception was tacitly granted to a hard-working young woman, her exceptional status only proved the rule. Some groups, perhaps because the draft is so obviously a male thing, were eager to find "equivalents" for women that went beyond supportive actions like burning a boyfriend's card. A few all-women sit-ins took place at draft boards and induction centers, and "Women Against Daddy Warbucks" staged an effective raid on a New York draft board. As long as the focus was the draft and the army, however, some women felt that the Resistance was not for them. When at the national Resistance conference in March 1969 a women's caucus confronted the men in a brilliant, tough, and compassionate way, many men responded well, and some projects were planned. But in local groups some women continued to feel strongly out of place, and before the broadening ideas of resistance took effect they drifted away. The New England Resistance, already weakened for other reasons, could not keep up with the women's caucus, and when it walked out, the group virtually fell apart.

Many people have been brought into the movement simply by a good long talk with someone already in it, and probably less by the content of the conversation than by the degree of communication. To talk and listen in an involved and authentic way is a liberating act, and in a society where talk is reduced to hollow bombast or merely functional symbols it can be the beginning of a political movement. If the movement is to be true to its initial insights it will maintain its direct and personal approach in speaking and living together. It was natural that resisters, asserting at once their individual humanity against an impersonal machine and their sense of world community with humanity in general, would turn to alternative ways of living, like work cooperatives and intentional communities. It was also natural to turn to one another for support during the uncertainty and loneliness that all resisters faced. But as with other Resistance undertakings the experiments in commmunity living, working, and decision-making tried to balance the competing demands of individualism and collectivism, to make, however unconsciously, what Buber calls the "third alternative." That alternative, says Buber, is grounded neither in the self nor in the aggregate, but in a series of honest dialogues between one person and another. "Getting your head out" was sometimes a vital part of Resistance work, for when someone in honesty responded, community was reestablished. Common antidraft work was the external basis for the commune, but authentic personal encounters were its life.

The Palo Alto commune was one of the most intense of the Resistance experiments in group living, but in varying sizes and for varying lengths of time (usually brief) communes flourished around the country. One hesitates to call them successful, but then they are not necessarily failures for lasting only a short time.

They were places where important things happened in the lives of those who tried to make them work, and their experiences may remain sustaining memories and sources of action in the future. As Susan Sontag wrote in her *Trip to Hanoi,* "Someone who has enjoyed . . . a reprieve, however brief, from the inhibition on love and trust this society enforces, is never the same again."

A group called Christian Resistance gave some serious thought to the question of community. They saw in the struggles of the Resistance and others the basis for a true *ecclesia* that would undertake the task of reconstructing the social order in the joyous spirit of the early Christians. In a statement put out in San Francisco early in 1968 the Christian Resistance wrote:

> We take this step of non-cooperation as an act of Christian witness and as a sign of our conviction that in America today religious obedience must, at some points, take the form of civil disobedience. We affirm, with Bonhoeffer, that our task is "participation in the suffering of God in the life of the world." . . . And yet, although we are painfully aware that the Cross stands at the center of the Christian life, we are not acting in quest of martyrdom. Rather, we are committed to the development of a Christian community with the intellectual and spiritual resources to maintain its independence of a national ideology and style of life becoming ever more callous to theological and humanistic values. We seek to discover and affirm that a life lived in the context of risk and suffering can also be a life which leads to the formation of joyous and vibrant community. We are attempting to face with equanimity, even with joy, the futuristic, open-ended dimensions of our situation, and to develop without abdicating our responsibility for rational analysis a new kind of realism that is appropriate to the openness of the future and the level of our commitment.

Its membership, never large, served as leavening in the rising loaves within the major religious denominations, extracting official support for draft resisters and deserters. They have been at the heart of the sanctuary movement and the campaign for amnesty for political prisoners. Some of them have joined in draft board raids like those in Catonsville and Milwaukee (see chapter 14).

Bruce Nelson, active San Francisco organizer for the Resistance, Christian and otherwise, wrote a short paper that ended with some remarks on community:

Many Resistance members are deeply concerned with the formation of community, and in some instances our common commitment is leading to the development of strong communal bonds. For at least two reasons this must continue to be a central concern. First, it would be impossible for most of us to face up to the tasks ahead, particularly the prospect of prison, were it not for the strength which derived from the experience of community. The Palo Alto Resistance, which has revolved around the life of a remarkable intentional community for more than a year now, is the clearest and most formal achievement of the community we seek. But, in less formal ways, the same patterns of interdependence are emerging elsewhere.

Secondly, the formation of community may bear an essential relationship to the shape of the future. Already, after only a few years of existence, the radical movement of the 1960's stands in danger of being consumed by its alienation from—and, in many cases, its hatred of—the old order. History demonstrates the paradoxical fact that those who are most intense in their desire for a freer and more humane order often fall victim to the dehumanizing aspects of their struggle. If radicals are to remain faithful to their own values, then they must create mechanisms in which those values can not only be expressed but also *experienced* in the present. As Richard Shaull comments in his essay in *Containment and Change,* "the shape of the new order becomes most clear, not through the definition of a set of ideals, but in a living community which expresses and at the same time points to a new reality of social existence, and provides a laboratory in which its diverse aspects can be experimentally worked out."

The "new reality of social existence" that Resistance communities expressed was not free of serious conflict, and we will conclude this chapter by acknowledging the deep difficulties that some groups encountered. Whether they were due to the inevitable stresses of Resistance work or to the fragile foundation—a returned draft card—on which in many groups high hopes were built, the defeats that Resistance communities met were often extremely painful. It was difficult for someone who was going to prison, no matter how strong he was, not to feel a sense of betrayal by those who were not, whether by their own devices or by the mysterious workings of the courts and draft boards. There was never a felt unanimity about the meaning of returning a card, though the "purist" line of total noncooperation dominated the rhetoric. Those who considered it a lesser act—as a risky protest, perhaps, but not a pledge of imprisonment or a fetish of manhood—felt coerced by the more militant line, while the purists often watched in dismay as their brothers launched legal suits, feigned disabilities at physicals, and accepted new cards. Some of the key organizers of the Resistance found for a variety of reasons that they could not maintain their commitment. For some the outcome was deeply disturbing to them and their groups, and they have been lost to the Resistance, and in some cases to the entire movement, by their guilt and grief.

Notes to Chapter Eleven

The principal source for the first few pages of this chapter is the conversation with members of CADRE cited in chapter 7.

The Philadelphia caroling is described in *Philadelphia Resistance Review,* February 1969. Alex Jack's story and FBI forms were both circulated widely in New England. War toys battle quoted from *Philadelphia Resistance Review,* December–January 1968–69. David Osher's quote is from his "Politics and Strategy of Resistance," *New Politics,* v. VII, no. 4 (Fall 1969).

For more on Buber's ideas on community see "What Is Man?" (in *Between Man and Man*) and *Paths in Utopia.* Bruce Nelson's paper is entitled "The Resistance" and was written early in 1968.

CHAPTER TWELVE

Community-Based Resistance

After the week of October 16–21, the relationship between SDS and the Resistance worsened. SDS members increasingly came to see the Resistance as a form of middle-class self-indulgence which they had once engaged in but since outgrown; and resisters responded by viewing the trend in SDS toward dogmatic theory and Leninist organization as a betrayal of the values which had drawn them into politics in the first place.

Yet the effort to combine the political perspectives of the two organizations continued for half a year longer at the national level, and longer still for many local groups. Shortly after the demonstrations of October 16–21 Carl Davidson described students' efforts to ban military recruiters and research from the university as "institutional resistance," and termed the student movement at large "an American resistance movement." Greg Calvert was still talking this language in November 1967, when in an interview with *The Movement* he emphasized the need for white radicals to discover their own identity and their own power to rebel.

I've always argued the student movement has to . . . develop an image of its own revolution, about its own struggle, instead of believing that you're revolutionary because you're related to Fidel's struggle, Stokely's struggle, always somebody else's struggle. . . . So much of the movement . . . has been whites in America who sensed that they weren't somehow whole, that somehow out of their experience they couldn't

164

build a revolution, trying to gain access to the possibilities of other people's revolutionary potentials. . . . We have to find the issues in our America which are real to us.

At the beginning of 1968 SDS still considered the draft its principal organizing target. National secretary Mike Spiegel called attention to the possibilities created by the revocation of deferments for graduate students. In a letter to Resist written on February 2, Les Coleman stated:

> The last SDS national conference mandated and authorized the national office to "up" its national draft program efforts as much as possible. The three focuses of the program are 1) the seniors program (which is off to a good start) 2) draft resistance counseling on the campus and 3) draft resistance projects in the community and in the high schools (which is going best of all).

As late as March 10, 1968, Sue Eanet and Mike Klonsky projected an ambitious draft program for Southern California in a letter to Resist requesting $16,000 for the next six months. The two SDS organizers claimed that there were ten traveling organizers coordinating draft resistance programs on nearly every campus in Southern California, in two-year as well as four-year colleges. Over twelve hundred high school students had struck and attended rallies protesting the draft in October 1967, they continued, a fact which encouraged them to build a draft coalition of white, black, and Mexican-American youth. "We have learned," they wrote, "that draft resistance can serve as a common denominator for uniting groups which would not ordinarily participate in common meetings or actions." To this end they sought funding for five community organizers, twelve campus organizers, two high school coordinators, and two office workers. Sue and Mike made their political perspective, the dominant one in SDS, explicit: "We encourage students to get out of the draft by any means necessary in order to remain where they are and to organize. We feel that we must stress going beyond individual non-cooperation into collective, political resistance." Yet there were overtones of Resistance rhetoric in the letter's summation:

Survival, in America, means organized resistance. We want to build a community of resistance and defense. The issues we choose are routes through which the community can deal with the larger problem on our hands—that of the antihuman society. So the draft, the police, and the repressive atmosphere and low quality of public education, are all issues which people can respond to because they threaten the very lives of our people. We view it as essential that our people recognize the interrelatedness of the survival of student radicals, community organizers, and working-class people. . . .

Greg Calvert caught the mood of those months a year later:

After the summer of '67, the Pentagon action and Stop the Draft Week which preceded it, it seemed to some of us that the time was rapidly approaching when the resistance notion of strategy could become the base for a new kind of radical solidarity among a variety of elements within the movement. I mean by "resistance strategy" a notion which included not only draft resistance and non-cooperation, but also resistance to Dow Chemical and other institutions of repression.

Rapprochement between SDS and the Resistance seemed possible after the indictment of Spock, Coffin, Raskin, Goodman, and Ferber in January 1968. Greg Calvert and Michael Ferber consulted by long-distance telephone about coordinating the rallies planned by the two national networks. In response to the indictments, John Fuerst wrote a pamphlet on "Resistance and Repression," which the SDS national office printed and· distributed, in which he tried to synthesize the personal and the political. John spoke of the need to make connections between political demands and "the sometimes unspoken personal needs for liberation which gave the spirit to the anti-war movement." The American university was characterized as "both an institution of political power and an institution of personal repression." Resistance, in John's view, was the bridge between the personal and the political:

The resistance movement on campuses has meant that the personal problems which confront students because of the social use they are put to become political problems of the first order. . . . And draft resistance has become a way of organizing people around their most immediate and personal troubles in a manner which directly relates those troubles to the harsh political power of a repressively run society.

The most sustained efforts to combine the insights of the Resistance and SDS were at a local level. Taking from the Resistance the idea that the draft affected persons in an intense and personal way which made it an ideal issue around which to organize, and from SDS an increasing emphasis on organizing which was multi-issue and oriented to the working class, a number of movement activists projected the strategy of "community-based resistance." In October 1967, Mike Spiegel and Carl Davidson of the SDS national office gave this concept their blessing, calling in *New Left Notes* for "organizing on the local and regional levels permanent, multi-issue, radical constituencies with a capacity for resistance rather than protest." The draft, SDS national draft coordinator Jeff Segal added, could be a "catalyst issue around which large and divergent amounts of community organizing work can be done. Organizers going into a community can start by talking about the draft, but stirring up people to move into other kinds of issues around local control and power."

The strategy of taking the draft as a catalyst or entering wedge for multi-issue community organizing received its definitive formulation in an article that appeared in *The Movement,* November 1967. It was written by Dee Jacobsen, who like Jeff Segal was from the SDS national office, but it grew out of discussions and early drafts in which SDS veterans Vernon Grizzard, Paul Potter, John Maher, and Les Coleman each had a hand. All of them, but especially Vernon and Paul, were experienced "ERAP workers": they had tried multi-issue community organizing in black and working-class white communities as a part of what was from 1964 to 1966 the main off-campus thrust of SDS, the Economic Research and Action Project. They felt it important to combine their skills and insights with the new and increasingly prominent issues of the draft.

The densely argued article, "We've Got to Reach Our Own People," developed a number of basic ideas:

1. Working-class people will not respond to "symbolic tactics" but want political action which will produce "real gains." (The article does not say what a "real gain" in the struggle against the draft might be.)

2. The war "hits hardest" among working-class people, and they know it. "Unlike some of the other things community projects have tried to work on, there is no need to produce 'consciousness' about this issue."

3. The draft "is the MOST IMPORTANT AND MOST TANGIBLE manifestation of the war." It is "important enough so that people will take a stand against his [sic] neighbor or his bowling team or the men he drinks with or works next to."

4. Opposition to the draft

> can strengthen the opposition to other institutions when they are used to suppress it. When the schools expel students for forming a high school draft resistance league, the general anger of the community about the school has a foundation and anchor that the abstractness of the "school problem" may have prevented from forming before.

5. Draft resistance may be nourished by the very alienation that dampens political participation through conventional channels. "Less than half of these communities vote because they don't believe political leaders will do anything for them."

6. Now, rather than after the war, is the best time to create political motion because "while the war continues, conditions in poor and working-class communities are getting tighter."

7. A draft resistance union can root itself in a working-class community because it will make sense to people accustomed to collective self-defense through trade unions.

8. A draft resistance union should exemplify solidarity. In words which recalled early movement rhetoric about "participatory democracy" and anticipated later talk about "affinity groups," the organizers wrote:

> You are a serious resistance: don't vote on issues, discuss them until you can agree. All the pain of long meetings amounts to a group which knows itself well, holds together with a serious, human spirit, and any member of which can step into a role of responsibility if someone

else leaves. Fight for that kind of group, because people will want to join with it: there are not many things in this country like that. Stand by each other.

As early as the spring of 1967 several local groups began to put into practice the ideas later elaborated in the article. New York City SDS tried to set up draft resistance unions on the Lower East Side and the Upper West Side in the hope, as they put it, that "collective community action against the draft can provide a good base for general political action." A Washington Draft Resistance Union sought to bring people together in such a way that "the members of the draft group will be forced to bring the issues raised by the draft into the context of their own lives, and begin to relate the unfreedom of the draft to the unfreedom in their own lives." But the largest and most influential of such groups were the Boston Draft Resistance Group (BDRG) and the Wisconsin Draft Resistance Union (WDRU).

BDRG

The Boston Draft Resistance Group grew out of the We Won't Go statements of Harvard and Brandeis in April 1967. For the first few weeks Bill Hunt, Tim Wright, and others who had collected signatures and published the statement spent their time trying to get established on more campuses. "For the past two weeks," an early newsletter declared, "we have concentrated on canvassing students. . . . We are assembling a fund of information on the legal aspects of draft resistance, and several of us are receiving training from the Friends in draft counseling. We have no intention at the moment of setting up a counseling service as such." They had an eye, however, toward moving into the community:

> Our concern now is to move off campus into high school and working class organizing. We are investigating the possibility of co-ordinating our draft resistance work with the community organizing projects of Michael Walzer and John Maher, which are serving as models for the national Vietnam Summer program. The attitude of national Vietnam

Summer towards draft resistance work is frankly ambiguous, although the steering committee has explicitly endorsed the concept and offered financial support.

In another few weeks they did move off campus and began to leaflet the neighborhood, give talks in schools, and seek out draftable young men in snack bars and pool halls. Like other groups they had heard about, such as the Milwaukee Organizing Committee, BDRG people attempted to locate those classified 1–A (whose names but not addresses are posted by draft boards) and offer them help. They also mounted periodic demonstrations at the Boston Army Base. Late in the summer, as increasing numbers of young men sought advice, they began a program of expert draft counseling, but for its first three or four months of community operation BDRG was mainly a "talking machine," as one worker put it, simply spreading the word in as many ways as it could to all the young men in the Boston area.

In September, Vernon Grizzard, Nick Egleson, and John Maher joined BDRG. Nick, like Vernon, had been both a national officer of SDS and an ERAP organizer, and had spent the summer with Vernon in Boston running a school for community organizers. John Maher had been working with Vietnam Summer. Their joining BDRG had the effect of shifting attention away from random outreach programs and demonstrations and more toward multi-issue community organizing. Counseling was one way to reach people, but it was slow, one-by-one, and only a fraction of the counselees were from working-class neighborhoods. They wanted other ways.

The plan they chose to concentrate on they called "The Early Morning Show": BDRG members were to meet at the boarding points for the buses that take the pre-inductees to the army base for their physicals, ride the buses with them, and talk to them about the draft and how to avoid it. It was described succinctly in an early newsletter:

> The program works as follows. Through some (forever secret) ploy, the BDRG Intelligence Squad gets the schedule of events. Then five or six BDRG members show up at the draft board at 6:30 A.M. to meet,

counsel, and organize the pre-inductees. (Often the BDRG squad stays overnight at one person's apartment and shares breakfast before setting off.) Once there, we circulate among the guys, explaining the possible alternatives to induction and offering them our support. Many of these guys want to talk; a good percentage of them are already consciously against the war, and a lot more are badly confused. We tell them about deferments, exemptions, and their right to refuse to sign the Security Questionnaire. We also hand out Draft Fact Cards with our address and phone and even make appointments for them to come in for counseling. Then we ride down to the induction center with them on the bus, wish them good luck, and catch a return bus back to town (usually by 8:00). All in all it's a pretty groovy way to start the day.

Occasionally BDRG members infiltrated into the base and posed as pre-inductees. When safely into the examination room they passed out leaflets and gave speeches against the war until they were evicted by Sergeant Brown. This particular operation was called "The Horror Show." "As the military-industrial complex goes, the Boston Army Base is a pretty bush-league operation, considering its crucial role in the lives and deaths of the young men of Boston." Thus began one of the first reports of The Horror Show in the BDRG newsletter (which was to become famous for its lively and literate prose style, thanks largely to Tim Wright).

Jutting out into the grim waters of Boston Bay, it's a conglomeration of warehouses, offices, recruiting and induction chambers. At ten minute intervals, a public bus leaves South Station, carrying army personnel, civilian workers, inductees, pre-inductees, and the Boston Draft Resistance Group to their appointed tasks. There is thus public access to the interior of the Base—a fact of considerable legal significance. . . . The security (!?) guards are civilians, with what seems to be a median age of 86, who can often be bullied and/or cajoled. So far we have allowed ourselves to be sluggishly evicted, although not without making a vivid impact on incoming draftees and passers-by. . . . (A snatch of dialogue from a recent raid may give a sense of the atmosphere. A civilian goon grabbed one of us by the shirt, muttering dire threats. GOON: "Listen, buddy. . . ." RESISTER: "If you don't get your hands off me in one second I'll have you booked for assault." GOON: "Well . . . don't get sore. But you guys better watch it." RESISTER: "We do.")

BDRG issued a cool, professional-sounding memo on "Anti-Draft Organizing at Pre-Induction Physicals," complete with a list of the eleven duties of an Early Morning Show leader and a suggested speech. It also printed large quantities of a small "Draft Facts" card to be handed out on buses and at physicals. One side of the card introduced the BDRG, quoting an antiwar GI; the other side listed nine classifications which would keep a man out of the army as well as the alternatives of Canada and induction refusal.

At its peak the BDRG was appearing regularly at the pre-induction physicals of twenty different draft boards. There were occasional arrests and minor hassles, but the reception by the pre-inductees grew more and more friendly, as Nick Egleson noted in the fall of 1968:

> [There is a] change in the mood of the young men threatened with the draft. They are no longer isolated and frightened as they were a year ago. . . . On the Early Morning Show we are almost never greeted by hostility as used to happen occasionally. . . . Just as there is trouble brewing in the Army, there are more and more men who will forcefully oppose the draft.

On the days Cambridge had its physicals the BDRG was almost always in a good mood. One day the BDRG nearly took over a physical, adroitly turning a menacing harangue by an army officer into a debate on the war, and calling for a straw vote on it. Of fifty pre-inductees, forty-eight voted against the war.

Although they prided themselves on their competence as counselors and could, as Nick later described it, "counsel circles around the army," BDRG members were not interested in it as a technical service alone. As early as August 1967 the steering committee concluded that:

> The AFSC [American Friends Service Committee] counselling course is no longer adequate for our purposes because it is non-political,

not aimed specifically at the War in Vietnam and, in consequence, somewhat out of date. In cooperation with Steve Hedger of the AFSC, we are therefore setting up our own counselor training program, as a means of providing BDRG with a reserve of people equipped to handle the specific range of problems we come up against most often at the River Street office.

The counselor training program grew rapidly to meet the sometimes overwhelming load. At one point over seventy-five men were coming to the office each week, all requiring at least a one-hour session, and usually more. But even with the increased demands on their time, the counselors tried to make each one aware of the larger causes of his plight, not to push him into one course or another with respect to the draft, but to encourage him to take some sort of action with others of his neighborhood.

BDRG also tried to reach GIs at Fort Devens and elsewhere, especially after the first Resistance sanctuary in Boston in 1968. Members leafleted at the Greyhound station, drove GIs from Boston to the base in a bus named Black Doubtful (which broke down on its first run), and worked in the underground that smuggled deserters to Canada or Europe. A coffeehouse was started for GIs and the movement, named The Sgt. Brown Memorial Necktie after a now-legendary incident involving Mike Mickelson of the BDRG and the black necktie (now hanging in the coffeehouse) that was once worn by Good Old Sgt. Brown, the officer in charge of pre-induction physicals. (In a later encounter, it is told, Sgt. Brown lost his shirt as well.)

With high school students BDRG had less luck. Everywhere the experience was the same: they were more concerned with their present repression in their schools than with their future encounter with the draft. "To them," Vernon Grizzard summed up, "the draft seemed far away—they knew that even as seniors their induction was probably more than a year away under the highest-age-goes-first draft guidelines." As another put it, "the draft is not an issue at high schools. It is only a second-hand trauma."

BDRG's relationship to the Resistance was often intimate and almost always cordial. There was some overlap in membership: Resistance members counseled and rode buses, BDRG members helped organize Resistance demonstrations, and several personal friendships existed between the groups. Until fairly late both groups kept free of dogmatic rhetoric. But as early as the fall of 1967 it was clear that BDRG would not advocate turn-ins or symbolic acts of any sort. Its target was the working class in the inner city, not the middle class in the suburbs and campuses, and it held to the belief that the tactics for organizing them were very different. BDRG did welcome the propaganda impact of the Resistance demonstrations (though it was critical of the manipulative potential of church sanctuaries) and at first it left open the possibility that turning in his card might help an organizer reach workers. "We learned," said the newsletter shortly after the conspiracy indictment against Spock and the others came down in Boston,

> that the Resistance tactic of returning draft cards and openly confronting the system is an idea that can make sense to working people, particularly when Resistance is explained as a repudiation of special privilege. Draft card burning, on the other hand, has had the effect of alienating working people from the peace movement, and we think it should definitely be abandoned. Card burnings are seen as a gesture of contempt directed at the guys who are already fighting, and people do not believe that card burners are exposing themselves to punishment: they assume that card burners are simply destroying the evidence.

A year later, the BDRG position had hardened. In a paper presented to the second national Resistance conference in March 1969 by Barrie Thorne, BDRG stated:

> The point remains theoretically as valid as ever, but it is unclear that turning in one's card has broken down any barriers between the working class and the student movement. There is little or no evidence to show that it is a significant action in these terms. In fact, card turn-ins may in some ways contribute to antipathies between these groups. Workers may see turn-ins, and especially card burnings, as unpatriotic efforts at draft dodging rather than as an action aimed at building a movement in the interests of the vast majority of Americans as well as the Vietnamese.
>
> Furthermore, card turn-ins sometimes create a false sense of moral su-

periority in students toward working class men who do not see non-cooperation as a real alternative to military service.

The paper gave some other reasons for opposing future turn-ins:

> The number of men willing to turn in cards and refuse induction is, and in the foreseeable future will continue to be, much too small to have any significant effect on the functioning of the military, the Selective Service System, or even the courts.

The number of men who were moved to action by the turn-ins was nowhere near as large as had been hoped. And, while large numbers of people—particularly academics—have moved to support draft resisters and to take public stands against the war, their support does not extend to the task of radically changing the American economic and political system. For example, many of those who supported draft resistance also contributed to the McCarthy campaign.

In order to stop the war in Vietnam and to prevent wars like it, we must build a movement to destroy American imperialism. Draft card turn-ins cannot create the mass base necessary to make that movement a success. . . .

Many men took non-cooperation as the ultimate in commitment. Some who turned in their cards did no other political work, having "done their thing to end the war." Despite efforts to overcome this tendency—through workshops, etc.—many who turned in their cards are "lost" to the Resistance.

In addition, a card turn-in is, by nature, a very personal thing. A number of men may turn in their cards together, but they are successfully isolated from movement-building by the courts and prisons. As a strategy, draft non-cooperation must rely on moral confrontation to persuade the government to end the war. It cannot be the basis for building a day-to-day movement with the power to challenge and defeat the entrenched business and government interests who profit from war and exploitation.

By this time the New England Resistance had itself abandoned turn-ins for many of the same reasons. Other Resistance groups, though they read the paper, continued to have them. The Philadelphia Resistance had a large turn-in in October 1969, getting most of its response, in fact, from working-class neighborhoods.

By this time too the BDRG was declining. After two years it still had not sunk roots into the community. Though hardly any young man in the Boston area who was called for his physical between the fall of 1967 and the summer of 1969 had escaped the attention of the Early Morning Show leafleters, only a few of them came to the BDRG for counseling, and almost none wanted to work in their own community. Perhaps, Nick later explained, "if we had had four times the manpower and ten times the will, we could have made it work, but since two years of hard work by dozens of talented people produced nothing, we felt justified in dropping it." Vernon Grizzard and John Maher, two of the most experienced, abandoned a project with blacks in the Riverside section of Cambridge.

Another problem BDRG faced, or failed to face, was the determined effort by the Progressive Labor Party (PL) to take it over and then either abolish it or drop the draft issue and turn it into a center for rent control, their current project. After the demonstrations at the Democratic Convention in Chicago (August 1968), the mood of BDRG began to change (as the mood did throughout the country). A kind of lethargy came over many of the workers, and as compensation for their inactivity they "politicized" their attitude and rhetoric, turning in some cases to PL for inspiration. In a group whose buoyancy and efficiency had depended on the cooperative and pragmatic style of its membership, the new tendency led to serious disputes. One of them was over the best approach to young men at the Early Morning Show. The PL-leaning members spoke frequently of the need for "struggle" against imperialism and capitalism, while most of the others tried to relate to the lives of those they met, dealing with individual problems, content to lead them a step or two toward political awareness. How one presented one's politics became a political issue in itself. Lines were drawn, meetings became polemical.

Nick Egleson feels that he and Vernon, among others of the non-PL block, failed to confront the PL threat as vigorously as they should have. It went against their experience in open, nonpolemical groups (both Nick and Vernon joined SDS in 1963 at Swarthmore, a very communal Quaker college), and they were already discouraged over the marginal results of their organizing efforts. After a while the PL faction questioned the continued existence of BDRG. The first important vote in the history of the group was taken: PL lost, and its supporters (about eight people) walked out. There were further encounters with PL, all of them unpleasant. A reconstruction of the counseling and Early Morning Show programs prolonged the life of the demoralized group, but in the fall of 1969, after two and a half years, it finally closed down.

In that time thousands of young men had been reached by a serious, friendly, and responsible antidraft group with a radical political perspective, and in that time the climate of opinion on the draft and the war reversed itself in Boston. But probably the most successful project of the BDRG, of those whose success can be measured at all, was one nobody had considered to be a separate project at all, the counselor-training program. Several hundred people went through the intensive course of instruction and apprenticeship. For dozens of them it was their first movement experience and led to their first serious movement work. A large number, after counseling for a while, went on to other projects, some having nothing to do with the draft. These facts were consoling to those who had spent so much time trying to build a community base. Vernon, reflecting on the demise of BDRG, refused to mourn:

> Our legitimacy as revolutionaries need not depend on our ability to create lasting organizations in communities which we set out to organize. Instead, perhaps, we should be content for the time being to create close-knit organizations of movement people which can reach out to new individuals and create more organizers in these communities. Success would not depend on their ability to form a trade union, community union, or community-based DRU.
>
> For example, the BDRG, or a group of radical teachers, a GI organizing committee or strike support group, or a propaganda group—all these centers of activity—could advance the movement without necessarily resulting in permanent organization. We should be realistic and recognize that centers of activity will arise, grow and die. The criterion for success should be whether or not they leave more people behind who can pick up on a new activity, build a new center of outreach, make a more incisive attack next time.

We ask so much that we can too easily think we are failing. The failure of the strategy of community-based draft resistance does not mean that it is impossible to build an effective organization which can reach most young people who face the draft. It only means that for now, the form of that organization will look more like the BDRG than a community union.

All those mornings on the bus, all those counselees streaming in and out of the office, all those confrontations with Sgt. Brown, may not have created a mass movement in the community, but it left several hundred experienced counselors and organizers as its legacy to the movement, along with a coffeehouse called Sgt. Brown's Memorial Necktie.

WDRU

The story of the Wisconsin Draft Resistance Union (WDRU) paralleled BDRG's in essentials. As WDRU member Jody Chandler tells it:

> In September 1966, four or five seniors at the University got together to discuss the anti-war movement and their own draft status. For eight weeks, discussion continued and the group grew to about forty men. The meetings were very good, very personal and intimate. People really came apart and talked about their lives and how their lives related to America. Out of those meetings developed a serious comradeship, and people saw that the only direction that could be taken was in terms of a union—some kind of collective action. But the meetings started to fall apart, because people had reached the limit, exhausted their souls, and they didn't know what to do. The draft was just this omnipotent thing that they really could not deal with.

Three or four people then took the initiative to write a We Won't Go statement. Forty-seven men signed that statement and it was published in the student newspaper. A public meeting was held, attended by over 150 people, and a loosely structured organization called the Wisconsin Draft Resistance Union was formed. Successful dormitory meetings followed and in May 115 men signed a second statement, supported by sixty women and men over draft age who signed a separate pledge.

Like BDRG, WDRU from the beginning looked outward toward the community. "We talked about the need to organize throughout the state and get to every high school in Madison," Jody Chandler says. "We, like others elsewhere," WDRU reported in midsummer 1967, "have been trying to get off campus and into the community. . . . And perhaps like others, our efforts are starting with a whimper not a bang."

An initial experience pointing toward off-campus work came on May 18, when three members of WDRU took their physicals at the Milwaukee induction center and about eighty more demonstrated in support. It was new territory for the movement (before BDRG had institutionalized the Early Morning Show) and so

the tactical debate raged. How does one support people who are being drafted? What does support mean? How do you go down and act in solidarity with your comrades? Don't you go in there and block all the doors and not let the Selective Service System take your people into the lion's den? Don't you chain up the bus doors and not let any of the people out of the busses? Don't we stop the busses from going in the first place? Don't we go inside and disrupt the whole thing and just tear the whole place down?

They asked themselves these questions but decided on a more low-keyed approach. Twelve people went to the bus station with donuts and leaflets to talk with the examinees, and carried on quiet conversation for forty-five minutes before the buses left. Inside the induction center, fourteen men not scheduled to take the physical gave speeches while the three from WDRU who were called for the examination talked and passed out leaflets. A picket line circled the building. Results were dramatic: eleven of the fourteen protesters within the building were arrested, a dozen of the eighty-eight inductees refused to sign the security questionnaire (four times the usual figure), and in the midst of a wrangle among the picketers as to whether their resistance should be more militant, "eight inductees held aloft a sign from the second-story window saying 'We appreciate you,' " and two more held up a sign which read, "Help us."

One WDRU worker concluded from this experience: "The main focus of our activities should be directed to . . . the fifteen to seventeen year old age bracket . . . and . . . the draft-resistance movement has to get off the campus to work with those who are *really* affected by the draft."

It made matters no easier that "the initial group consisted almost solely of upper-middle-class students from the large metropolitan areas of New York, Washington and Chicago." Dan Swinney, for instance, was the son of "an executive who privately opposes the war but does not want to rock the boat." But the small group of organizers who stayed through the summer in Madison persisted in their efforts.

A breakthrough came at a speaking engagement at a church coffeehouse in Williams Bay, a small conservative town in southern Wisconsin. As Bob Gabriner and Barbara Baran recall,

> Sixty high school students and 30 John Birchers showed up to hear the DRU speakers. The Birchers threatened to bomb the coffeehouse, but the kids were not to be intimidated and really responded to the talk. They invited the DRU back. The evenings spent in Williams Bay pointed out that the very presence of DRU polarized the group and that in such a polarization most of the young people sided with the young organizers against the adults.

It was particularly important that this success took place outside Madison, which student radicals at the University of Wisconsin "generally conceived of as an oasis in a desert of backwoods conservatives."

In the fall of 1967 WDRU organizers began work among high school students in communities such as Eau Claire, Superior, and Janesville. Dan Swinney reported to the national Resist office in February 1968:

> The WDRU has been working on community based draft resistance since late last summer. We now have a full-time staff of about 10 people who are working with a number of different constituencies in

Madison and around the state. We have found the concept of draft resistance useful in creating a political consciousness in the community. Most of our work has been with high school students creating programs such as draft information centers, guerrilla theaters, high school reform, etc.

By the summer of 1968 WDRU had grown to the point where they could project a "Summer Offensive," involving teams of organizers in various communities, a touring guerrilla theater company and a statewide underground newspaper. According to one leaflet:

> We are ready, willing, and able to travel anywhere in the Wisconsin-Illinois-Minnesota-Iowa area to speak on draft alternatives and draft resistance, to do individual draft counseling, to set up draft information centers, and to train draft counselors. We are the proud possessors of a 1960 Dodge Stationwagon, known as the Draft Caravan. It is capable of parking in any city or town.

Resistance organizing in medium-sized Midwestern cities, however, was often disheartening. In Sheboygan, for instance, WDRU was handed the apparent gift of three induction refusers. One was a garbage collector, another a student, the third a young college professor. But as it turned out,

> the fact that we had several men who refused induction made it more difficult to organize in Sheboygan. These men became living examples of how you can be destroyed—socially and economically—if you decide not to go, to resist the draft. Instead of being able to show other young men how their lives could be different, how they could, through building the draft resistance movement, confront the oppressive institutions which affect their lives, they re-inforced the idea that such institutions, and particularly the Selective Service System, are invulnerable, omnipotent, and it is best to submit passively to their authority.

In Waukegan WDRU had its first experience with non-college-oriented working-class youth. A letter from Bill Drew, one of the Waukegan organizers, suggests the repression encountered in trying to reach these youngsters.

Our first leaflet offering draft counseling got us busted for distributing without a permit. We have broadened our scope in order to most effectively capitalize on the tensions which our presence in Waukegan has produced. We have trained 2 draft counselors and use our apartment as the base of operations for a newspaper and as a place for discussions. Last night we were busted on a disorderly conduct charge for selling our newspapers at a lakefront dance.

Experiences like these, as well as the changing ideological climate of the larger movement, led WDRU to reevaluate its politics. The first summer's work had made clear the "necessity to develop programs which were *not* directly connected to the draft. We found that high school students are more directly affected by the authoritarian nature of their high school experience than they are by the draft." The Summer Offensive a year later called into question, for at least some WDRU organizers, the correctness of organizing even around antiauthoritarianism. An issue such as a high school dress code came to seem to these organizers an aspect of "youth culture." Insisting on an orientation toward the class interests of workers, they preferred to agitate on the issue of tracking in the public schools.

At the same time, "the old idea of a union which combined the subjective and personal needs of people with the struggle against objective conditions began to fade." And as in these different ways the elements which had distinguished WDRU from SDS began to disappear, the need for a separate organization became less compelling. In the early summer of 1969, WDRU dissolved.

Dan Swinney, a central figure in WDRU's entire history, argues that the dissolution was in reality a regrouping which permitted the group to continue work on the draft in a new political context. Looking back over the three years, Dan saw WDRU's evolution this way:

The more we became involved in people's lives outside of the liberal university community, the more we were faced with the need for power based in the people, not dependant on any aspect of the system. So you broke down the conditioning and when a guy from Williams Bay or Sheboygan faced induction he was still faced with the army, prison, or exile and for him those alternatives were much more limited than a guy who went to Wisconsin or Harvard. Moral integrity just didn't make it when faced with the material necessities of the people we met. People responded to us from the most incredible places and we had a set of basic programs that could start a growing movement in any community, but something was still missing. A furniture repairman in Eau Claire, whose son led the high school movement and later became an organizer for us, wanted to support his son, to become involved but if he did he could be crushed financially within a month. He demanded more disciplined and serious organization. In our high school work we found that the poorer the kids were, the more serious, disciplined and militant they were; the more we dealt with abstract issues like the draft (which is an abstract issue until 17 or 18), violence vs. non-violence, etc., the more we attracted bourgeois kids who usually were the worst organizers, being isolated socially and intellectually from the students and not concerned with their isolation; the more we dealt with anti-authoritarian issues, we had sporadic struggles but never the development of serious organization or struggle. We also faced the fact that this level of work was not keeping up with the pace of events in this country and around the world. So we were forced to begin to deal directly with the class structure of this society and world. We began to see ourselves as Marxists and to begin to raise issues of class oppression and how they related to us as a draft resistance union, and how we saw a revolution as the only way to deal with those problems. A guy would come to our office for draft counseling, we would counsel him and then explain why the only real way to deal with the draft was to make the revolution. . . .

We held a meeting in Appleton, Wis. early last spring of all the full-time organizers for WDRU from around the state and made the decision to concentrate all of our people in the industrial belt between Milwaukee and Chicago in order to give us the opportunity to deal with the problems of developing new forms of organization and programs that would potentially develop the base necessary for real resistance to the draft and other forms of oppression as well as the ability to create a new society. WDRU was dissolved to create three projects in Milwaukee, Racine, and Lake County.

Nationally, SDS and most of the radical movement dropped a focus on the draft and on (in Greg Calvert's words) "resistance and resistance themology" much earlier than BDRG and WDRU. The change coincided with another week of dramatic events, March 31–April 4, 1968. During these days President Lyndon Johnson delivered the "April Fool" speech in which he withdrew from the 1968 presidential race, declared a partial halt in the bombing of North Vietnam, and announced the readiness of the United States to attend peace talks; about 1,000 more draft cards were turned in on April 3; on April 4, Martin Luther King was assassinated, and riots occurred in cities all over America.

Two movement conferences just prior to these events indicated the new course. Meeting near Chicago, many SDS activists joined with Tom Hayden, Rennie Davis, and members of the National Mobilization Committee in planning a demonstration at the Democratic Party national convention in August. Meeting in Lexington, Kentucky, the SDS National Council heard former SDS president Carl Oglesby urge that the movement had done all it could to end the war and should make its first priority assistance to black liberation. These new targets and strategies replaced the draft in the minds of most student radicals. "In retrospect," Noam Chomsky wrote in January 1970, "it seems possible that the war could have been ended if popular pressure had been maintained. But many radicals felt that the war was over, that it had become, in any case, a 'liberal issue,' and they turned to other concerns."

Notes to Chapter Twelve

On SDS thinking in the winter of 1967–1968 about resistance: Carl Davidson, "Toward Institutional Resistance" and speech of October 27, *National Guardian,* November 11, 1967; interview with Greg Calvert on November 17, 1967, *The Movement,* December 1967; SDS pamphlet, "Resistance and Repression" [January 1968]; Greg Calvert, "A Left Wing Alternative," *Liberation,* May 1969.

On the concept of community-based resistance: Carl Davidson and Mike Spiegel, "SDS & Oct. 21st: Repression and Resistance," *New Left Notes,* October 9, 1967; Jeff Segal, "Against the Draft," *The Movement,* October 1967; Dee Jacobsen and others, "We've Got to Reach Our Own

People," *The Movement,* November 1967; New York Regional SDS Staff to "Dear Friend," Summer 1967; "Tentative Summer Program Outline for the Washington Draft Resistance Union–Summer 1968."

On BDRG: BDRG leaflet, May 1967; *BDRG Newsletter,* June 29 and August 1967, February 1 and April 1968, February and April 1969; Nick Egleson in the *Old Mole,* October 5, 1968; Vernon Grizzard, "How It Worked in Boston," *The Movement,* January 1969; Nick Egleson to Michael Ferber (January 19, 1970); David Washburn and Charlie Fisher to Ferber (February 25, 1970). Washburn and Fisher are at work on a comprehensive history and analysis of BDRG.

On WDRU: Bob Gabriner and Barbara Baran, "WDRU from Conscience to Class," *The Movement,* April 1969; "WDRU," *Resist* [published by the Draft Resistance Clearing House], Memo #4; Jody Chandler, *Wisconsin Draft Resistance Union* [Fall 1967]; *Wisconsin Draft Resistance Union* [four case studies of organizing efforts, Spring 1968]; *What Is Guerrilla Theatre, Anyway?* [Fall 1968]; *Capital Times,* July 25, 1967; *WIN,* June 30, 1967; various issues of the underground newspapers: *Fresh Air, Connections, Sheboygan Pressed, The Open Door* [Milwaukee], *Tradition* [Eau Claire], and *Links;* Bob Weiland to National Mobilization Committee (July 6, 1967); Sidney Glass to Alice Lynd (June 15, 1967); Dan Swinney to Resist (February 11, 1968); Bill Drew to Resist (July 22, 1968); Dan Swinney to Staughton Lynd (January 7, 1970).

Noam Chomsky is quoted from his article, "After Pinkville," *New York Review of Books,* January 1, 1970.

 CHAPTER THIRTEEN

Sanctuary

As interest in draft resistance and in the war itself declined among civilians in the spring of 1968, resistance within the armed forces grew by leaps and bounds. The full story of GI resistance will have to be told by others, hopefully by those who organized and experienced it. Here we can only sketch its dimensions, and then explore the contribution to the GI movement made by the Resistance.

The draft resistance movement had begun with isolated acts of defiance, and resistance within the armed forces first expressed itself in the same way. Thus Privates Dennis Mora, David Samas, and James Johnson (the "Fort Hood Three") publicly announced their refusal to go to Vietnam in July 1966; and Captain Howard Levy refused to give medical training to Green Berets and was court-martialed in May 1967. A year later, just as in the case of draft resistance, hundreds of servicemen were in motion. On October 12, 1968 several hundred active-duty servicemen took part in an antiwar march in San Francisco. Two days later, October 14, twenty-seven servicemen imprisoned in the nearby Presidio stockade sat down in protest against the shooting of an unarmed fellow prisoner. *Resist* said of the march that it marked "the coming of age of the American servicemen as active participants in American politics," and *Hard Times* commented on the Presidio mutiny:

186

The Presidio mutiny of Monday, Oct. 14, marks a turning point in the movement of GIs against the war and against military authoritarianism. Until that point, the publicized cases all involved individual acts of witness by well-educated, or highly political people. . . . The only collective action had been done by blacks—the uprising (close to a race riot) in the Long Binh Jail, and the refusal of 43 black soldiers at Fort Hood, Tex., to accept duty in Chicago at the time of the Democratic Convention.

The men who sat down and sang "We Shall Overcome" at the Presidio, like the bulk of military deserters, were working-class whites.

Military resistance in 1968 and 1969 grew enormously, and began to compare in numbers with draft resistance and evasion. Desertion (AWOL over thirty days) rose from forty thousand in 1968 to 53,000 in 1969, a rate of one deserter every ten minutes. Brigs were filling up, re-enlistment rolls were emptying.

Several dramatic events in 1969 corroborated the testimony of the statistics that there is a grave crisis in the morale of American servicemen. At Fort Jackson in Columbia, South Carolina, where Levy had made his solitary protest two years earlier, twenty servicemen were arrested on March 20 for attending an antiwar meeting. On June 5 a rebellion broke out at the stockade in Fort Dix, New Jersey after prisoners had been made to stand in the hot sun for five hours. In August, media featured the refusal of soldiers in Company A of the 196th Light Infantry Brigade of the Third Battalion to continue fighting in the Songchang Valley of Vietnam. Reporting the incident under the caption, "A Whiff of Mutiny in Vietnam," James Reston of the *New York Times* commented: "There is a breaking point where discipline, duty and even loyalty to the men at your side are overwhelmed by fear and death and a paralyzing feeling of the senselessness of the whole bloody operation." In October and November, 1969, servicemen found a variety of ways to take part in the massive moratoriums on October 15 and November 15. Near Camp Pendleton, California, 500–750 active-duty GIs led a parade down the main street of a neighboring community. A full-page advertisement, taken in the *New York Times* by 1,366 active-duty GIs, said in part: "We are opposed to American involvement in the war in Vietnam. We resent the needless wasting of lives to save face for our politicians in Washington. We speak, believing our views are shared by many of our fellow servicemen." It was reported that in South Vietnam there were platoons which went on combat patrol wearing black armbands in solidarity with the moratorium.

It is difficult to assess the impact made by draft resistance on the soldiers' revolt. Of course the Resistance provided an important model of insubordination, but most GIs found it hard to identify with the middle-class students who joined it. Some servicemen admitted they were impressed by the seriousness of the acts of refusing induction or returning a card, as opposed to picketing and sitting-in, and some appreciated the gesture of solidarity in renouncing student deferments, but many felt condemned by draft resisters for being in the armed forces at all. In any case, the influence was not direct; far more immediate and influential were the projects of other sectors of the movement, who were helping with underground newspapers and setting up coffeehouses near the bases. More important too was the decision by a number of dedicated organizers to enter the army in order to organize, a policy the Resistance did not condemn but could not encourage. But the Resistance did make one tangible contribution to the GI movement, though it was not originally conceived mainly for them: the practice of publicly sheltering a serviceman in a church, or "symbolic sanctuary."

On May 20, 1968, the day the Spock Trial opened in Boston, the Arlington Street Church offered "symbolic sanctuary" to two young men: Bob Talmanson, 21, whom everyone called "Tally," the first organizer of the Resistance in New England and a draft refuser who had just lost his appeal to the Supreme Court, and Bill Chase, 19, an AWOL soldier and veteran of Vietnam. They were allowed to remain in the church building with some supporters from the congregation and the New England Resistance until they were arrested or they turned themselves in. Tally was arrested after a few days. He passively resisted and was carried to a police car, where dozens of supporters sat in the way; they were forcibly removed and the car took Tally to jail. He began serving a three-year sentence at Petersburg penitentiary (he was released in December 1969). Bill gave himself up to the army after he was promised a psychiatric examination and fair treatment. He got them, and a few days later he was discharged.

This was the first sanctuary in the east, probably in the country (there were reports of a sanctuary on the west coast the previous winter which were not confirmed). It was appropriate that it should occur in the Arlington Street Church: it had been the first church in the country to hold a draft card turn-in, an event that had led to the draft conspiracy trial that was in progress a mile away in the Federal Building. At the very moment Tally was carried out of the church, in fact, the prosecutor was showing films of the turn-in of October 16.

One of the earliest advocates of symbolic sanctuary was one of the Boston defendants, Rev. William Sloane Coffin, Jr., Chaplain of Yale University. His sermon during the October 16 service in Arlington Street Church included a history and defense of the concept:

When an issue is one of conscience then surely it is one we may not wish to seek but it is one we cannot properly avoid—particularly the synagogues and churches. So what are they to do?

"Thou spreadest a table before me in the presence of mine enemies."

As men have always felt certain times to be more sacred than others, for example, the Sabbath, so they also have felt certain places to be more sacred, for example, the home, the temple, the church. And closely associated with these more sacred places has been the belief that there a man should find some sort of sanctuary from the forces of a hostile world. "Thou spreadest a table before me in the presence of mine enemies." These familiar words from the twenty-third Psalm refer to an ancient desert law which provided that if a man hunted by his enemies sought refuge with another man who offered him hospitality, then the enemies of the man had to remain outside the rim of the campfire light for two nights and the day intervening.

In Exodus we read that the altar of the Tabernacle is to be considered a place of sanctuary, and in Numbers and Deuteronomy we read of "cities of refuge," three in Canaan and three in Jordan.

Then during the Middle Ages all churches on the continent were considered sanctuaries, and in some instances in England the land within a mile of the church was included. And according to the Justinian Code sanctuary was extended to all law-breakers, Christian, Jewish, and non-believer alike, with the exception only of those guilty of high treason or sacrilege. Now if in the Middle Ages churches could offer sanctuary to the most common of criminals, could they not today do the same thing for the most conscientious among us? And if in the Middle Ages they could offer forty days to a man who had committed both a sin and a crime, could they not today offer an indefinite period to one who had committed no sin?

The churches must not shirk their responsibility in deciding whether or not a man's objection is conscientious. But should a church declare itself a "sanctuary for conscience" this should be considered less a means to shield a man, more a means to expose a church, an effort to make a church really be a church.

For if the state should decide that the arm of the law was long enough to reach inside a church there would be little church members could do to prevent an arrest. But the members could point out what they had already dramatically demonstrated, that the sanctity of conscience was being violated. And further, as the law regarding "aiding and abetting" is clear—up to five years in jail and a fine of ten thousand dollars—church members could then say: "If you arrest this man for violating a law which violates his conscience then you must arrest us too, for in the sight of that law we are now as guilty as he."

What else can the churches do?

No one claimed that sanctuary had a legal basis, as it did during the Middle Ages, or even that it should have. It was a way for a religious community to make a moral and religious declaration both in support of the young men who claim sanctuary and against the policies they would be ordered to carry out. Sanctuary may in fact be illegal, though there have been no prosecutions yet for "harboring" AWOLs or "aiding and abetting" resisters in a sanctuary. It is certainly the willingness to risk indictments that has lent so much gravity to the decision of a church to grant it.

The entire process (granting sanctuary, the days of waiting, press conferences, and final arrest) is a little like a Morality Play, with the weaknesses and strengths of any symbolic drama. It is only "play," a ritual, for no one supposes that the police will actually stop at the door upon command of God or the minister of the church. But it is a clear symbolic lesson that can hardly be misinterpreted even by a hostile press, and as a way of educating the public about resistance, desertion, and the extent of community support for them it has been remarkably successful.

During the symbolic drama some very real experiences happen, and many who are now active in the antiwar movement trace their involvement to their experiences at a sanctuary. The first Boston sanctuary declared itself a Liberated Zone, and interpreted liberation broadly. Long personal raps and patient justifications alternated with poetry readings, folk and rock concerts, be-ins, and religious celebrations. Sanctuaries became little oases of the "new life," partly to cheer up the resister or deserter during his grim vigil, but mainly to do what is natural, to get practice living a free and natural life in the midst of struggle, to show grace and humor in the teeth of the dragon.

Most sanctuaries have been in churches (nearly always Protestant), for it is there that the symbolism is clearest. But the New England Resistance wanted to broaden the concept by placing it in a secular context where it would find new support communities and spark new forms of "institutional resistance." As a kind of transition, two sanctuaries were held in college chapels in the fall of 1968, one at Harvard Divinity School and one at Boston University's Marsh Chapel. The latter made such an impact on campus that two more were held shortly thereafter, one at Brandeis and one at MIT, neither of them in chapels. (Some suggested the name be changed to "asylum," but "sanctuary" it has remained.) The MIT sanctuary did much to awaken students to their unwitting complicity in the military-industrial-research complex. Several groups were formed, some of which a year later were carrying out actions against counterinsurgency research.

Meanwhile church sanctuaries were going strong. The "Nine for Peace," all servicemen (AWOLs from all four main branches of the Armed Forces) took sanctuary in the Howard Presbyterian Church in San Francisco on July 15, 1968. They all made brief public statements, of which the following two well express the mood of struggle and the mood of celebration that make up most sanctuaries:

I must disavow myself from any organization that commits murder in the name of a political delusion. I am not a murderer, and under no circumstances can I ever delude myself into becoming one. I enlisted in the Marine Corps unaware of the true implications of the military service. Once training had begun, I was confronted with the realities of the military machine: the insidious dehumanization process, its total disregard for human life, and its inherent need to perpetuate the very conditions it supposedly seeks to destroy in order to sustain itself. Seeing the military for what it really is has served as an even greater revelation to me, it has given me an awareness of my responsibility, I will not be a party to the rape of this humanity, I will not kill for my country.

(Jack Robinson, Westport, Connecticut)

I'd like to be in a rock band.

I like beautiful sleep dreams in color.

I like trees, Albert Camus, and Jungle Jim.

I like children with red rosie faces and beautiful eyes that sparkle in time and rhyme with heaven.

I love my family, my country, and Igor Stravinsky.

I like windy beaches, fiery sunsets, Margaret, and lace.

I like private thoughts that usually come to nothing.

I like Henri Rousseau, Greek music, Norma's spaghetti, and Bertrand Russell.

I love Russians, Vietnamese, and George Wallace.

I love plains, mountains, deltas, rice paddies, and peace.

I love Gandhi, Socrates, Jesus, and you.

I like machines that make good things.

But I hate machines that make machines out of people who make machines out of others.

I am not a machine, I am a man.

(George Dounis, Atlanta, Ga.)

There have been problems. The Unitarian Universalist Church of Buffalo, after much agonizing, agreed to grant sanctuary to Bruce Beyer and Bruce Cline, both draft refusers, on August 8, 1968. For ten days members of the church and the Resistance maintained a relaxed vigil—speeches, songs, and picnics amidst sleeping bags and leaflets—and on August 19 the police and FBI suddenly arrived, clubs swinging wildly. Insufficiently prepared perhaps, and certainly provoked, a few demonstrators threw punches at the police. Nine demonstrators were arrested and charged with assault, including Beyer and Cline. Four of the "Buffalo Nine" eventually came to trial (March 1969): the jury was hung on three of them, but it convicted Beyer, who was then given three years in prison. Meanwhile the church congregation, aghast at the sight of blood on the pulpit, bowed to the will of the older and more conservative members, revoked the offer of sanctuary, and publicly apologized to the FBI.

The most remarkable sanctuary began a year later, August 6, 1969 (Hiroshima Day), in Honolulu, and developed into what might be called a "mass sanctuary": about three dozen servicemen, including thirteen Vietnam veterans, went AWOL at various times to join the sanctuary, occupying four churches and the University of Honolulu. It was the culmination of a prolonged confrontation between the military and the Hawaii Resistance, which came into being as a protest against the activation of the Hawaii National Guard one week after the assassination of Martin Luther King. Members of the Hawaii Resistance tell the story as follows:

> Throughout the weekend following King's murder civil disturbances swept the country. . . . There was a report that the Hawaii National Guard would be called up to help suppress the racial disorders on the mainland. Governor John Burns of Hawaii, a few months earlier at the Western Governors' Conference, had boasted about the 50th State's Guard units to his colleagues and offered use of his troops to the other states in time of need. That Hawaii's boys had received riot-control training, and could serve as a neutral force coming from out-of-state was his rationale for his offer. Needless to say, this upset many people in Hawaii who felt Hawaii's National Guard should neither be sent to the ghettos to oppress their black brothers, nor be shipped to Asia to oppress their yellow brothers in Vietnam.
>
> On April 11, SDS called a noon meeting in Hemenway Hall to discuss solutions to racial problems in the United States. . . . About mid-way through the two hour meeting, word was received that the Hawaii Na-

tional Guard and U.S. Army Reserves had been called up to active duty.

Richard Tanimura arose before a crowd of 500 people and said, "The time has come for me personally to take a stand as a member of the National Guard."

"I find myself compelled to oppose any participation of any units of the Armed Forces of the United States in either Vietnam or in quelling racial disorder on the mainland." . . .

"I do not know what the solution to the problem is, but if I am asked to suppress any people of any color, I cannot in good conscience reply, I will." Everyone rose to applaud Tanimura's action. He sat quietly on stage, wiping tears from his eyes.

This was a major breakthrough in Island history. The Japanese-American community, who in World War II had produced young men willing to sacrifice themselves in combat to show their loyalty to America, had now nurtured a new breed willing to risk everything to build a new order based on justice and peace.

Following Richard's emotional statement, George Sarant asked the crowd who had just given Tanimura a standing ovation: "What are you going to do? It's up to you. Are you going to let Richard be dragged off to jail or are we going to fight?"

Bill Smith, SDS President, and a 1–O (Conscientious objector) got up and said, ". . . If he (Richard) goes to jail, I'm going with him because that's where my place is." Up in flames went Smith's draft card.

John Witeck, founder of SDS on campus, went up, embraced his good friend, and lit his own draft card . . .

Smith and Witeck were followed by ten other young men who also burned their draft cards that day. They included a Navy veteran, two fellows with 4–F classifications (physically unfit for military service), an ex-Marine, and six others who held student deferments.

On the morning of May 3, 1968, the newly activated Hawaii National Guard assembled at Ft. DeRussy to hear their governor and their generals ceremoniously send them to active duty. . . . Ft. DeRussy, located near the heart of Waikiki, serves as the induction center for draftees in the state. It also serves as the processing station for troops on R & R from the Far East. On this particular morning, members of the Resistance were up early picketing, leafletting, and rapping with the troops and their families. Following the official ceremonies, as the Guard rolled out of the Fort in troop trucks, a group of Resisters stepped out into Kalia

Road and sat in the path of the convoy. The demonstrators were quickly surrounded by city police and carried out of the road.

Ironically, several nights before, the Resistance had voted against any organized act of civil disobedience. The twenty or so who staged the sit-in responded spontaneously to the callous lack of concern shown by the Governor and the generals for the welfare of our Guardsmen—although Hawaii has only 1% of the national population, her 4,600 newly activated Guardsmen made up 17% of the total national call-up. . . .

Even before the Kalia Rd. case had been settled, the Resistance voted to support a sit-in planned by the University of Hawaii's student government . . . to protest the move by the Administration to oust political science professor Oliver Lee [an opponent of the war]. . . .

At the climax of the sit-in 154 students and faculty were arrested by police for trespassing on school property. The case was subsequently dismissed. The American Association of University Professors investigated the Lee case and found the university in error. Lee was re-instated.

During the confusion of the sit-in, Richard Tanimura, leaving his family, his friends and his country behind, sought asylum in Sweden. Richard's choice of exile as an alternative to prison generated considerable discussion around the prison-vs.-exile debate among Resistance members. The Resistance supported Richard's act of conscience, and argued strongly that either alternative was deserving of support. . . .

In November [1968], two Marines, Gary Gray and Tom Met, picked up a copy of the *Roach*, Hawaii's first underground newspaper, in Waikiki's International Market Place. They had both found the Marine Corps oppressive and had developed grave doubts about the Vietnam war. They were seeking outside help. They contacted the *Roach* staff who in turn contacted Resistance organizers. After initial discussions with Jim Douglass, the Rev. Gene Bridges and other Resistance leaders, the two young men decided to make public their opposition to the military system by seeking "sanctuary."

The Resistance arranged for the two marines to appear at a rally on the U.H. campus where before T.V. and other media representatives, they made public their grievances.

For several days the two Marines, chained to Resistance supporters, locked in a physical and spiritual bond against a common oppressor, lived in sanctuary, at first in the student union building

and then at the University branch of the YMCA. In justification
of the university as sanctuary the Resistance stated:

> *Why sanctuary here?* Hemenway Hall is the student's building, a
> youth center, the site at which two young men of the Marines cemented
> their commitment. It is our right as students and as young people to
> afford protection in our building for those who seek to protect us from
> suffering what they have suffered. The University is committed to the ex-
> change of ideas and to criticism of the existing order. This is precisely
> what these men seek to do, and their place is rightly found in a Univer-
> sity. The University, with Churches just entering a "Christian convales-
> cence," must serve as social conscience and sanctuary for those who are
> fighting injustice; there is simply no other place. With Marine recruiters
> enjoying easy access to campus, why not Marine resisters? Truly the
> coming days will show the real nature of the University's commitment,
> whether to war or to peace, and if it is to war, then it shall have no peace.

During the sanctuary several local churches began examining
their contemporary obligation to offer sanctuary. The discussions
that followed led to the eventual passage of resolutions by the
Church of the Crossroads, the Unitarian Church, and the Society
of Friends, to give sanctuary to objectors on religious or moral
grounds.

Tom and Gary turned themselves in to Marine authorities at
the climax of a march to the Kaneohe Marine Corps Air Station
on Sunday, November 17. Subsequently both were court-martialed and given prison terms.

"This first sanctuary experiment left many Resistance people
feeling rather helpless," the Honolulu Resistance reported. "The
war machine mechanically and unresponsively kept grinding
away. We had largely responded to its initiative. We had to take
the offensive." They resumed militant demonstrations at army
bases, held more turn-ins, spent more time in jail.

Then on Hiroshima Day 1969 a new sanctuary began. One resister described the beginning:

> The age-old concept of sanctuary experienced its most recent
> revival on August 6 in Honolulu, Hawaii when Airman Louis D. "Buffy"

Parry made a statement of conscience upon entering the Church of the Crossroads. Parry chose the day that commemorates the bombing of Hiroshima to tell the people of America, "I have concluded that further co-operation with the U.S. military on my part would be to commit crimes against humanity. The Germans smelled the burning flesh of the Jews and passed it off as their patriotic duty to remain silent. Bullshit! When humanity's head is on the guillotine and it takes individual commitment to remove the head before the blade falls, I say to hell with patriotism. Above all laws, above all patriotic duty is the duty to preserve human life."

Another account continued the story:

> After Buff and John Catolinotto of the American Serviceman's Union spoke to a rally following the G.I.–Civilian Walk for Peace on Sunday, August 10, five more servicemen announced they were joining the sanctuary. Military police on hand refused to accept the men's I.D. cards and were startled when one of their plainclothesmen blew his cover and joined the sanctuary.
>
> The crowd returned to the church, and the small band grew as Bob Matheson of the Navy "joined up."
>
> The next day organizational meetings went on while the community waited to hear word from a Marine who had said he was coming as soon as he collected his pay-check. He was having trouble getting out of Kaneohe Marine Corps Air Station. All liberties had been cancelled and entry to the station was restricted in the wake of fighting between black and white Marines. He had to jump the fence and arrived at the church late Monday night.
>
> The next morning an army private on R&R from Vietnam (the sanctuary had renamed the Army's Rest & Recreation period "Rethink and Resist") came for counselling and stayed. As the week went on hundreds of servicemen stopped by the sanctuary for counselling, to rap or to look around. By August 20, more than 20 had decided to stay.
>
> The military's strategy seemed to be to avoid a confrontation, perhaps in the hope that the sanctuary would fall apart or that the men would reconsider their decisions. An Army spokesman said, "If they think that we are going to send down a couple of squads of soldiers to arrest them, they are out of their minds. This is precisely what they want us to do—a pretty

demonstration of violence at the church in front of a battery of television cameras."

One sailor, Arthur Parker, did turn himself in after a talk with a chaplain. He said the sanctuary was not what he had expected. "It's not a sanctuary any more. It's a move to overthrow the government and I don't stand for that."

Another resister, Marine Vince Ventimiglia was turned in by his parents, who flew in from New York. When they failed to talk him out of his decision, they invited him to their hotel for lunch and informed the military. He was arrested by the military police at the hotel.

The communal spirit which prevailed at the Pentagon demonstration and in a number of sit-ins during the grim years 1967–1969 was evident in this sanctuary.

> The spontaneous growth of a loving community of people who cared about each other was the central experience of the early weeks together. We all had a sense of hope, a sense of being a tiny model for a possible future. . . . Spontaneous new-style communion services were held at midnight, with the whole assemblage rising from the floor, shouting and dancing, as an announcement came in of new men entering sanctuary, or of a new statement of support, or a heartening newscast.

When military police broke into the four churches on September 12 a number of the servicemen they expected to find there had already left, or escaped during the raids. Buff Parry and Lou Jones, a Marine with five and one-half years service who was wounded in Vietnam, appeared at the General Convention of the Episcopal Church in South Bend, Indiana, on September 2, seeking "symbolic sanctuary." When it was requested that all those supporting the two men stand up, over six hundred of the eleven hundred delegates rose and about four hundred came forward to surround the servicemen. Those who fled to the mainland ten days later, on September 12, left behind a statement. "We are not fleeing sanctuary," they began,

> we are extending it. We are on the way to the mainland to spread the concept of sanctuary as far as we can. We will continue to tell

the story of GI's who are resisting the injustices and the immorality of the US military system and its involvement in Vietnam. We are not fleeing but entering an even more active phase of development. Sanctuary is on the move. Buffy and Lou carried it to South Bend and Canada. Many of our brothers are already on the mainland carrying on what Buffy and Lou began.

Notes to Chapter Thirteen

Sources drawn on for GI discontent include the *New York Times,* April 28, 1969, August 27, 1969, Jan. 22, 1970; *The Movement,* July 1969; *National Guardian,* June 14, 1969; Flora Lewis in the *Chicago Sun-Times,* Sept. 9, 1969; *Chicago Daily News,* Jan. 20 and 30, 1970; *CCCO Newsletter on Military Law and Counseling,* December 1969, which cites the Department of Defense for numbers of deserters and the *Navy Times,* Nov. 16, 1969, for the number of men in military prisons; *Student Mobilizer,* Jan. 21, 1970; numerous issues of *Hard Times,* which of all movement publications has covered resistance within the armed forces most fully; a special issue of *WIN* on GI resistance (Dec. 21, 1969) that among other things lists the forty-eight underground papers for or by GIs being published at the beginning of 1970; and materials released by defense committees for the Presidio 27, and for defendants at Fort Jackson and Fort Dix.

The statements of the San Francisco servicemen are in a pamphlet, *The Nine for Peace,* copyrighted 1968 by the San Francisco Resistance.

Details of the first Boston sanctuary can be found in the *Boston Globe,* May 20, 1968, and the ten days or so following; and in the first few issues of the *Boston Free Press* (which began publication with the sanctuary and Spock Trial).

Coffin's sermon was reprinted in the *Boston Free Press,* May 20, 1968, and in Jessica Mitford, *The Trial of Dr. Spock* (New York: Knopf, 1969; Vintage, 1970).

For more historical background, see articles by Joseph Harvey, *Boston Sunday Globe,* May 26, 1968; and by Edward B. Fiske, *New York Times* (Sunday), June 2, 1968. For a strategic discussion, see two articles by

Rev. Richard Mumma in *Resist* newsletter, #14 (July 29, 1968) and 17 (October 14, 1968).

In describing Hawaii Resistance we were fortunate to have access to an unpublished manuscript by Wayne Hayashi, "Roots of Resistance," and to additional pages written by John Witeck and Stephen Kubota, with supplementary paragraphs by Jim Douglass. These friends also provided the documents quoted: Young Claude (Gary) Gray and Tom Met, "A Call To Join Us" and "A Declaration Of Sanctuary." The sanctuary of August–September, 1969 is recounted in "Army Invades Hawaii Churches," *Plain Rapper*, August–September 1969; Ben Norris and Anthony Buxton, "Bust in Hawaii," *WIN*, October 15, 1969; and *Peacemaker*, September 27, 1969.

As this book went to press a splendid first installment of the history of GI Resistance was published: Fred Gardner, *The Unlawful Concert: An Account of the Presidio Mutiny Case* (New York: Viking, 1970).

CHAPTER FOURTEEN

The Ultra Resistance

For those who were excluded by sex or age from direct resistance to the draft but who wished to advance from a supporting role to protagonist, there were several recourses. We have already described the many statements on behalf of resistance, demonstrations where women and undraftable men relayed draft cards, and symbolic sanctuaries in churches. But on October 27, 1967, a few days after the week of the Resistance and the Pentagon march, four men in Baltimore committed an act which was clearly as serious as draft resistance and which seemed in many ways to be "the next step" beyond it. Francine du Plessix Gray, writing in the *New York Review of Books,* named the Baltimore Four and the groups which followed them the "ultra resistance."

On that day in October, Fr. Phillip Berrigan, S.J., Rev. James Mengel, Thomas Lewis, and David Eberhardt walked into the Selective Service offices in the Baltimore Customs House and poured blood over the files. They did not try to escape; they stood quietly until they were arrested. A few days later they were arraigned on charges of damaging government property, mutilating government records, and interfering with the functioning of the Selective Service System.

In a leaflet they handed out inside the Customs House the four men declared their solidarity with American servicemen and asked the Selective Service employees to resign from their jobs. "We quarrel with the idolatry of property," they added, and the war machine that makes property of men. We confront those countrymen to whom property means more than human life. We assert that property is often an instrument of massive injustice—like these files. Thus we feel this discriminate destruction for human life is warranted.

Their press statement, which included the text of the leaflet, finished with a simple invitation to emulate them: "We invite friends in the peace and freedom movements to continue moving with us from dissent to resistance."

Within the next two and one-half years there were at least a dozen more "actions," as they are simply called, against draft boards or other institutions.

The Catonsville Nine (May 1968): Phillip Berrigan and Thomas Lewis again, with Phillip's Jesuit brother Daniel and six other Catholic priests and laymen destroyed 378 draft files "with napalm manufactured by ourselves from a recipe in the *Special Forces Handbook,* published by the U.S. government."

The Boston Two (June 1968): Frank Femia and Suzi Williams, both about twenty, poured black paint on several hundred draft records.

The Milwaukee Fourteen (September 1968): Some ten thousand draft files were burned by this group of almost entirely Catholic men, including several priests.

The DC Nine (March 1969): A predominantly Catholic group again, including former priests and nuns, destroyed files of the Dow Chemical Company in Washington, D.C.

The Pasadena Three (May 20, 1969): Three Resistance workers burned about five hundred draft records.

The Silver Springs (Maryland) Three (May 21, 1969): Three resisters mutilated several hundred draft files with black paint.

The Chicago Fifteen (May 25, 1969): About twenty thousand draft files were burned by this younger, largely non-Catholic group.

Women Against Daddy Warbucks (July 1969): Five women mutilated several thousand draft records and stole the "1" and "A" from the typewriter in a New York board.

The New York Eight (August 1969): A group of four women

and four men (three of them priests) staged two raids, destroying seventy-five thousand draft files in the Bronx and several thousand more in Queens.

The Akron (Ohio) Two (September 1969): A resister and a Navy veteran set fire to an office housing five draft boards, destroying or damaging about one hundred thousand draft records.

"The Beaver Fifty-Five" (October 1969): Not fifty-five but eight, and not from "Beaver" but the midwest, they struck a set of draft boards in Indianapolis and the Dow Chemical Company in Midland, Michigan.

The Boston Eight (November 1969): Four draft boards were struck and about one hundred thousand files destroyed by this group of three women and five men, including several Catholic clergy.

The East Coast Conspiracy to Save Lives (February 1970): Eleven, including four priests and two nuns, destroyed many thousands of draft files in three buildings in Philadelphia, and many files of the General Electric lobbying offices in Washington, D.C.

To this list we should add The Big Lake (Minnesota) One, Barry Bondhus, who on Washington's birthday 1966 dumped two large buckets of his own and his family's excrement into the 1–A files of his draft board. Hardly mentioned in the American press, he was lionized by the European student Left (especially the anarchists). From his fertile mind (or whatever) came "the movement that started the Movement."

Many of the younger participants in the ultra resistance had also been in the Resistance, and many who had not had been inspired by it. Several of the latter, like the Berrigan brothers, had also been active in the civil rights movement in the south, where they came to respect the tactic of open, nonviolent civil disobedience. Most of the older ones, and several of the younger, moreover, were dedicated Catholics, and so they were open to a range of experiences and influences not available to the rest of the movement.

One such influence, in Dan Berrigan's words, was

the influence of the worker-priests, especially as they had gone through the Algerian experience and the French experience of colonialism and helped, I think, France understand herself as a post-colonial power. I think their contribution solidified my idea that perhaps we had accepted a kind of Marxist mystique without analyzing it, and that we ourselves were unconsciously and perhaps in a betraying sense dedicating our conscience to an ideal of warfare as inevitable.

Dan had met several dedicated worker-priests during an assignment in France.

Several of the priests and nuns of the ultra resistance had worked in Latin America, the Algeria of the United States. John Hogan, Marjorie Melville, and Thomas Melville (of the Catonsville Nine) had been expelled from Guatemala after seven, fourteen, and eleven years of work among oppressed farmers. Dan Berrigan had been briefly assigned to Mexico as a punishment for his antiwar activities, and George Mische (also of the Catonsville Nine) resigned from USAID in Latin America in protest against United States' policy there. Arthur Melville (Thomas' brother) and his wife Kathy (both of the DC Nine) had also worked in Guatemala. They could not avoid the appalling sight of American imperialism in action, nor, most of them, the appalling conclusion that armed struggle by peasant guerrillas was necessary to defeat it. Back home they translated their anger and solidarity into unarmed and at least half-symbolic raids against the war machine and the corporations whose interests it protects.

There was in fact some dispute within the Catholic action groups over the advocacy of eventual violence. George Mische and the Berrigans were at odds over it, and when the *National Guardian* quoted Art Melville as saying that they "have to do certain things that will lead to the beginning of . . . armed struggle" it provoked a flurry of confusion and dismay among other ultra resisters and their supporters. Art has since explained that he was misquoted, that he is not building for armed struggle but for nonviolent revolution, and only if there were no other hope would he advocate violence. He and many other ultra resisters would probably agree with the Catholic priest and writer Thomas Merton, who advocated a "theology of resistance which is at the same time *Christian* resistance and which therefore emphasizes reason and humane communication rather than force, but which also admits the possibility of force in a limit-situation when everything else fails," and with Gandhi, who said it is better to resist violently than not at all. Initially differences like these melted in the process of acting. "For a growing number of us," the Milwaukee Fourteen said, "the problem is no longer that of grasping what is happening. We know it by heart. Ours is rather a problem of courage."

Dan Berrigan named the civil rights movement, the experience of the worker-priests, and the writings of Thomas Merton as the strongest influences on his radical beliefs, but those are not the only events that shook the Catholic church in the 1960's. The encyclicals of John XXIII, *Mater et Magistra* and *Pacem in Terris,* and the deliberations of the Second Vatican Council, have had an impact that is still reverberating. So had the series of revelations by historians (and by Hochhuth's play *The Deputy*) that the Nazi policy of genocide had the cooperation and even the blessings of the German Catholic hierarchy, and perhaps of the Pope. These discoveries came at a time when America's own most powerful Catholic official, Cardinal Spellman, was loudly sanctifying America's policy in Vietnam. An almost unique counterexample, the Austrian Catholic peasant Franz Jägerstätter, who was beheaded in 1943 for refusing to wear a German army uniform, was made known by Gordon Zahn in his biography, *In Solitary Witness.* The book made a deep impression on Fr. Jim Harney, who recounted it in a preface to the new edition a few months before he became one of the Milwaukee Fourteen:

I had read Gordon Zahn's book, written of a man and a war past and gone, and was now confronted with the horrible war taking place in Vietnam. It was necessary that I put my priorities in order. It came to this: was I going to remain silent when what I loved so much, the family of man, was made a mockery of? Or would I be willing to join the Resistance and pay the price for something I believed in: the price was going to jail and possibly being expelled from a seminary, possibly not serving the Church as a priest? Would I remain silent when the very survival of an entire people is at stake? In October of 1967, at the anti-war rally held at the Arlington Street Church in Boston, I joined my voice with the 2,500 ministers, priests, and rabbis who urged President Johnson, "In the name of God, Stop It!" and, further than this, I severed my ties with the Selective Service System.

The examples, chastening or inspiring, of German complicity and Third World revolution, the precepts of Pope John, and the moral issues of contraception, abortion, and clerical celibacy, combined to shift the growing edge of Catholic theology toward a concern for the worldly condition of the soul and away from doctrinal detail. Several theological trends came together in the 1960s to provide a rich and coherent frame of reference for the revolutionary Catholic, of which the most important were the Christian-Marxist dialogue, secularization theology (popularized by Baptist Harvey Cox), the idea of the Death of God, and the Theology of Hope. As Tony Mullaney, probably the ablest scholar of the ultra resistance, explained it before standing trial for his part in the Milwaukee Fourteen raid, these new influences have challenged the traditional Christian view that history is beyond the control of man, and that man's only concern should be the preparation of his soul for death and heaven or hell. On the contrary, God has left man's fate, individually and in the mass, in his own hands. We are historical agents, with greater or lesser impact on history's direction according to how well we interpret the cues or clues to the future. We can, and we ought to, carry out Christ's mission in history to establish the Kingdom of Heaven on earth. To do this we may take clues from Christ's example, and from the Bible generally.

Christ was neither a nationalist zealot seeking to liberate Judea from Rome nor a religious mystic seeking personal liberation through transcendent revelation. He was a practitioner of salvation personal and social, he assumed that the state of the soul and the state of society were interdependent, and he sought ways to help men's lot in this world as well as the next. We who wish to fulfill his mission should, like him, side with publicans and prostitutes, lepers and sinners: with the outcast of the world, victims of racism, imperialism, and genocide. The Christian revolutionary agrees with the Marxists that the springs of historical change are found among the blacks and poor in America and the entire Third World. They must be treated with deference, as Hebrews were commanded by Yahweh to regard the *anawim* (widows, orphans, cripples) with deference. More than that, they must be joined and supported in an alliance for revolutionary change.

The Bible provides suggestions for tactics as well as general historical truths. Tony was encouraged in his decision to join the Milwaukee Fourteen, for example, by the *parresia* or "bold speech" from the disciples and apostles in the face of hostile authorities, as when Peter spoke before the Sanhedrin (Acts 4: 1–23). Such outspokenness, like the Quaker tradition of "speaking truth to power," became a model both for the bold courtroom behavior of the Fourteen and for their original act of Christian witness.

Many of the Catholics were in their mid-thirties when they joined an "action," but some, as we said, were younger and had gone through draft resistance themselves. The late David Darst, a Christian Brother, lost a request for Conscientious Objector status in September 1967, returned his draft card in December, repeated the act in January and again in February, refused induction in April, and joined the Catonsville Nine in May. At least five of the Milwaukee Fourteen were draft resisters. One of them was Michael Cullen, whose individual maturation recapitulated the phylogeny of resistance: he signed the We Won't Go statement of the University of Wisconsin, returned his card in January 1968 (after watching his friend and seminary roommate Bob Gilliam stand trial for refusal), burned another in August, and joined the Milwaukee Fourteen in September. Another was Jim Forest, who had helped to found the Catholic Peace Fellowship with Dan Berrigan. Not at first a resister—he was discharged from the Navy as a CO—he had been working with Resistance groups and from the work grown frustrated at the repetitive and sterile quality that he felt attended draft resistance. He did not at first see any improvement with the Baltimore action: when Phil Berrigan wrote to say he was considering joining another action, "I wrote him a long letter about why he shouldn't get involved again." When Jim learned that Phil and the others had nonetheless acted in Catonsville, he took a week off, "looking at the trees and the bears, thinking about the action," and decided at least to help organize the Catonsville defense committee. While in New York for that purpose he had a long talk with Dan Berrigan, who was depressed because no one had yet come forward to take the next action. Catonsville was not meant to be just a "futile and beautiful witness, in which you didn't expect anything to happen, and indeed, were rather opposed to anything happening," but was meant to "open up a new phase of resistance."

       I was suddenly flabbergasted that I hadn't grasped the need for a break of the resistance movement into a new kind of strategy, and that this was perhaps part of the answer to the kind of wall we were running into with the draft card business. Not that this would be the total face of the thing, by any means. This could be an important new aspect.

Jim brooded some more, and then decided to join the Milwaukee Fourteen. "The whole thing just blossomed in my head."

  The first Boston action, the actions in Pasadena, Silver Springs, and Chicago were carried out largely by resisters, but they were a different breed, younger and predominantly non-Catholic. The Silver Springs group, for instance, consisted of an induction refuser, a nonregistrant, and a nonregistrant-apparent (not yet eighteen). The remarkable John Phillips, a member of the Chicago Fifteen, was also one of the March 1966 draft-card burners known as the South Boston Four (one of whose members, David O'Brien, lost his appeal to the Supreme Court in May 1968). After serving fourteen months in prison John founded the Prisoners' Information and Support Service (or PISS, named apparently in honor of Barry Bondhus), a news and training center by ex-cons for prisoners-to-be. He also wrote to his local board to remind them of his existence and to declare his intention to refuse cooperation with the draft. Less than twenty-four hours after his probation period elapsed, John was burning draft files in Chicago. Charlie Muse, then twenty-one, joined the Chicago 15 after serving twenty-seven months for refusal to register.

  Like Pietro Spina, the revolutionary in Ignazio Silone's *Bread and Wine,* who put on the garb of a priest to disguise himself from the fascist police, Catholic radicals in the ultra resistance have sometimes used the forms of the church to conceal their mission.

In Chicago, for example, Father Nick Riddell rented an office ostensibly as a religious book outlet in the shabby old office building at 2355 West 63rd Street where there were thirty-four local draft boards, covering all of Southside Chicago with its primarily black, Latin, and working-class white registrants. Late on a Saturday afternoon, most of the group moved into the rented office on the same floor as the draft center. At about 4 A.M. the next morning (Sunday) they entered the SSS office through a broken window, filled more than 40 burlap bags and waste cans with at least 20,000 records, took them out into the alley, and burned them.

The "ideology" of the ultra resistance has always been radical. The Catonsville Nine statement, echoed by those of several later groups, succinctly declared their attitude toward America's most sacred institution: "We believe some property has no right to exist. Hitler's gas ovens, Stalin's concentration camps, atomic-bacteriological-chemical weaponry, files of conscription and slum properties are examples having no right to existence." Anti-imperialism was also present from the first. At his sentencing in May 1968 Phil Berrigan said:

> Our country now stands at the pinnacle of world power—we are history's most powerful empire, and perhaps its most dangerous one. We are richer than all the rest of mankind, and our military power surpasses that of all the rest of mankind. The equation between the two, wealth and military power, is not an idle one. As President Johnson has said on a number of occasions, "the rest of the world wants what we have, and we're not going to let them take it."

But as action followed action anticapitalism became more and more explicit, while religious and moral language slowly disappeared. Three of the raids were against corporations (Dow twice, General Electric once), and in their statements the groups who carried them out were unequivocal in their condemnation. The entire DC Nine statement was devoted to condemning "you, the Dow Chemical Company, and all similar American corporations. . . . We are outraged by the death-dealing exploitation of the people of the Third World, and of all the poor and powerless who are victimized by your profit-seeking ventures." They extended their sacrilegious contempt for "some property" to some corporations:

> We deny the right of your inhuman corporation to exist:
> —you, corporations, who under the cover of stockholders' and executives' anonymity, exploit, deprive, dehumanize, and kill in search of profits;
> —you, corporations, contain or control Americans and exploit their exaggerated needs for security, which you have helped to create;
> —you, corporations, who numb our sensitivity to persons, capitalize on our concern for things.

The East Coast Conspiracy to Save Lives summed up their reasons for striking at General Electric in a sentence of classic brevity:

> We have destroyed General Electric files because GE is the second largest war contractor in the United States, because GE exploits its workers both at home and overseas, and because we wish to point out the collusion between the military system, giant corporations, and government.

Two days after they invaded the midtown offices of thirteen Manhattan draft boards in July 1969, the New York Five (or Women Against Daddy Warbucks) appeared at Rockefeller Center, which houses the offices of several major corporations, and tossed shredded 1–A draft files into the air amid lunchtime crowds. They also sent over ninety copies of their statement, with its indictment of corporations,

> to the president, chairman of the board, and members of the board of directors of Dow, Chase Manhattan, General Dynamics, Standard Oil, etc.—corporations with offices in Rockefeller Center. With that letter, we sent the "cover sheet" of a "deceased" file (i.e., not the file itself), carefully cut so that the man's name was missing and could not be used offensively.

Following this precedent, the New York Eight in August returned complete 1–A files to the top executives of the Grace Lines, International Telephone and Telegraph, Standard Oil, and Anaconda. (All the executives promptly forwarded the files to the Selective Service System.)

When they made themselves public at Rockefeller Center, the five Women Against Daddy Warbucks also addressed themselves to the reigning deity of the place, John D. Rockefeller. In Maggie Geddes' words:

> When we arrived at the rally at Rockefeller Center, we gathered at the large marble placque which stands at the entrance to the pit area of the Plaza. The placque is officiously large, and has a John D. Rockefeller, Jr., quote emblazoned upon it: "I BELIEVE . . . that law was made for man, and not man for the law; . . . that government is the servant of the people and not its master; . . . that love is the greatest thing in the world." Before we began tossing the confetti-ed files to the people who'd gathered, we taped a large sign we'd made over the placque—"You can fool some of the people all the time, . . . etc."—and then poured a mixture of oil, pieces of draft files, and torn dollar bills over the placque.

The reasons for joining an action, personal and political, religious and secular, were often marked out among possible participants at retreats held several weeks before a projected raid. Here was where a community was born that would withstand the ordeal ahead and serve as a model to the rest of the movement of what men and women could create. At the first of two retreats before the Milwaukee action Dan Berrigan stressed the necessity of "opening our lives to each other and to the edge we have to walk together, and will hurt us." We must face the breaking up of our lives, he went on, face the reality of our situation in the world, not withdraw from it. We are not tourists. It is our task to hasten history's outcome, help the birth-death to happen. Where do we begin? By saying No on every front where man is destroyed and defeated. Supporting him, mere "airlift programs," are not enough. Something deeper, more painful and mysterious, is required: we must ourselves become the victims, place ourselves at his side.

America is a new Roman Empire. In it love has lost its central-
ity, a loss symbolized in secular society by the draft. The state
seeks to place its stigma on young soldiers, making a total claim
on them, aping God. But a new community can be born. Its signs:
freedom, poverty, love. In jail, without freedom, you must rely on
love. In poverty, without possessions to cling to, you must cling to
one another. "I want to be able to confront the draft with the evidence of a community of people who are doing something else."

After his talk there was a discussion of tactics. Almost exactly
two years after the proto-resisters' meeting in Des Moines had decided against a "big bang" strategy (see chapter 4), the ultra resisters made the opposite decision. They could be most effective,
they felt, by concentrating their forces.

The imperative to act was intensified by the news from the
Democratic Party Convention in Chicago. On the second day of
the retreat one of their number "invited the community to action." Those prepared to act were asked to meet the next morning
in an old barn nearby. Eighteen came. Of these, fourteen acted in
Milwaukee.

The spirit of community based on individual commitment grew
stronger in the jail and court. After the arrest Fr. Larry Rosebaugh wrote from the Milwaukee County Jail Annex:

> Now the external action is accomplished. We are gathered now
> in a room sleeping the fourteen of us, separated from the other inmates.
> In this room is where the action lies. Never before have I experienced the
> lives of individual men so personally, so deeply. All in such a short span
> of time. Maybe the reason is: Never before in the life of each of us, have
> we made a decision that would affect our lives, as this decision.

Another of the Fourteen, Doug Marvy, a twenty-seven-year-
old mathematician, smuggled a poem from the jail:

> I am not a poet, but what has taken place in the Milwaukee
> County Jail Annex since Wednesday, September 25, defies the logic of
> my more usual methods of communicating. I therefore offer:

FOURTEEN FREE MEN

We have been nourished without food,
Cried out of joy
And read in the darkness.
We are free.

We have held conversations in silence,
Lost self by asserting ourselves
And lost fear by finding it.
We are free.

We are beginning to know what's unknown,
Share what's unsharable
And watch what cannot be seen.
We are free, we are free.

Doug's wife Andrea is a professional dancer. When the $95,000 bail set on the Fourteen had been raised, she was seen "dancing for her husband on the sidewalk outside the County Jail, while the fourteen above, silhouetted against the bars, sang alleluia for joy."

A brief description of the ultra resistance can only hint at its vitality and variety. Some day its members will have to tell their own story, but until they do a couple of episodes from their adventures can serve as samples of their spirit.

The draft board in Milwaukee had been well "cased" by the raiders, but there was one hitch in the operation: there were two cleaning women in the hall rather than one. Jim Forest described the scene:

We had just about finished cleaning out the boards we were hitting when I heard this shriek in the hallway. I opened the door and there was this huge cleaning woman running down the corridor being chased by two of our guys, two priests in clericals. I grabbed her from behind. I put one hand over her mouth and another over her belly, and walked backwards to the door with her. I was kind of up tight and nervous, but I tried to explain what we were doing. I said, Maybe you have a son and maybe you're worried that they will take him to Vietnam. Maybe you know people who have boys in Vietnam. And all of a sudden, her body, which was this rigid plank of pine, just relaxed. And I let go of her.

She was shaking a little bit. And she said in this thick, maybe Central European accent, "Why didn't you tell me?"

Once in jail the first act of the Milwaukee group (as it had been also of the Catonsville Nine) was to send flowers and candy to the cleaning women.

Toward the end of the trial of the Catonsville Nine an incident occurred that has already passed into the folklore of the movement. As Barbara Deming told it:

> When Judge Thomsen suggested that they should bring things to a close, Dan asked, "May we finish in prayer, Your Honor? I would like to recite 'Our Father'." The judge sat for a long moment and then replied that he would have to ask the government (the prosecution) whether it had any objections. The prosecution replied, "The Government has no objections and rather welcomes the idea." And so judge, prosecution, and a large number of marshals who had been brought into the courtroom in case of trouble, stood and recited with the defendants—clearly would have felt embarrassed *not* to recite with them: "Our Father who art in Heaven . . . *Thy* will be done . . ." And again the defendants stood there at ease—what they believed, what they said and how they acted clearly in harmony—and again those who were bringing them to justice, as it is called, stood there clearly in contradiction to themselves.

Another story will have to be written some day about political trials during the last few years. The Chicago Eight, or The Conspiracy, will be remembered as the most spectacular, and probably the most important, of the trials, but displays of unmannerly tactics in the face of judicial repression developed out of the experience of several groups of defendants. Of these the best known, of course, are Dr. Spock and his four co-conspirators, whose cautious style provoked criticism from the movement, much of it deserved. They did in fact take greater risks, legally, than the less well-mannered Oakland Seven conspiracy defendants (organizers of Stop The Draft Week), but the latter set the precedent for vigorous political education as an integral part of a legal defense (and an effective part, for they were acquitted). Equally important were the trials of the Resistance and the ultra resistance. It has become more and more characteristic of Resistance trials for the defendant to defend himself, relying on a lawyer only for technical matters, if at all. David Harris caused his jury to deliberate over eight hours in an open-and-shut refusal case, thanks to the eloquence of his personal defense. As a resister refuses to play the role of "soldier," he also refuses to play "defendant"; instead he confronts judge, jury, and prosecutor as human beings, frail like himself, but like himself also capable of seeing through the roles they are expected to play and rejecting them in favor of a deeper vision of what is human.

Resister Joe Maizlish of Los Angeles explained why he entered no plea and turned down all offers of counsel:

> I have found that deputy marshals, probation supervisors, judges, deputy U.S. Attorneys, clerks of the court, indigent panel attorneys, other defendants not only in selective service cases, secretaries in the court clerk's office, are puzzled and interested when they run into someone who is not denying the charge against him, but instead is telling them "where he's at" and expressing politely the deepest doubts about where *they're* at.

The Milwaukee Fourteen chose to dismiss their lawyers. One of them was William Kunstler, and had they known what style of defense he was capable of (which he displayed in the Chicago Conspiracy Trial) they might well have retained him. But they had been discouraged by the confined style he and the other lawyers showed in Catonsville and in the Boardman case in Boston. In the latter Kunstler stood by helpless as the judge harassed CADRE organizer Rick Boardman throughout his attempts to explain to the jury his reasons for noncooperation, and with little ado the jury convicted him.

How the clerical "lay advocates" conducted their case has been well presented by Francine du Plessix Gray. It might be summed up in a statement they issued just before they stood trial: "We remain men of hope. We invite everyone—prosecuting attorneys, jury, sheriffs, brothers and sisters in the resistance and even Judge Larsen—to join us."

The ultra resistance, then, raised several issues for the movement: nonviolence versus violence, the destruction of property, and lay advocacy. But by 1970 probably the greatest controversy was over anonymity. Why stand around and get caught? Why not split, and hit another board later? One answer was given by John Phillips in a letter from Cook County Jail, May 31, 1969:

> The one point on which we are at odds with other movement people as well as other prisoners is over whether we should have split the scene. I had a hard time understanding the rationale for this, myself; I certainly don't want to be in prison. We don't want our support community to be based on the fact of our sacrifice, suffering, etc., but on the action itself. I know all through this INSIDE that we were right in standing around and not attempting to elude capture, but only now am beginning to discover words that can adequately convey what that feeling was. It has to do with marking the act in a very personal, human way—shouting out may be the most important thing in what we did: that HERE WE STAND, ordinary people, fearful people yet not forced by fear into concealment, people daring to challenge more than the law we broke, but its authority-of-fear that drives people to secrete themselves and keep running. . . . THERE IS NO POINT TO RUNNING, REPRESSION IS CERTAIN: IF DEPERSONALIZED, REPRESSION WILL BE GENERAL. The brunt of our attack is that we 15 weak human types, with fear and trembling, had the audacity to stand there and say that we have done this and that no power of government can erase that fact; we take responsibility, we identify ourselves in the act we performed; no more schizophrenia; schizophrenia, double agents and the rest of the game are all rejected here. If we are punished, we are punished for the act itself and not for getting caught in the act of trying to elude the law. There is never a real escape, and I don't like being a fugitive anyway. The revolution proclaims: We are sick of living in fear. By remaining on the scene, we have an important leverage. All this may be bullshit. Anyway the work goes on.

But John has since jumped bail. Indeed by the end of their trial seven of the Chicago 15 had given up on using the court as a political forum and gone underground.

There were in fact disagreements over anonymity among the ultra resisters, or at least different degrees of receptivity to it.

Claudette Piper, for example, though she had no regrets over her involvement in the Boston Eight, nonetheless hesitated to urge others to follow suit. A clear and eloquent defense of voluntary surrender came from Ted Glick, a draft refuser who joined the East Coast Conspiracy to Save Lives:

> As I see it there are two primary reasons why we and others before us have revealed our identities. The first is that without doing so, we would not be able to speak publicly to other people about what we did and why; that is, we would not be able to educate other people. Without this education and public exposure, it is doubtful that the draft file destruction and corporate disruption movement would have grown as it has.
>
> Secondly, in taking public responsibility for our actions, we are saying that we are not acting in the manner of the present system—a system in which no one is responsible for the destruction and dehumanization of life. Instead of saying that we are anonymous, faceless, and only parts in a machine, we are saying that we are human beings, individuals, part of a community, and willing to take responsibility for our lives and for the lives of our brothers. We feel that only in such a way will the movement reach other people and succeed in reaching its goal—a society in which people can be humane and loving towards each other.

The greatest gift the ultra resistance has given the movement for social change in America may be a joyous and personal way of doing serious work, a way that will dispel, and not just rearrange, the lineaments of the old order and set an example that will call forth the new. From their rhetoric, theology, and tactics, with which much of the movement disagrees, the ultra resisters seem to emerge as real people, messengers to the whole movement with tidings of courage and good cheer. About them we feel as Dan Berrigan felt about the others who preceded him: "We think of such men, in the world, in our nation, in the churches, and the stone in our breast is dissolved; we take heart once more."

POSTSCRIPT

Something new happened at the hour appointed for the surrender and imprisonment of the Catonsville Nine (now only eight because of David Darst's death in a traffic accident). Half of them, the Berrigans, Mary Moylan, and George Mische, refused to turn themselves in and went underground. After two weeks, Phil Berrigan and David Eberhardt of the Baltimore Four, also a fugitive, were caught by the FBI in a rectory in New York. Dan was captured by the FBI after four months of pursuit.

A few days before his brother was caught, Dan Berrigan made a spectacular public appearance at Cornell, where he had once been chaplain. Seven thousand students and a few FBI agents filled the university gymnasium for an evening of revolutionary drama and religious ceremony. It was still Passover, so part of the program was devoted to a Freedom Seder, adapted by Art Waskow from the traditional Haggadah. At the customary pause for the appearance of the prophet Elijah, Dan walked on stage and took his place at the table. After the service he spoke; then the lights dimmed for a rock concert, Dan slipped off stage, dressed himself in a costume belonging to the Bread and Puppet Theater (which had performed earlier), left the gym, climbed into a truck, and rode off into the night. The costume was one of the twelve apostles.

Michael Ferber had a chance to talk to Dan a few weeks after his incarnation at Cornell. (Dan Berrigan held a series of meetings, interviews, taped and filmed discussions, and surprise appearances ever since he first eluded capture.) He described his underground mission as an "experiment" to "open up possibilities," just as Baltimore and Catonsville were designed to provoke new and more serious acts of resistance. What changed his mind about surrender? The country has changed: we are becoming an "occupied people" in a police state and we must have an underground to survive. Nonviolence is still the best approach to political action—draft refusal, draft raids, sabotage of corporations— but the traditional association of nonviolence with the willingness to go to prison must be broken. If it is right to resist an "illegal" law then it is right to resist "illegal" imprisonment. What does he hope to accomplish? The demystification of governmental power: the FBI is not omnipotent, they can be kept off balance, outwitted, embarrassed. The continuation of ultra resistance: not imitations of Catonsville, perhaps, but deep and risky acts of resistance nonetheless. (No doubt Dan felt called to carry on the work of his brother, for it was Phil's energy and moral pressure that had spurred several of the later groups to action.) The exploration of the possibility that useful movement work can be done underground, in America, by a well-known and widely sought activist. And the invocation of the unexpected: a deliberate challenge to himself and his community to make happen, or let happen, something that we cannot in our ignorance predict. It may be the birth of a new idea, or a new strategy, or a new resistance community. It will come of honest dialogue about our own lives and how they can be put to the uses of God and mankind. "I do not expect ever to return to a normal life."

Notes to Chapter Fourteen

Francine du Plessix Gray, "The Ultra-Resistance," *New York Review of Books,* September 25, 1969, which deals mainly with the trial of the Milwaukee Fourteen, is still the best article on the ultra resistance as a whole. Another important source of information is the book, *Delivered into Resistance* (New Haven: Advocate Press, 1969), compiled by the Catonsville Nine–Milwaukee Fourteen Defense Committee. It includes an introductory essay by Jim Forest, the statements of the Catonsville Nine and Milwaukee Fourteen, and a meditation by Dan Berrigan from which the closing quote of this chapter was taken. See also Paul Velde, "Guerrilla Christianity," *Commonweal,* December 13, 1968.

Of the Baltimore Four, Catonsville Nine, Milwaukee Fourteen, DC Nine, Women Against Daddy Warbucks, Boston Eight, and East Coast Conspiracy to Save Lives we had copies of most leaflets and press statements. Michael Cullen kindly made available to Lynd his tapes of talks by Dan Berrigan in August and November 1968. Tony Mullaney shared his board as well as his learning with Ferber in May 1969. Ferber also had talks with Jim Harney (May 1969), Art Melville (August 1969), and Claudette Piper (February 1970). Lynd and Ferber talked with Jim Forest in March 1969. Correspondence: Bob Graf to Lynd (January 29, 1969); Maggie Geddes to Lynd (January 2, 1970).

More accessible are the following:

Baltimore Four: Dee Ann Pappas, "The 4," *Baltimore Peace and Freedom News,* March–April 1968; "Our Friend Has the Equipment to Understand Better," Liberation News Service Report of the statements made by Berrigan and Lewis at sentencing; "Phillip Berrigan Writes from Jail," reprinted by *PISS News Notes,* January 1969, from *Commonweal,* December 6, 1968; and Phillip Berrigan, *A Punishment for Peace* (New York and London: Macmillan, 1969), especially pp. 145–155.

Catonsville Nine: Among accounts of the trial are those by Florence Howe, *Resist,* October 28, 1968; Dan Finnerty and Mike Sherwin, *Philadelphia Resistance Review,* October 1968; Paul Mayer, *Renewal,* November 1968; and Barbara Deming, *Liberation,* December 1968. Dan Berrigan has turned the trial record into "factual theater" under the title *The Trial of the Catonsville Nine* (Boston: Beacon, 1970). See also the *Catholic Radical,* December 1969, for Dan Berrigan's remarks about David Darst at a memorial service after David's tragic death in an automobile accident.

Another splendid article by Francine du Plessix Gray, "Acts of Witness," *New Yorker,* March 14, 1970, appeared too late for us to use here. It is a long and fascinating biography of the Berrigan brothers with details of their actions in Baltimore and Catonsville. James Finn, ed., *Protest: Pacifism and Politics* (New York: Random House, 1967) has interviews of both Berrigans before their acts of ultra resistance. Daniel's words about worker-priests, which we quote, are from here. For background on other participants see Marianne Hinckle, "Lives of the Baltimore Saints," *Ramparts,* August 28, 1968.

Milwaukee Fourteen: See the *Catholic Radical,* published monthly from September 1968, especially October 4, 1968, with the group statement and biographies of the Fourteen, and the communications from jail by Larry Rosebaugh and Doug Marvy which we quote; and the *Milwaukee 14 Newsletter,* appearing monthly from December 1968 until the trial the following May.

DC Nine: "Interview with Art Melville," *National Guardian,* April 12, 1969.

Chicago Fifteen: John Phillips, "On Facing a New Term in Prison," *PISS News Notes,* June 1969; David Moberg, "The Chicago 15," *Liberation,* Fall 1970.

Women Against Daddy Warbucks: *New York Times,* July 3 and 4, 1969; *Chicago Action Community Newsletter,* July 25, 1969; *National Guardian,* July 12, 1969.

On Joe Maizlish: "Defending Yourself in Court: The Joe Maizlish Story," *WIN*, October 15, 1968.

Gordon Zahn's book, *In Solitary Witness*, with a new preface by Jim Harney, was reprinted in 1968 by Beacon Press, Boston.

The quote from Thomas Merton is from an essay called "Toward a Theology of Resistance" which introduces his last collection of essays, *Faith and Violence* (Notre Dame: University of Notre Dame Press, 1968). The collection also includes an essay on Franz Jägerstätter, and it is dedicated to Phil Berrigan and Jim Forest.

For Dan and Phil Berrigan's latest adventure, see *National Catholic Reporter,* May 1, 1970.

CHAPTER FIFTEEN

The Corporation as Target

The pressure to strike out in new directions grew as the tactic of draft card return began to lose momentum. Between twelve hundred and fifteen hundred persons returned their cards in October 1967. On December 4 at least 375 more cards were returned, according to the *Resistance National Newsletter*: 89 in New York City, 36 in Chicago, 89 in San Francisco, 22 in Los Angeles, 26 in Buffalo, and smaller numbers in widely scattered locations. (In Boston, at least forty cards were returned and eight burned in a ceremony held on November 16 rather than December 4.) About a thousand cards were returned on April 3, 1968 and about 750 on November 14. These totals did not, however, represent a nationwide grass-roots upsurge. Boston accounted for almost half of the cards returned on April 3. After the November 14 turn-in, David Spittlehouse of the Philadelphia Resistance commented that only twelve groups in the United States and one in England had participated, and that half the cards returned came from the west coast. (The TCDIC newsletter put the ratio at three-fourths.) The Philadelphia Resistance was one of the few groups for whom the turn-in tactic still had meaning after November 14, 1968. There were more than thirty cards returned in Philadelphia on April 3, about the same number on November 14, 285 on May 1, 1969, 87 cards returned and thirty-odd burned on October 15, 1969 (the first national Moratorium), and eighty turned in on March 19, 1970. Elsewhere turn-ins became practically nonexistent. Having condensed its strategy into a single tactic, and made of that tactic a fetish and badge of manhood, many Resistance groups paid a price when under new circumstances the tactic no longer seemed appropriate.

Restlessness with the already classic model of national draft card turn-ins was apparent at the first national Resistance conference held April 30–May 3, 1968, in southern Wisconsin. A paper called "Hasty Notes on Strategy" written for the conference by Paul Rupert of Palo Alto Resistance and CADRE three times mentioned "socialism" as the goal of the Resistance movement. Rick Boardman's notes on the reports of local Resistance groups included the following entries:

Washington, D.C. Did not hold draft card turn-in on April 3d "because it alienates constituency."

Detroit. Leaving question of noncooperation "open" for individuals.

Seattle. Has not stressed noncooperation.

New York. Goal orientation toward draft card turn-ins destructive.

After the conference the newsletter of the San Francisco Resistance commented: "A few groups (e.g. Buffalo, Detroit, and Washington, D.C.) found themselves moving away from an emphasis on noncooperation, and many individuals expressed the feeling that Resistance activities should encompass a good deal more than noncooperation with the draft."

A year later, at the second national Resistance conference, the same questions were felt more keenly by more groups and individuals. CADRE's call to the conference began:

There seem to be a lot of reasons to gather. Anon: 1. Noncooperation has been questioned sharply outside and inside the Resistance. People want to hear, for example, where Boston is at. 2. People are broadening their idea of Resistance to go beyond the draft, to include new allies, and new issues.

NER: FROM SANCTUARY TO SDS

It was understandable that CADRE called attention to the experience of "Boston," that is, the New England Resistance. Boston had been the focus of national media attention on October 16 at the Arlington Street Church turn-in. Boston had outproduced even the San Francisco Bay Area in draft cards returned. Yet Boston had declined to participate in the fourth turn-in of November 14. Why? Was Boston ahead or behind the evolution of other Resistance groups? Could it even still be considered part of the Resistance? Within the national community of resisters "Boston" became a symbol in the continual debate over the adequacy of Resistance strategy.

When it began, the Boston resistance movement had been as explicitly nonviolent and as religious in tone as any in the country. "God Isn't Dead," asserted one NER leaflet, "He Joined The Resistance." At a "service of rededication" in the Arlington Street Church on January 29, 1968, Neil Robertson read a selection from Gandhi, and the meeting sang "Once To Every Man And Nation Comes The Moment To Decide," as it had on October 16. That same month in the first issue of the *New England Resistance*, Joel Kugelmass reported on an afternoon of talk between Dennis Sweeney, Rick Boardman, and nine members of the Boston resistance group.

> For the first time, we took up as a group some of the more general questions of Resistance; we wanted to ask what the meaning of resistance can be, why people turn in their draft cards, and what sort of direction resistance might take in the future. We agreed that, all the rhetoric aside, resistance is above all a gut declaration of freedom, a primary act of personal liberation. Resistance continues to be an expression of conscience, but the expression involves the whole person—not just his politics and morality.

Thus, as of New Year 1968, if the assumptions of October 16 were being questioned at all, that questioning appears to have thrust in the direction not of politics but of personal liberation.

The reorientation of New England Resistance toward a more class-conscious, political view of resistance began with the assassination of Dr. King. In the last issue of the *Resistance* prior to April 3, nonviolence was still prominent: the cover featured "It's

Your Choice" by Joan Baez, and the inside matter Jim Bevel's December 1966 speech to the Chicago We Won't Go conference. The May 1 issue of the same newspaper, however, carried articles on racism and the meaning of Dr. King's death, including these remarks by Neil Robertson:

> To the white community King represented non-violence, a civilian patrol, but he did not represent non-violent social change. As long as King arrested violence, he was relevant to the white community as a policeman; eloquent, intelligent, but nevertheless, a policeman. And like any policeman, he was irrelevant until "business as usual" was disrupted. He was called out, business went back to normal, and he again became irrelevant.

By midsummer Bill Hunt, in a speech on Boston Common, was praising the Black Panthers and calling policemen "pigs." This was indeed a change from the thoughtworld of October 16, 1967, after which the New England Resistance had thanked the Boston police force for being different from Berkeley's.

The experience of sanctuary, however, was probably the most traumatic for NER, and caused a number of its members to question nonviolence. Before the first sanctuary in Boston a press release asserted that "The New England Resistance has pledged to deny the arrest of these two men." After it ten NER members christened the Arlington Street Church the "first liberated zone" and stated:

> Resistance announced victory Wednesday when we nonviolently obstructed the arrest of Robert Talmanson. We exposed the necessary reliance upon violence and the threat of violence that underlies all Federal claims to legitimacy and power. As we predicted, the authorities were subjected to moral humiliation.

But if moral humiliation was the objective of sanctuary they should not have announced beforehand that they would prevent arrest. If, on the contrary, the objective of sanctuary *was* to prevent arrest, the moral humiliation of the government did not signify victory. Neil Robertson probed these inconsistencies in an essay on the "Politics of Sanctuary" the following November. "A deeper implication of non-violence is a kind of supercilious moralizing," he wrote, "in which a naive proportion emerges: authorities (violent)—evil; sanctuary participants (non-violent)—good." Others both within and without the Resistance developed the critique of sanctuary, stressing in particular its deceptive theatrical character, its potential for manipulating the one who seeks sanctuary, and its pacifist basis. Their arguments had a dampening effect on NER, especially after the fifth or sixth sanctuary, when the excitement began to pall.

Barbara Deming tried to combat the discouragement felt by the Resistance itself after the first sanctuary:

> When the government came for Talmanson—"Tally"—his comrades sat in front of, behind, on top of the police car into which he had been put by federal marshalls (limp and holding a volume of Lao Tze). Things stood still for about an hour, and then the police decided not to make the arrests that everybody had expected, but to beat people. Two people were sent to the hospital. This violence brought about a crisis of thought among those involved.

> The director of the church, Victor Jokel, shocked by the bloodshed, felt that the attempt at obstruction had been a mistake, and that only spiritual means of resistance should have been resorted to. Spokesmen for The Resistance declared that in the light of the police action they would have to review among themselves the whole question of nonviolence. Before this, they had been able to assume that if they remained nonviolent, the police would respond without violence, too. Now they could no longer make that assumption. "Nonviolent protest has two functions—to keep the participants from committing violence and also to keep the whole situation from becoming violent. If the second function is lost, the first is far less meaningful."

> My hope is that all concerned will reconsider their appraisals of what occurred. I would call the action taken an eminently right one. It was in the first place simply a very logical extension of the statement all were concerned to make to Tally—of our community with him. It was a way of managing to be with him that much longer. Jim Havelin, a young poet in The Resistance, wrote a poem immediately afterwards that communi-

cates the spirit of the action. ". . . When I kneeled behind the car and saw his face in the window he wrote love in the back window of the police car. . . ." It was also a very logical extension of the statement all were concerned to make to the government authorities: That if Tally didn't want to go, we denied their right to coerce him. This was a way of making it not only embarrassing but difficult for them to take him.

One of the Resistance spokesmen put it very well: "We no longer feel the need to cooperate at any point . . . If we can make it as difficult for them as this every time (that they come to take a man away), it could change the political complexion of the country." I agree that it could. But *if* it could, how can those beginning to raise such difficulties expect to remain unscathed? Nonviolence is not a magic spell that one can cast over the antagonist—the psychological equivalent of one of the new paralyzing drugs. One of its functions is to minimize—*in the long run* the violence an antagonist will feel justified in using; but it can hardly be expected to prevent retaliation altogether. One of The Resistance people declared that the police action had "destroyed nonviolence as we have known it." If nonviolence as they have known it—that is, a relatively calm response to their nonviolence—is likely to become rare now, is it not precisely because they are beginning to challenge the war machine with much more vigor, beginning to show that they are capable of hampering it? To have violence come down upon one when one is not oneself violent is a very special shock. It is also the classic testing point for one trying this way. If they will persist in the face of unfair retaliation—persist both in their disobedience and in their refusal to use violence themselves—then, I propose, their nonviolence will become not less but far more meaningful.

Sanctuary was also significant for the New England Resistance in that it opened up communication with GI and working-class resisters. The first sanctuary was a joint action by a civilian resister (Bob Talmanson) and a serviceman (Bill Chase). Of the subsequent Wellesley sanctuary of Al Loehner, a "Resistance Statement" asserted: ". . . for the first time in our generation, a real bond is forming between the college-educated and the working class in America. . . . The Resistance movement began on the nation's campuses, but the growing number of men seeking sanctuary are from working-class backgrounds." Subsequent second thoughts about sanctuary as a tactic did not diminish the felt need for outreach beyond the middle class. The *New England Resistance Newsletter* for January 1969 offered the generalization that the peace movement had been "elitist" in supposing that the middle class could end the war, but now saw the need for "the GI and the working class from which he so often comes."

Work with AWOLs in sanctuaries led naturally to questioning not only the previous aloofness of the Resistance from dissenters within the armed forces, but also an organizing style which centered on dramatic public acts. At the November 1968 teach-in on resistance in the military which the New England Resistance substituted for a November 14 card turn-in, there was a division of opinion as to whether two AWOL Army privates should turn themselves in. Some Resistance workers felt "that such individual actions gain a major amount of the attention and distort the real priorities in GI organizing, i.e., the need for primarily quiet and collective discussion and action by enlisted men."

Besides work with GIs, the New England Resistance began working with high school students. This stimulated similar reappraisals. An announcement of proposed activity with Concord area students during the summer of 1968 stressed that "it is neither advisable nor desirable to emphasize the non-cooperation aspect of our previous programs." After the summer, an assessment of "Summer Organizing in the Suburbs" concluded that not only noncooperation but the draft itself had been too much emphasized. "Organizing on the draft was considered paramount without the initial realization that it would be most fruitful if it was the [sequel to] work on the high school as a social institution," this organizer wrote. Fall 1968 issues of the *Journal of Resistance* paid much attention to a rebellion against dress codes in East Boston high schools which had brought together black and working-class white students.

The intellectual reorientation of NER might also be characterized as a changing answer to the question: What is the main problem? In the winter of 1967–1968, New England resisters would have answered that the main problem was militarism. Even when, after April, they began to reach outward toward blacks, GIs and high school students, they at first tried to fit these programs into the older rhetoric. The ghetto was termed "the most terrible, miserable channel of all." In addressing the issue of racism after Dr. King's murder, the New England Resistance called for a card turn-in as "a minimal assault upon white racism," and offered the analysis that "the degradation of the Vietnamese and the despair of the American blacks are two sides of a single continuing force, militarism."

By March 1969, when they presented their position to the second national Resistance conference, NER answered this question little differently than SDS. The main problems were racism, imperialism, and capitalism. Their summary of their own development began this way:

> After April 3 we found ourselves with a great number of people clamoring for something to do. Everyday, new people came into the office saying that they wanted work, a surprising number of them said they were prepared to work full time. Forced to find work for everyone we drew up a number of projects, few of which lasted even through the summer and none of which are in existence today. We were producing work for people to do without giving any good reasons for doing it. In one sense, we "had no politics," as the saying goes. What we had, in fact was an inconsistent mixture of political and nonpolitical ideas, great ambitions plus half-baked plans, brilliant theorizing and inept practice, all welded into an apparent collective by the euphoria plus fever of that amazing month. And we had some 800 guys who had turned in their draft cards but only a handful of whom were interested in extending their commitment to radical social change beyond that single act. A great many were not interested in changing [anything] but the draft laws. We found that we could not organize them into any kind of meaningful group, partly because we had only the vaguest conception of what that group should do, and partly because the reasons for committing this act were as varied as "to change the draft law" and "to destroy the whole fucking system." The question of our responsibility to them still remains, as does the question of their responsibility to the movement.

The NER position paper went on to describe how the Arlington Street Church sanctuary led to "our rejection and mistrust of the liberals who formed our constituency." The paper emphasized work with GIs and high-school youngsters, and the abandonment of nonviolence which followed this immersion in working-class constituencies. It concluded:

> Our departure from non-violent strategy plus style, our increased emphasis on lower middle class and working class kids, our drive toward greater collective decisionmaking plus responsibility to the group —these are some of the processes we are in the midst of, not goals achieved. Problems plus tensions are still very great, our existence is precarious, but our collective sense of purpose is greater than it has been in a year.

The NER delegates to the March 1969 Resistance conference (Penny Kurland, "Walrus," and Michael Ferber) expected their group's position to be denounced by resisters from other parts of the country. Nothing of the sort occurred, because the experience of other groups was parallel. As the three reported in the NER newsletter:

> We need not have felt defensive . . . for while we may have developed farthest from our original tactics and style, nearly all the other groups have taken steps in the same direction. Most groups are also de-emphasizing turn-ins, though none have abandoned them altogether. Many people were interested in the specifics of high school and military work.

NEW YORK: AN ELEGY

Only a few Resistance groups survived the demise of the turn-in tactic. In the spring of 1969 there was a depressing similarity to the newsletters in which a number of Resistance groups reported a falling-off in draft card turn-ins, financial contributions, and morale. "From where we're sitting," the New York Resistance wrote in April, "things look pretty bleak." It was not only that the war went on. Also:

> Most of the guys who call us first and want to come down to the office have to be turned away and referred to another counseling service

because we have only 2 or 1 or no draft counselors available. We have hardly any money left in our checking account, and certainly can't afford to pay staff and counselors—so in order to subsist they have to go out and get part time jobs—which means that they can't be in the office when they are needed.

The few mornings that we do make it down to leaflet Whitehall Induction Center with information about the draft mainly for pre-inductees, we speak to countless guys who tell us "It's too late, I'm being inducted (enlisting) this morning, why didn't you guys talk to us before?" How do we tell them that the movement isn't able to have two people down at the two induction centers . . . for an hour or so every morning—to say nothing of having people at the draft boards to talk to guys who register or come down to talk to a clerk about their draft problems?

In the same tone the newsletter remarked: "You may never get another mailing from us. . . . Our unpaid bills almost equal our bank balance. A mailing costs over $100. . . . We have a very good brochure on what the Resistance is about. However, we haven't had the time to print it up or the money to buy the paper. . . . P.S. At least four of us are on the verge of nervous breakdowns. Also, next week will be the trials from the Sanctuary bust at City College. If we are sentenced, the whole staff may be in jail for a while."

San Francisco Resistance reported much the same situation in June. They too budgeted $100 for a newsletter, and they too commented that this might be their last. "There comes a time when the situation is so bad, so depressing that all we can say is that there is no money and that the future of not only Resistance activities, but of the office itself is at stake." Moreover, "It's been a long time since Resistance people have gotten together just to be together. Pot-lucks seldom draw more than a half dozen people."

And yet, in the Bay Area at least, this same newsletter asserted that "induction refusals are at an all time high." It would seem that while the Resistance was dying, resistance was very much alive. The office itself closed with a bang rather than a whimper on November 21, 1969 when San Francisco police and MPs raided it in search of servicemen Absent Without Leave. The Resistance had offered hospitality to G.I. Help, an operation "devoted to counseling GI's in trouble with the military, finding them lawyers and psychiatrists, places to crash, giving them information about the alternatives of exile to Canada or Sweden, open resistance to the military, going underground, or seeking various kinds of discharges." Early in the week of November 21 G.I. Help had reluctantly agreed to let four or five AWOLs sleep in the office. The authorities found almost a dozen when they broke in.

The New York Resistance marked a similar terminus in a letter dated October 7, 1969, which began: "The New York Resistance office has closed," but stated near the end: "Our folding is hopefully only a step in the growth of a strong movement of resistance to militarism, imperialism, and capitalism." In this moving but tranquil document, Marilyn Albert, Ed Fields, Ronnie Lichtman, Meyer Vishner, Lenny Brody, Debby Carter, Jill Boskey, and Bob Kowalik sketched a historical analysis of the Resistance. The period of decline began in the late spring of 1968, when

> Resistance in larger cities began to lose steam. (Although it was about this time that Resistance groups started to spring up in small towns and in the Midwest.) We had been successful in helping to move the middle class significantly: McCarthy and Kennedy entered the presidential race, the government was pushed into negotiations, and Johnson was forced to step down. But it was precisely these events which pulled the political rug out from under us. Many people were temporarily removed from radical action by the McCarthy campaign. After McCarthy lost the Democratic nomination at Chicago, and with a growing awareness of the true nature of the Paris talks, we had an opportunity to regain the initiative. Most people felt, however, that draft card returns had served their purpose as a means of moving the middle class. We had reached the point of "diminishing returns"—increasing the number of draft resisters would do little or nothing to move people. A new tactic to further radicalize the middle class had to be found. Also, the "repressive tolerance" of the government and the selectivity with which it prosecuted resisters helped destroy the psychological momentum of noncooperation. The drama was taken out of it, and the media lost interest. While at one time, turning in one's draft card was the only example of a politics of risk, in the past year other groups have offered tactics that also involved risk— "streetfighting," campus confrontations, etc. People no longer felt a

need for noncooperation as a means to personal radicalization. Staying out of prison to organize and going into the Army to organize GI's became the favored tactics.

In New York, the letter continued,

> our greatest failures were our inability to broaden our tactics to meet both the political climate and our anti-imperialist analysis, and to define our constituency beyond white, middle class, male college students. After the summer of 1968, old organizers drifted into other things —some returned to school, others formed guerrilla theater groups or rural communes. Many organizers came to feel that, partly because Resistance no longer had the potential for being the mass movement we once aspired to, they couldn't ask another man to risk prison.

At the second national Resistance conference, the eight went on, "it became clear to us that if Resistance was to survive as an organization, we would have to make the transition from a single-issue, single-tactic orientation to a multi-issue one." Some groups, such as Palo Alto Resistance, had been able to do this. New York had not. Recognizing that their group, "rather than being a living, flowing, growing community of activists," had become "an office and little more," they decided to abandon "the Resistance 'shell' (the name, reputation, office, mailing list, etc.)."

Yet the eight New York resisters affirmed: "We don't think people should be overly sentimental about obsolete organizations dying, because that is a natural process in a changing scene, and new movements develop." And also: "We feel that the common experience of trying to build an alternative to American 'life'— some of us facing prison in the process—has bound us together in such a way that although we may drift into different things, we will always maintain our sense of fraternity."

PALO ALTO: SYNTHESIS AND SUCCESS

Even for those Resistance groups which successfully moved beyond the draft issue, local organizing came into tension with the movement's increasing awareness that the structure of power it confronted was national and international in scope. SDS and then the Resistance had named "imperialism" and "capitalism" as the most fundamental causes of the Vietnam war. How could agitation around tracking in public high schools or low-keyed communication with servicemen in movement coffeehouses add up to mass power which could take on the "power elite" or "ruling class"? This was the fundamental frustration of movement activists in the late 1960s. A way forward began to be found by identifying the enemy as a series of very specific institutions run by a group of very specific persons.

The direction of the most creative Resistance groups (as of the ultra resistance) was toward direct action against corporations. The *Plain Rapper,* published in the Bay Area by Bruce Nelson and others, stressed the corporation in issue after issue. David Greenberg of CADRE moved to Pittsburgh and wrote a brilliant power structure analysis of the corporate ties of Carnegie-Mellon University. In the spring of 1969 resisters in Palo Alto and Minneapolis, two of the oldest and strongest centers of Resistance activity, joined with local SDS chapters in creating anticorporate programs. This work held out hope that the impulse of resistance could be translated into programs of day-to-day action for large numbers of people which would tangibly affect corporate power.

The "April 3 Movement" at Stanford in the spring of 1969 was an atypical amalgam of SDS analysis and initiative and Resistance political style. In October 1968 the SDS chapter at Stanford demanded that the university and its wholly owned subsidiary Stanford Research Institute (SRI) halt all economic and military projects in Southeast Asia. The boards of trustees of Stanford and SRI presented a target which the following remarks by Jim Shoch only begin to indicate.

> The Stanford Board of Trustees is a microcosm of the American ruling class. As individuals, they have important economic interests in the Third World. Union Oil, represented on the Stanford board by a director, Arthur Stewart, and on the SRI board by its president Fred Hartley, has a drilling operation off the Thai coast and owns the concessionary rights to all 55,000 square miles of Northeastern Thailand, the area where the Thai insurgency has its greatest strength. Shell Oil, whose

president Richard McCurdy is a trustee, runs the largest oil refinery in Southeast Asia, in Thailand. Tenneco, the massive conglomerate whose president Gardiner Symonds is both a Stanford trustee and an SRI director, moved into the Indonesian oil business after the right-wing military massacre of 300,000 Indonesian and Chinese leftists in 1965.

Castle and Cooke, owner of 55% of the Thai-American Steel Works, is represented on SRI's board by its president Malcolm MacNaughton. Castle and Cooke is also developing a $50 million operation in the Philippines.

Stanford trustees and SRI directors have broad economic interests in Latin America. Utah Construction and Mining owns the controlling interest in the Marcona Mining Corporation, an iron firm located in Peru. Utah has recently begun operation in Chile as well. Trustee Ernest Arbuckle and Stanford's Vice-President for Business Affairs, Alf Brandin, are both Utah directors. Arbuckle is also a former executive with the W. R. Grace Corporation, a firm with extensive sugar and shipping interests in Latin America.

Not surprisingly, the students discovered that Stanford harbored classified research on radar jamming over bombing targets at the Applied Electronics Laboratory later occupied by the movement, while SRI did research on chemical and biological warfare and counterinsurgency research, for instance in Thailand.

In January 1969 a number of SDS members entered an on-campus meeting of the Stanford board of trustees where they presented a list of demands, including the resignation of several trustees. In February twenty-nine persons were tried for this action by a university disciplinary committee. They responded by demanding an open meeting of the trustees.

At this point one faction of SDS organized a new group called the SRI Coalition. The Resistance was included in this coalition, and (in the words of *The Movement*) "Paul Rupert of the Resistance, a pacifist, was the central figure." When the trustees responded to the SDS demand by arranging a March 11 forum between five trustees and six students, Paul was one of those who presented the case against SRI so forcefully that the trustees lost an initially neutral audience of fourteen hundred. What the meeting showed, Rupert wrote gleefully afterward, was "what happens when the rulers are caught in someone else's context."

Influenced by the Resistance, the SRI coalition (in the words of *New Left Notes*) "avoided rhetoric and did not substitute militancy for politics." On April 3 a meeting of seven hundred students called for an end to chemical and biological warfare, counterinsurgency, Vietnam-related and classified research at Stanford and SRI, and demanded an open decision-making meeting by April 30. On April 8 the trustees rejected the demands. On April 9 a meeting of over nine hundred students voted to occupy the Applied Electronics Laboratory indefinitely. They did so from April 9 to April 18.

Sit-ins tend to be joyous and communal happenings; even so, the special impact of the Resistance on this one is apparent. Guidelines voted on April 9 included: no harm to persons, no property destruction, an open door policy in the building, and no tampering with files. On April 14 the fifth issue of *Declassified,* a newsletter printed in the occupied laboratory, reported that 605 signatures had been collected on the following "statement of complicity and solidarity": "I am sitting in at the Applied Electronics Laboratory. Wish you were here." The previous day Paul Rupert had moved that the sit-inners divide themselves into small groups for discussion. "In an informal survey, *Declassified* learned that the most frequently discussed topic was the question of moderates and radicals in our movement and their fears of each other. A student who considered herself a moderate said that the small group meeting was helpful in resolving the problems of political v. moral issues in her mind."

Consistent with this tone was the sit-in's response when faculty members came through the building in pairs to identify students for subsequent disciplinary action. A leaflet observed: "It was also suggested that calling the faculty cops a bunch of motherfuckers was not the best tactic, whatever our personal feelings about them. A restrained, earnest attempt to win them to our cause can only work to the benefit of the movement."

The sit-in won extraordinary support from those outside the building. Resolutions of support were forthcoming from Theta Delta Chi, Concerned Asian Scholars at Stanford, El Tigre Club,

Phi Gamma Delta, and five residential halls. Representatives of the sit-in also took their case to university employees and three neighboring high schools. Women were invited to join the sit-in by their "sisters at AEL," who noted that "to make it possible for you to come to AEL we have established a co-operative child care center, staffed by both male and female volunteers."

As at Columbia there was a wedding in the occupied building. *Declassified* began its seventh issue with a poem "To Carrie And Marc" ending:

> "We join in Solidarity Forever
> Your union makes us strong."

In rhetoric reminiscent of Greg Calvert's speech at Princeton two years before, the same issue of the newspaper tried to place the Stanford protest in the context of the larger student movement:

> This has been the historical trend of the student movement—from symbolic protests of society's injustice to others in expiation of the supposed guilt of privileged students, we have moved to the perception that we too are a part and victims of a society in which we do not share control. . . . Our step from attacking symptoms to attacking the economic roots of social ills is just beginning.

The union of personal and political was also sustained in the following manifesto in *Declassified*, entitled "Love":

> A new community is forming in the bowels of the university. People are learning to reject the alienation and separation which Stanford fosters in us. We are really beginning to relate to each other and trust our brothers and sisters. We are realizing that we can create a new world which is run on our love and trust, rather than on the buying and selling of people. Through our actions, we challenge the values and assumptions of the men who run Stanford. It is only now, as we break out of the routine and structure of our lives as Stanford students that we can really begin to change our lives. We cannot be judged by the assumptions of a dying system. We are responsible to our new community, our form of communication and life. We are together, we can share and smile, and we reject the death-style that pervades the society all around us.

The trustees are men of death and oppression. We reject this, and call for life and love. Join us in creating a new community and a new world.

The spring ended, many meetings and another sit-in later, with partial victory for the students. Chemical and biological warfare research was ended and SRI sold.

MINNEAPOLIS: GOING FOR THE JUGULAR

The Honeywell Project in Minneapolis launched a similar campaign off the campus. Here the target was the twentieth-largest defense contractor in the United States (in fiscal year 1968), manufacturing antipersonnel bombs for use in Vietnam. About a third of Honeywell's annual sales are to the Defense Department. The corporation has four ordinance plants in the Twin City area, the largest of which employs four thousand workers.

In December 1968 Marv Davidov, an organizer with the Twin Cities Resistance group, called together about twenty-five persons from "clergy, students, SDS, Draft Resistance, Women's Liberation." One of the group's early efforts was an appearance at the annual shareholders meeting on April 29, 1969. A former Honeywell employee, Evan Stark, addressed the shareholders meeting on behalf of the Project, and called on the corporation to abandon defense work. The basic Project leaflet featured pictures of children killed and wounded by antipersonnel bombs, and repeated the demand that Honeywell "cease all aspects of defense production" and use its resources "for the creation of goods valuable to humanity."

The Project sought to reach a variety of constituencies. The church committee sent speakers to various denominations "urging them to take public positions of opposition to fragmentation bomb production by Honeywell, to raise funds for the project and to visit members of the Honeywell board of directors." Campus groups were formed at four colleges, including a study group on the problem of reconversion to peaceful production. One Project worker tried to organize Honeywell scientists and engineers. A ward club in the neighborhood of a Honeywell plant "met with members of the city council there and demanded that the plant be zoned out of their area." As of fall 1969 plans were underway "to create national and international demonstrations perhaps during one designated week at Honeywell plants and sales offices everywhere in the world," to "demonstrate at the churches and homes and country clubs of local directors," "to create a situation where Honeywell recruiters have a tough time on campus," and perhaps to initiate a selective consumers' boycott.

Of particular interest was the attempt of the Project to join forces with industrial workers inside the Honeywell plants. After the shareholders meeting, according to Davidov, "we got a call from two very sympathetic union people, a white woman who is part-time recording secretary with the union [Local 1145 of the Teamsters] and a black man who is a plant steward in aerospace." Although the two callers did not wish to identify themselves publicly with the Project, they agreed to give advice as to the content of leaflets. A first leaflet to Honeywell workers began:

TIRED OF BEING PUSHED AROUND?

Why all the pressure on employees to make the quotas set by Honeywell bosses? Who benefits from the speed-up in production—the men and women making the products or the big executives? Binger gets a raise from $147,000 to $213,000 and an $83,000 bonus. What big raise and fat bonus did you get? When assembly workers and a shop steward speak out, what happens? Who gets pushed around?

Who gets pushed around with property taxes, sales taxes, and income taxes? Honeywell executives and stockholders hide behind loopholes and tax shelters. A Minnesota legislator reported that companies like Dayton's, 3M, Hanna Mining, and Honeywell get enormous tax breaks. And who pays through the nose for these taxes?

Who gets pushed around by inflation? Wage-earners pay the bulk of the surtax. Why is it that Honeywell's profits soar while the real wages of its employees sink into higher costs? What caused inflation in the first place—overpriced spending of under-paid wage-earners or the squandering of money by undertaxed corporations like Honeywell?

Toward the end the leaflet recognized the fear that if Honeywell gave up defense work many jobs would be lost.

What would happen to your job if Honeywell dropped its contracts? Honeywell dropped all its war work in 90 days after World War II and its profits went up 25%. No one needs to lose his or her job if proper planning is done and if the company respects the rights of its employees. One group in the Honeywell Project is studying economic possibilities for employees, including reconversion methods and upgrading skills.

A later leaflet addressed to Honeywell workers attempted to generalize these observations, offering the following "pocket analysis" of the American economy:

> Over the last decade the average wage earner has been plagued by high-rising costs. For example, costs of home ownership went up 31%, and medical services zoomed up 60%. Wages, for the most part, have not kept pace with rising costs. Moreover, the rise in the consumer price index (our daily bread costs) resulted in a 5–10% increase in 1968. And wages, particularly those without a cost-of-living clause, were eaten up by these costs.
>
> However, the biggest burden on wage earners is the inequality in the tax structure. The working family that makes between 7,000 and 15,000 dollars a year gets hit the hardest by local and national taxes.

This second leaflet also referred to a recent accident at one of the four Honeywell plants in the area, in which a young woman's hands were severely mutilated by the accidental explosion of a bomb. "No attempt was made to adjust the speeded-up rates in order to insure the safety of employees."

The Honeywell and April 3 projects, however, were exceptions to the rule. Typically, Resistance groups quietly broke up and individual resisters joined persons from other movement organizations in anticorporate actions. Dick Freer of St. Louis Resistance, for instance, joined a demonstration at a trustees meeting of Washington University in St. Louis. The students demanded the withdrawal of investments of Washington University funds in munitions corporations and in companies that have holdings in the Republic of South Africa; they also asked that certain members of the board of trustees resign because of their affiliations with companies such as McDonnell Aircraft. In addition, the protesters asked that all board of trustees' meetings be open and public. Dick himself wound up with four days in jail when he attempted to restrain a guard from pushing a fellow-demonstrator through a glass door. The special attention he received resulted, Dick believes, "from a remark typed on the warrant: 'Alleged to be a member of SDS.'"

Notes to Chapter Fifteen

The number of draft cards returned on the four turn-ins is a matter of controversy. For instance, New York Resistance estimated 1400 on October 16, 600 on November 16 and December 4, and "close to 1000" on April 3 (*The Resistance: Where It's At, Where It's Going*). The TCDIC newsletter for April 1968 also states that "more than 3,000" men had noncooperated during the first three national days. We have followed somewhat more conservative estimates. David Spittlehouse's total for November 14 was "approximately 450" (*Philadelphia Resistance Review*, February 1969).

Sources drawn on for the New England Resistance include *Resistance National Newsletter*, *Resistance* and *Journal Of Resistance*, all edited by members of NER in 1967–1968, as well as the *New England Resistance Newsletter* and a collection of press releases, prospectuses, newspaper clippings, and the like, preserved by Neil Robertson. See also "What's Happened in New England Resistance," *WIN*, May 1, 1968, and Barbara Deming in *Pittsburgh Draft Resistance*, n.d.

On the demise of New York Resistance, see also "New York Resistance, R.I.P.," *WIN*, November 15, 1969, and for San Francisco, *WIN*, February 1, 1970.

The April 3 Movement at Stanford is described in *Peninsula Observer*, "through March 31," 1969, *New Left Notes*, April 26, 1969 and *Plain Rapper*, June and July, 1969. Members of the movement sent us a full collection of its mimeographed fliers, along with *Declassified*, Volume I, Numbers 1–7, and two pamphlets, *SRI* and *The Goods On AEL*. The *New York Times*, January 14, 1970 gives details on the outcome of the struggle.

A conveniently available account of the Honeywell Project is Marv Davidov's "Letter to the Movement" in *Liberation*, October 1969. Richard Freer described his experience in a letter to Neil Robertson (June 5, 1969).

CHAPTER SIXTEEN

The Resistance Mentality

Someday a learned book will be written on the factors that produced "the Movement." Unless it is written by someone who grew up in the fifties and early sixties, it is likely to miss a vital cluster of images and ideas that helped make up the world view and sense of self of vast numbers of young people. Central to the cluster is the motorcyclist, either alone or part of a gang: Marlon Brando in *The Wild One*. Thom Gunn was more prophetic than he knew in his 1957 existentialist motorcycle poem, "On The Move":

> One joins the movement in a valueless world,
> Choosing it, till, both hurler and the hurled,
> One moves as well, always toward, toward.

There are related characters in the western cowboys of countless movies and the alienated rebel, James Dean. These archetypes found natural literary counterparts in the rebel and Sisyphus figures of Camus, and a natural philosophical rationale in existentialism generally. Put a gun in his hand, and this archetypal figure becomes the movement hero of the late 1960s: Che Guevara, or Bonnie and Clyde, or the protagonists of *Wild In The Streets*. But the movement hero of the early 1960s, both in fact and fantasy, was unarmed. He was, for example, Bob Moses of SNCC, a reader of Camus, and a legendary practitioner of participatory democracy and nonviolence.

The Resistance was that portion of the movement in the second half of the 1960s in which the spirit of SNCC and SDS in the early 1960s was still, for better or worse, most evident. It was evident for instance in these words of David Harris in August 1967:

> To choose resistance means that there are no longer simply issues, there are no longer simply problems to argue solutions to; beyond innuendo and beyond observation and conclusion, there is an act with the totality of our lives against the machines of the state. The act begins with a refusal to cooperate with conscription; as long as America continues to mean oppression, the act has no end.

Lennie Heller had been under similar influences. In their speeches and writings both spoke of acts, of lives, of commitment, not of calculations of moral options or strategies for social change. In early October Lennie wrote:

> You can't rationalize your way out of this one. This is not the subject for a term paper. You must begin to answer that question, What will I do? Most people who claim to be in the opposition just aren't doing anything. Maybe handing out leaflets, maybe giving moral support to the noncooperators. Well, that simply isn't enough. The only way out is the hard way. That means incurring personal risks. That means attacking the machine with your minds, your bodies, and inevitably with your lives.

The personal style of speaking that once characterized the New Left was retained by the Resistance when most other groups went ideological, abstract, and "political." A typical Resistance "rap," especially on the west coast, would include the story of how the speaker came to the decision to turn in his card and refuse to cooperate with the draft. Some might be mystical: "I had a vision that afternoon, and somehow I knew I would." Or humorous: "The other day a bar-tender refused to accept my draft card as valid proof of age, so what good was it to me? Maybe my draft board will have better luck with it." Or defiant: "No goddam government is going to make me carry no goddam piece of cardboard in my goddam pocket." Or existentialist: "There it was, staring at me, and there I was, staring back. It was absurd. While I stared, people were dying in Vietnam." Or male-chauvinist: "I found I wasn't a man until I said 'Fuck you' to the draft. Besides, girls say yes to guys who say no." Usually the tone was modest, even diffident, but always the personal touch was present.

This Resistance spirit—understated, humorous, tied to the specifics of an experience—is perhaps best communicated by the poetry resisters quoted and wrote. Just as the song "We Shall Overcome" in many ways summed up the atmosphere of the Southern civil rights movement, so Resistance poetry is a clue to Resistance ideas.

A CADRE leaflet for the November 14, 1968, day of noncooperation consisted of five poems. One, by Robert Peterson, was entitled "Dear America":

> Dear America you worry me
> Our friendship (& that's all it ever was)
> is shaky. . . .

Another, by Olga Cabral, reported cosmic rebellion against the American empire:

> This morning the sun
> for the first time in 7,000,000 years
> reported late
> for work. . . .
> The stones hate us.
> The eyes are bitter.
> Every tree is out to strangle us.
> The grass mistrusts us. . . .

Then there was Joseph Langland's lullaby "for Sadako Sasaki, dead of leukemia in October 1955 at the age of twelve. A few months before her death she tried to fold 1,000 paper cranes, which according to Japanese legend would protect her health; she had reached 964 when she died." A fourth was by Vietnamese Buddhist monk Thich Nhat Hanh. It closed by asking:

> If we kill men, what brothers will we have left?
> With whom shall we live then?

A similar leaflet by the Ann Arbor Resistance used quotations from the wall slogans of the May 1968 events in France. "Do not free me. I will do it myself." "A man is not stupid or smart; he is free or slave." "From a man, one can make a cop, a vegetable, or a marine; why not make a man?" It also included a French song from the Algerian war period:

> Gentlemen, who are called great, I am writing you a letter that you will perhaps read if you have time.
> I have just received my draft notice to report for duty before Wednesday evening.
> Gentlemen who are called great, I don't want to do it.
> I am not here on earth to kill poor people. . . .
>
> Tomorrow I will leave, I will close my door in the face of the dead years. I will go along the roads.
> I will live by begging on land and on the sea, in the eyes of the new world, and I will tell the people
>
> Profit from life, banish misery, we are all brothers, people of all countries.
>
> If you must spill blood, spill your own, gentlemen the good apostles, gentlemen who are called great.
> If you pursue me, inform your gendarmes that I will not be armed, and that they will be able to shoot.

The Ann Arbor leaflet also contained a poem by Barbara Gibson which reflected the increased awareness in the Resistance of "the system."

> Damn the cages, and the keepers
> and those who come to stare and those

who are the agents of the blinding
and the maiming of the animals
and damn the zoo.

And both the Chicago and Ann Arbor leaflets included lines by
Rainer Maria Rilke, entitled "A Dedication of 1924":

As nature leaves whatever lives to face
the venture of blind pleasure, without
freeing a single one to find a hiding place,
we too are to the ground of our being
in no way dear, it ventures us. Yet still
much more than plant or beast, we will
this venture, move with it, and sometimes even
are more venturous (and not from selfishness)
than even life itself, by a breath more
venturous. . . . This fashions us, though shelterless,
safe dwelling at the core of gravitation
amid pure forces, what brings us salvation
is that, confronted with the threat, we dare
to turn into the open, shelterless,
till in the widest spaces, anywhere
where the law touches us we may say Yes.

In the poems of the resisters themselves we see political commitment emerge from a background of connection with nature.
Jeffrey Shurtleff of Palo Alto wrote in the summer of 1967:

Amidst the summer and autumn grasses
Children flourish at the breast of the coast.
In the brief season of war,
We mourn the death of the fisherman's son.

Later that year he found new ways to speak of the "Yes" to life
which, for resisters, was the context of their "No" to so much of
our society. These are phrases from his "Three Poems" of December 1967:

Do not fear a place for lack of air,
    flowers live there,
and though few, are well tended. . . .

Penitentiary is quiet place,
being last and closest to Death.
Its thoughts are timeless,
like a clock without a voice.
The convict Penitent at night,
drifts among the blue shadows
harboring no malice. . . .

The flower has no shame,
    it never blinks its eyes,
not even in the face of the fire.

Resisters even wrote poetry to their draft boards. A Long
Island resister, Doug Baty, had this to say to his local board
under the title "Brother Doug Baty Replies":

people
do u really know what ud do?
do u really understand what u ask? . . .

    You see this picture.
that was your mother
    and mine.
the baby was u
    and me.

i am u
    and u are me
    and what have we done to each other?
i am in a monastery of joyful mind
    and will remain here for my life
    even if I am placed in jail.

u do not have the right to order me
    nor anyone else. . . .

u are a draftee
i am a chairman
what does that do?

should I hit you?
or should i laugh
and let us both
go free?

i am neither mentally, morally, nor physically fit to kill.
i am also grateful to you
for helping me come to my senses.

In June 1968 the newsletter of the Berkeley Resistance published an anonymous poem which ended:

this was the time of love's body politic
you lived in the forest and
sought refuge in the village
where you taught the younger brothers
to make sounds and to be silent
to think and to have faith in the unthought
you dance and there is calm on the other side.

Love's body politic was as good a way as any to describe the Resistance. Writing, in September 1968, in *The Northwest Resistance,*
Ann Fetter spoke of the resisters' concern to keep alive the purpose of the revolution in their way of making it:

We have grown so used to war,
to hatred, to strife, to injustice,
perched like terrible, invisible birds of prey
on all the trees of our landscape,
that we can no longer see the sun
save through the darkness made by thin stretched wings.

We have put our lives in abeyance
on account of this dreadful reality.

We can no longer take time, it seems,
to be simple or uncaring,
except in small mouthfuls, moments
snatched, always guiltily, from the demands
of the cause grown great as life to us.

Our arms have grown stiff from bearing banners,
politics dictate our choice of friends,
our voices are hoarse from pleading with our patron saints:
    small, bearded tartar, great Lenin;
    Gandhi, gentle wraith with holy eyes;
    lion-headed Trotsky;
    beautiful black Martin;
with whose names we hope to exorcise
the terrible vultures from our skies.

And yet, if the millennium did arrive
and we could see the coming of our gentle revolution
like small white birds everywhere descending,
what then would become of us?
Could we then see the sun, would our arms
grow again supple and our voices soft?
Or would we be lost, immobile with confusion,
not knowing what to do with our lives,
having seen the attainment of our great goals.

Oh brothers, sisters, pray that we be able
to lay aside, with thanks, our patron saints
and take up the business of living.

Some have argued that the Resistance had nothing else to talk about except personal commitment, "sentiment," or "moralism," and that it was a sign of maturity in SDS, for example, that it could stick to strategy in its speeches and debates. David Loy argues forcefully that the absence of an ideology made it more difficult for the Resistance to expand into a multi-issue orientation:

The draft card has been our natural "tool." But when we expand beyond an anti-draft approach to an anti-capitalist one, difficulties arise. Refusing induction is adequate as a means to the end of abolishing the draft; we know very immediately what is wrong with the draft, its direct infringement on our freedom, and our end is negative, involving simply the destruction of a particular institution for which we need no replacement. But when the end becomes broader and more ambiguous, the status of the means must become questionable too. Being anti-capitalist implies a more precise analysis of what is wrong with capitalism and the substitution of an alternative economic and political structure. Turning in one's draft card, even if done as a consciously anti-imperialistic act, does not in and of itself provide that analysis or propose a social alternative. As an anti-draft action, it is ideologically complete and self-sufficient; as an anti-capitalist one, it is not. Because we're not sure exactly what we are against, much less its origins, because we're not sure what alternatives to propose, we can't be certain about our means.

There is truth in this but the alternative is not self-evident. Surely for every apolitical and "sentimental" speech or pamphlet from the Resistance, SDS produced a dozen long theoretical treatises constructed out of abstract categories (with quotes from Marx or Mao as cement) and almost no connection to real experience. Which is the more useless is anyone's guess, but a personal rap from the Resistance is at least an expression of someone at the point of action (and an expression that may inspire others to act), whereas theoretical analyses have a way of engendering only more theoretical analyses. Obviously the truth lies somewhere in between. Theory should be ahead of practice, but still attached to it; it should start from where people are now and lead to where they might feasibly go, but not so far that unexpected events would make the course unrecognizable. Above all it should be grounded in the actual experience of those that are to carry it out, not imposed by self-appointed theoreticians who have mastered the "science" of revolution. On the largest scale: we need the traditional theoretical classics, of course, but even more we need to have confidence in our own perceptions of the affluent, technologized, H-bomb-brandishing society we live in, so different from those the classics were about, and our ability to put together a program for transforming it.

The Resistance mentality also expressed itself in the omega.

The Greek capital letter omega is as close to an official Resistance symbol as anything can be in a group where nothing is official. How it came to be associated with the Resistance, however, no one seems to know. In Boston, shortly after October 16, Alex Jack returned from a seminarians' conference in Cleveland with the symbol; its dual significance made it catch on, a thousand buttons were printed of a black omega (designed by Harvard student James Smith), and within a couple of months most Resistance groups in the country had adopted it. It is now a generalized resistance symbol, common among antiwar groups outside the original Resistance, though it has always been more popular in the East than in the West.

In physics, the capital omega stands for Ohm, the unit of electrical resistance. It suggested to the draft resisters the very metaphors they had been using—friction in the machine, attrition of the supply lines, turbulence in the conduits to Vietnam—metaphors endorsed by no less an authority than the Selective Service System itself in its classic memorandum on "channeling." A neat and clever symbol of the tactic, though perhaps too mechanically conceived, the Ohm's very remoteness from historical or political reality appealed to the whimsy of the Boston group and of nearly everyone who came across it. Groans of recognition, like those that greet a pun, echoed across the country as initiates were instructed in the dark lore of draft resistance. The groans grew when an MIT student pointed out that electrical resistance, measured in Ohms, can be construed, very vaguely, as a kind of opposite of the property of electrical inductance, symbolized by a capital L. Inductance, which the NED defines as "self-induction," is a process whereby currents are generated or changed by magnetism. Under certain conditions it can act as a sort of forward inertia; under others it can communicate a flow of current from one wire to another. It is a kind of lemming effect for electrons: alienated, rootless, without a sense of community, they herd mindlessly together and flow or oscillate at the command of those who control the channeling system. (The Resistance has been accused of lemming-like behavior itself, of mutual inductance by animal magnetism into early martyrdom.) Since the Resistance opposes induction, it was suggested, its buttons should say "L no—We won't flow!"

As the last letter of the Greek alphabet, the omega can mean simply the end—of the draft, of the war, of all war. For the same reason it has been associated for the last two thousand years with Christian eschatology. In the Revelation of John (22:13) Christ says: "I am the Alpha and the Omega, the first and the last, the beginning and the end." The end or last (*eschatos*) came to mean the Second Coming, the final Apocalypse, where all accounts are squared, history ends, and the Kingdom of Heaven begins. For the orthodox seminarians in the Resistance this symbolism was significant. They were performing an act of religious witness, a prophetic act, guided perhaps by a desire to imitate Christ, certainly also by a vision of what it will take to usher in the Kingdom. The Resistance was criticized for its "apocalyptic style," by which was meant a confusion of inner need with outer reality and the resulting conviction that an individual act will make a difference in the world.* Most Resistance groups tried to play down the Christian aspect of their symbol, or at least to detranscendentalize it to refer to the possibility someday of a new community here on earth, the product of men and women working together. It is no accident that several of the priests and nuns who destroyed draft files in Baltimore, Milwaukee, and elsewhere, were profoundly influenced by a similar detranscendentalizing process. The Theology of Hope, the Death of God, and secularization theology (the latter popularized by Harvey Cox, a Resistance supporter) converged into the notion that the Kingdom will be built in history, on earth, and by men. The omega is a direction, a set of cues to action, and symbolized the hope, if not the faith, that in the fullness of time man will fulfill his divine promise and build a new community.

* Another feature of the omega symbol, seized on by the more poetic resisters, is the homonym of Ohm in the sacred Hindu syllable "Om" (or "Aum," according to purists), the peace that passeth understanding.

Wisdom on Brando et alii came from a conversation between Greg Calvert and Michael Ferber (March 1969), and from ten years of conversations, motorcycle rides, and movies shared by Jeremy Taylor and Ferber. Thom Gunn's poem occurs in *The Sense of Movement* (Faber and Faber: London, 1957). David Harris and Lennie Heller are quoted from the *Resistance Newsletter,* nos. 2 and 3.

David Loy's paper "An Alternative to Marxism" has not been published. Sources for poems are the *Resistance Newsletter,* vol. I, no. 2, August [1967]; *Resist,* December 1967 and April 1968; [Berkeley] *Resistance Newsletter,* no. 2, June 1, 1968; *Northwest Resistance,* September 16, 1968.

EXCURSUS: RESISTANCE EPISTEMOLOGY
(by Michael Ferber)

Underlying some of the disputes in the movement are differing views of man and how he comes to know his world. In the pages that follow I will trace some of the history of the nature-nurture controversy and its political implications. It is presented as a set of problems in historical perspective that point generally toward a certain kind of politics, not a set of answers accumulating in history toward an ultimate "science" of revolution. In fact its presentation is part of the point: man has the capacity to be free, to free himself, to transcend his conditions and remake history. It is, I think, part of the Resistance tradition.

Locke and Hume
In 1690 John Locke published two books, *Two Treatises of Government* and *An Essay Concerning Human Understanding*. Both, but especially the latter, were influential sources of eighteenth-century ideas on government, natural rights, psychology, and epistemology, and they are a convenient place to pose the problems that have recurred in various guises for the last three centuries or more.

In the *Two Treatises* Locke presents his doctrine of "natural rights," including liberty, equality, and property, which he assumes occur in a "state of nature" and which he therefore takes as the basis for his political theory. As men contract out of nature and into society they relinquish certain rights in order to make others more secure. Not all rights are to be thus "alienated": some cannot be willingly surrendered without violating Reason (or God's will). To posit a state of nature and natural rights, however abstract and undefined, is to limit the right of any person or government to control any other person: it presumes an innate and inviolable dignity. If there is a natural condition of man, then there is a standard against which to judge all social and political arrangements. The long-range implications of such a standard are subversive—democratic, egalitarian, even anarchistic. But Locke, of course, was no subversive.

Locke nowhere clearly specifies the natural qualities of man which entitle him to natural rights. In *Two Treatises* he appeals to Reason, or Nature, or self-evident facts, or divine revelation as the sources of his assertions about man, but they remain abstract and undefined. He believed that God endowed man with Reason and so arranged Nature that man can reason his way toward correct knowledge of Natural Law. Or at least some men: Reason, it seems, requires leisure and education for its proper functioning, and (as Locke says elsewhere) "the greatest part of mankind want leisure or capacity" for it. The equality of men by nature is outweighed by the inequality of men by nurture. Though all men have natural rights, in society only the few, the propertied gentlemen, are properly rational, and fit to rule.

The tension between the egalitarian and libertarian implications of Locke's doctrine of natural rights (by itself) and the antidemocratic, elitist implications of his reliance on Reason (and its slow cultivation) as their foundation has troubled many readers of the *Two Treatises*. The tension widens to a contradiction, many readers believe, when the natural rights doctrine is compared with the epistemology and psychology Locke espouses in *An Essay Concerning Human Understanding*.

In the *Essay* Locke entered the nature-nurture controversy over human knowledge and its sources. In refuting the doctrine of "innate ideas" (held by the Cartesians of France and the Platonists of Cambridge), he gives to man only the most meager natural (or innate) mental equipment. He claims that man is born with no innate ideas ("idea" can range in meaning from "primary notion" almost to "sense-impression"): the mind is a *tabula rasa* (blank slate) or waxed tablet that passively receives and records (perceives and remembers) sensations from the world. It has the innate capacity to make only a few operations on its present or past impressions: it can intuit general relations, like similarity or simultaneity, and it can make complex ideas out of simple ones by compounding them, comparing them, or abstracting one of them from a cluster. Capable only of shuffling and shunting what happens to come its way, the mind is almost entirely a creature of its conditions.

The consequences of this passive, meager, and atomistic model of the mind for Locke's own doctrine of natural rights and natural law are grave. If man's mind can be built up almost entirely by the accidents of his environment, then to what universal standards of truth or morality can we appeal? If all is nurture, what is natural? Some modern scholars (Aarsleff) think they can extricate Locke from this difficulty, but others (Laslett) point out that Locke himself was aware of the problem and, suddenly famous for his *Essay,* was reluctant to be known as the author of *Two Treatises.* In any case, the difficulties were acutely felt by political and moral philosophers, both British and American, in the eighteenth century.

By itself, Locke's environmental epistemology can point in either a revolutionary or conservative political direction. Negatively, as a corrosive solvent of ideas for which there is no empirical basis, it has been well used against political and religious superstition. The tradition of British empiricism has always been iconoclastic, and sometimes revolutionary. On the other hand, Locke's epistemology can serve the *status quo.* It supports the notion that only the leisure class can rule, for their blank slates are the only ones to have been properly nurtured (presumably by those whose own blank slates were properly nurtured) to become rational. If the mind is a mirror of its environment, then its social views are reflections of the society it grew up in, and from here it is a short step to ethical relativity.

Together the two tendencies can produce trenchant critiques and withering satire, but very little (except Reason) on which to base an alternative vision of man and society.

David Hume, the most rigorous and honest of the early empiricists, was both an iconoclast in theological matters and a conservative in political. In his epistemology he resorted to "instinct" to account for our sense of causality (not derivable from sense-impressions alone), but said nothing about what instinct is or where it comes from. To account for our belief that our impressions of the world are not subjective idiosyncrasies but true reflections of universal nature, Hume relied on the equally vague "feeling": an idea is true if we feel it forcefully or firmly. Needless to say, "instinct" and "feeling" are no more satisfying than Locke's "Reason" as answers to the deep problems of true knowledge.

Hume was an ethical relativist. He argued that "this is good" means "this is approved of." He is responsible for the notion that has come to be called "Hume's Guillotine": that one cannot argue logically from statements of fact to principles of morality. One could say that for Hume, then, principles of morality *are* statements of fact. It is the fact that certain things are approved of in Hume's milieu (his milieu being gentlemen of breeding and taste like himself), and since there is no logical or rational way to negate or transcend the environment he is in, he might as well relax and adopt prevailing custom as his moral norm. "Custom" plays a role in his ethics rather like "instinct" and "feeling" in his epistemology: all are resting points in Hume's otherwise relentless examination of principles and foundations. Left unexamined, they remain indigestible elements in an otherwise smooth and well-honed system.

Herbert Marcuse has well summarized the situation after Hume:

If Hume was to be accepted, the claim of reason [not Locke's Reason] to organize reality had to be rejected. For as we have seen, this claim was based upon reason's faculty to attain truths, the validity of which was not derived from experience and which could in fact stand against experience. " 'Tis not . . . reason, which is the guide of life, but custom." This conclusion of the empiricists' investigations did more than undermine metaphysics. It confined men within the limits of "the given," within the existing order of things and events. Whence could man obtain the right to go beyond not some particular within this order, but beyond the entire order itself? Whence could he obtain the right to submit this order to the judgment of reason? If experience and custom were to be the sole source of his knowledge and belief, how could he act against custom, how act in accordance with ideas and principles as yet not accepted and established? Truth could not oppose the given order or reason speak against it. The result was not only skepticism but conformism.

Dissenters

Locke, Hume, and other empiricists provided a set of concepts and metaphors that dominated eighteenth-century thinking on the nature of man and society, so the conflicting tendencies within empiricist thought, especially Locke, engendered a pervasive intellectual crisis. Much of the century's political, social, and epistemological writing, in both England and America, seems like a set of quarrels with Locke. Among the chief quarrelers—chief in the depth and extent of their critique and in their influence on the American Revolution—were the Dissenters: Thomas Paine, Priestley, Burgh, Price, Cartwright, and others. They attacked or revised Locke on both his epistemology and his natural rights, and where they resolved his inconsistencies it was in a steadily more radical, egalitarian direction.

The doctrine of natural rights, it was recognized, is a liberatory idea but is inadequate as explicated by Locke. Some rights, for example, cannot be bartered for others. Priestley and Price claimed that certain rights are inalienable not because Reason declares them so but by their very nature: there is no equivalent for them. It is not that society works best when some rights are retained, but that man cannot surrender them and still be man. Among these are the right of conscience and the right of revolution.

Locke's right of property came under steady attack by such writers as Priestley, Burgh, Cartwright, and Thomas Paine. Together they shifted the doctrine of natural rights away from a focus on property to a focus on conscience. Out of their critique of the accumulation and exploitation of God's earth came the view (later espoused by Jefferson) that the state may regulate private inheritance for the public benefit.

But if the critique of natural rights was basically friendly, that is, if the aim was revision and extension rather than refutation, the critique of environmental epistemology was hostile. Burgh argued that moral truths are directly self-evident, that one need not rely on Reason or custom, and that "moral truth is in no respect more vague or precarious than mathematical." Price gave to the mind a faculty that could generate new ideas not received from outside, that "power within us that *understands,* the *Intuition* of the mind." Against Locke's metaphors of mirror, slate, or waxed tablet Price likened the creative faculty to an "eye of the mind" and an "innate light." The faculty of perception Locke ascribes to the mind Price said "sees only the *outside* of things," not their true natures, and it "lies prostrate under its object."

Some of the critics, moreover, insisted that the faculty of perceiving moral and intellectual truth was present in all normal humans, even the meanest classes, and was not restricted to Locke's cultured gentlemen. Since an intuition is direct, it takes no time, so no leisure is required for its use. If Locke's epistemology tended to support his political elitism, Cartwright's belief in "common sense" supported his egalitarian view that natural law was available to the "laboring mechanic and the peasant." The shift from Reason to common sense as the basis for political fitness converged with the shift from property to conscience as the basis for human dignity.

The New Left in general (at least until recently) and the Resistance in particular have sided, of course, with the egalitarian and humanistic ideas of the Dissenting critics of Locke. It may seem absurd to mention Locke and the Resistance in the same breath, but it is part of the point of this essay that epistemology, broadly defined, is important. In fact the crux of the debate on tactics between the Progressive Labor faction and the "New Left" faction of SDS in 1967 and 1968 was the question (as Nick Egleson put it), "How do people learn—by being told the answers or finding them out for themselves?" And the rest of this essay will try to show that similar disputes occurred within and between the Marxist and anarchist traditions, which we do relate to, and that the quarrel with Locke (by Chomsky, Marcuse, and others) is still going on.

Moreover, certain specific influences are indeed traceable to the Dissenters. Price's "innate light" is in many ways related to the

"inner light" of the Quakers, who today constitute or have influenced a large portion of the draft resistance movement. It was
Price, too, who set free the mind of William Ellery Channing from
the constrictions of Locke's philosophy. Channing, among his
other accomplishments, founded the congregation that became
the Arlington Street Church, the first church in the country to
hold a draft card turn-in and the first to offer symbolic sanctuary
to a resister and a deserter. And Burgh was an influence on Thoreau, whose civil disobedience against the Mexican War (in the
words of Rev. William Sloane Coffin, Jr.) "put something in the
mainstream of American conscience that over a century later is
nourishing us today."

Kant

Immanuel Kant, the founder of idealist philosophy, was provoked
by Hume to develop his monumental work on epistemology, *The
Critique of Pure Reason.* He disagreed with the contention that all
knowledge comes from sense-data, arguing instead that man's
field of perception is a joint product of sense-data from the world
and *a priori* categories from the mind. These *a priori* categories are
not innate ideas that precede sensory experience but something
like forms or modalities through which sensations must be experienced: unity, causality, space, time, etc. Our experienced world is
not an accidental construct, for our human nature imposes form
and coherence on our experiences. We perceive objects on our
terms, not theirs; the mind is active and creative, not passive or
prostrate.

This shift in terms from object to subject Kant likened to the
Copernican revolution in cosmology, and there is no question that
in Germany at least he established a wholly new model of the
mind and the world that all later philosophers had to confront.
The work of Hegel, Feuerbach, and Marx could not have occurred without the prior revolution of Kant.

Kant's ethical philosophy, though not derived from his metaphysics and epistemology, is congruent with them. Thus he lays
great stress on the dignity of the individual rational creature and
enjoins us to treat him always as an end in himself, never merely
as a means to our ends. And he believed firmly in inalienable nat-

ural rights which "man cannot surrender even if he so wills" and before which all politics "must bend the knee."

Theodore Parker

The Unitarian minister Theodore Parker is worth citing as an example of a radical social reformer influenced by both the German and the Dissenting traditions. Parker took part in an armed raid on a Boston courthouse to set free a captured fugitive slave, he campaigned for women's rights, penal reform, and economic equality, and during the war with Mexico he, like Thoreau, issued a call to resist illegitimate authority: "What shall we do in regard to this present war? We can refuse to take any part in it; we can encourage others to do the same; we can aid men, if need be, who suffer because they refuse." As a Unitarian theologian Parker was the leader of the radical party, arguing against the belief (which conservative Unitarians shared with Trinitarians) in miracles and the unique revelatory basis of Christianity. He insisted that God was incarnate in all men, not just in Christ, and that all men possess by nature the capacity to apprehend directly the existence of God and the truths of basic Christianity, "the primitive gospel God wrote on the heart of his child." This capacity relies on a faculty of intuition (enlightened by reason and empirical induction) which gives ideas "that transcend sensational experience; ideas whose origin is not from sensation, nor their proof from sensation." The matrix of Parker's social ideas as well as his theology was the idealist heritage he shared with Channing, Emerson, Thoreau, and the other Transcendentalists. He wrote that "the sensational system so ably presented by Locke in his masterly Essay, developed into various forms by Hobbes, Berkeley, Hume, Paley, and the French Materialists . . . gave little help." Instead "I found most help in the works of Immanuel Kant." The sensationalist epistemology, he saw, leads to ethical relativity, to a denial of universal laws in favor of expediency, whereas the transcendental/idealist approach provides a basis for morality in the intuitive promptings of man's universal nature, in "the law which God wrote ineffaceably in the hearts of mankind."

Marx

In Karl Marx the fairly clear choices between nature and nurture, active and passive, subject and object become much more complicated. He was not a traditional philosopher concerned with traditional problems; in fact, he was concerned to show how pointless traditional philosophy was, in the face of the great historical movements of classes and their ideologies. Nonetheless something like an epistemology and anthropology, I think, can be extracted from his largely historical and economic theories.

From one viewpoint Marx went further than Kant in giving to man a creative function in the process of perception. For Marx both the idealists and the empiricists were limited by their chosen mode of access to the object, namely conception or contemplation, whereas in real human life we encounter objects actively. In his *Theses on Feuerbach* Marx wrote:

> The chief defect of all previous materialism [empiricism]—including Feuerbach's—is that . . . reality, sensibility is conceived only in the form of the object or as intuition, but not as human sensory activity, *praxis,* not subjectively. That is why it happened that the *active* side, in opposition to materialism, was developed by idealism—but only abstractly, for idealism, naturally, does not know real sensory activity as such. . . .
>
> Feuerbach, not satisfied with abstract thinking, appeals to sensory thinking [or intuition]; but he does not conceive sensibility as a practical, human-sensory activity.

One might expect, then, that Marx conceived of a richly endowed human nature, capable of holding its own identity against the pressure of reality, but in fact he was at pains to deny any concept of general human nature. Human nature is only the sum of all concrete human "natures" throughout history. Man is a social creature who must work to survive: his "nature" is a function of his social relations and his social relations are a function of his society's pattern of labor, its economy. And since work and society have changed drastically over the ages, man's "nature" has changed drastically as well. About the only generalization we can draw is that human nature—except for biological drives like hunger and sex—is highly malleable. Conscience, dignity, freedom,

Reason, "instinct," or *a priori* categories, all are contingent on social relations.

Moreover, it seems to be man's practical activity itself that puts him at the mercy of economic conditions. Alienated by his labor, exploited by the capitalist classes, he becomes deformed into an appendage of his tools. Even the owner of the tools is a creature of his class, and all the ideas and beliefs of owner and worker alike are ultimately functions of their material situation, and their material situation is the outcome of an immense and inevitable historical process in which man's individual will counts for nothing.

Although Marx's own views were not this simple, we can find in his basic metaphors a kind of contradiction between his revolutionary communism and his reduction of ideas to mere reflexes of economic reality. It is not clear how anyone can transcend his class interests and biases and seek the truth instead; in fact it is not clear what truth is, since all ideas are historically relative. But apparently some truth is absolute and eternal—science, for instance, and dialectical materialism, or Marxism. By becoming a Marxist, and only so, one can overcome his class background (usually petit bourgeois) and master history. In some ways this process resembles the initiate's sloughing off his material and time-bound self when he discovers the eternal *gnosis,* but it also resembles Locke's view that only those who have cultivated Reason are capable of self-rule and rule over others.

Marx's writings can support a less elitist interpretation. It is not that individuals are absolutely incapable of liberating themselves, but that it is futile to try to liberate whole segments of society until history has come round to the ripe moment. (The idea of the ripe moment provoked much controversy, especially among anarchists and Russian Jacobins, because of its chilling effect on liberatory impulses.) But Marxism generally tended toward the elitist view that only Marxists are fit to govern the working class and its revolution. This tendency, along with Marx's authoritarian personal style, drew the implacable opposition of the anarchists, who invoked some of the same values as the Dissenting critics of Locke.

Marxists and Anarchists

Michael Bakunin, the anarchist rival of Marx in the First International, concentrated most of his fire on the Marxist view of the state. The Marxists agreed in principle with the anarchists that the state must be abolished, but for the Marxists the state must first be given to the newly liberated proletariat as a tool for the forcible consolidation of the classless society. The anarchists were for doing away with it right away, preferring the chaos that might follow to the accumulation of power in a few hands, no matter how benign.

The particular form of the state that Bakunin feared from the Marxists was the bureaucracy run by a managerial elite. In a highly prophetic paragraph he wrote:

> But in the People's State of Marx, there will be, we are told, no privileged class at all. All will be equal, not only from the juridical and political point of view, but from the economic point of view. At least that is what is promised, though I doubt very much, considering the manner in which it is being tackled and the course it is desired to follow, whether that promise could ever be kept. There will therefore be no longer any privileged class, but there will be a government, and, note this well, an extremely complex government, which will not content itself with governing and administering the masses politically, as all governments do today, but which will also administer them economically, concentrating in its own hands the production and the just division of wealth, the cultivation of land, the establishment and development of factories, the organization and direction of commerce, finally the application of capital to production by the only banker, the State. All that will demand immense knowledge and many "heads overflowing with brains" in this government. It will be the reign of *scientific intelligence,* the most aristocratic, despotic, arrogant and contemptuous of all regimes. There will be a new class, a new hierarchy of real and pretended scientists and scholars, and the world will be divided into a minority ruling in the name of knowledge and an immense ignorant majority. And then, woe betide the mass of ignorant ones!

Bakunin wrote little from which we can extract an epistemology or view of man's nature, but what he wrote is quite clear on the question "How do people learn?": by themselves, by the free use of their natural faculties, if not immediately, then soon enough, if they are left alone and not troubled by an intellectual elite.

When . . . tutelage is attempted upon adult persons wholly deprived of education, or the ignorant masses, and whether that tutelage is exercised in the name of higher considerations, or even of *scientific reasons* presented by a group of individuals of generally recognized intellectual standing, or by some other class—in either case it would lead to the formation of a sort of *intellectual aristocracy,* exceedingly odious and harmful to the cause of freedom.

. . . While definitely rejecting any tutelage (in whatever form it asserts itself) which the intellect developed by knowledge and experience—by business, worldly, and human experience—may attempt to set up over the ignorant masses, we are far from denying the *natural and beneficial influence of knowledge and experience* upon the masses, provided that that influence asserts itself very simply, by way of the natural incidence of higher intellects upon the lower intellects, and provided also that that influence is not invested with any official authority or endowed with any privileges, either political or social. For both these things necessarily produce upon one hand the enslavement of the masses, and on the other hand corruption, disintegration, and stupefaction of those who are invested and endowed with such powers.

. . . Man is not free in relation to the laws of Nature, which constitute the first basis and necessary condition of his existence. They pervade and dominate him, just as they pervade and dominate everything that exists. Nothing is capable of saving him from their fateful omnipotence; any attempt to revolt on his part would simply lead to suicide. But thanks to the faculty inherent in his nature, by virtue of which he becomes conscious of his environment and learns to master it, *man can gradually free himself from the natural and crushing hostility of the external world—physical as well as social*—with the aid of thought, knowledge and the application of thought to the cognitive instinct, that is *with the aid of his rational will.*

Lenin's extension of the elitist tendencies of Marxism into his theory of the vanguard party with control over all aspects of the revolution was severely attacked by Marxists (Plekhanov, Luxemburg) and anarchists alike. After the Bolsheviks took power, the anarchist Emma Goldman accused them of treating humans as means to their own ends (state power), of outraging basic human rights, and thereby wrecking the revolution:

> It is at once the great failure and the great tragedy of the Russian Revolution that it attempted (in the leadership of the ruling political party) to change only institutions and conditions while ignoring entirely the human and social values involved in the Revolution. Worse yet, in its mad passion for power, the Communist State even sought to strengthen and deepen the very ideas and conceptions which the Revolution had come to destroy. It supported and encouraged all the worst antisocial qualities and systematically destroyed the already awakened conception of the new revolutionary values. The sense of justice and equality, the love of liberty and of human brotherhood—these fundamentals of the real regeneration of society—the Communist State suppressed to the point of extermination. Man's instinctive sense of equity was branded as weak sentimentality; human dignity and liberty became a bourgeois superstition; the sanctity of life, which is the very essence of social reconstruction, was condemned as unrevolutionary, almost counter-revolutionary. This fearful perversion of fundamental values bore within itself the seed of destruction. With the conception that the Revolution was only a means of securing political power, it was inevitable that all revolutionary values should be subordinated to the needs of the Socialist State; indeed, exploited to further the security of the newly acquired governmental power. "Reasons of State," masked as the "interests of the Revolution and the People," became the sole criterion of action, even of feeling. Violence, the tragic inevitability of revolutionary upheavals, became an established custom, a habit, and was presently enthroned as the most powerful and "ideal" institution. Did not Zinoviev himself canonize Dzerzhinsky, the head of the bloody Tcheka, as the "saint of the Revolution"? Were not the greatest public honors paid by the State to Uritsky, the founder and sadistic chief of the Petrograd Tcheka?

Paul Goodman and Noam Chomsky

Paul Goodman's work in education and psychology is well known but his production has been so various that certain of his assumptions might be missed. Many of them occur explicitly in the opening pages of *Growing Up Absurd,* a book that had a major impact on the New Left of the early sixties.

Growing up as a human being, a "human nature" assimilates a culture, just as other animals grow up in strength and habits in the environments that are for them, and that complete their natures. Present-day sociologists and anthropologists don't talk much about this process, and not in this way. Among the most competent writers, there is not much mention of "human nature."

. . . growing up is sometimes treated as if it were acculturation, the process of giving up one culture for another, the way a tribe of Indians takes on the culture of the whites: so the wild Babies give up their "individualistic" mores and ideology, e.g., selfishness or magic thinking or omnipotence, and join the tribe of Society: they are "socialized." More frequently, however, the matter is left vague: we start with a *tabula rasa* and end up with "socialized" and cultured. ("Becoming cultured" and "being adjusted to the social group" are taken almost as synonymous.) Either way, it follows that you can teach people anything; you can adapt them to anything if you use the right techniques of "socializing" or "communicating." The essence of "human nature" is to be pretty indefinitely malleable. "Man," as C. Wright Mills suggests, is what suits a particular type of society in a particular historical stage.

This fateful idea, invented from time to time by philosophers, seems finally to be empirically evident in the most recent decades. For instance, in our highly organized system of machine production and its corresponding social relations, the practice is, by "vocational guidance," to fit people wherever they are needed in the productive system; and whenever the products of the system need to be used up, the practice is, by advertizing, to get people to consume them. This works. There is a man for every job and not many are left over, and the shelves are almost always cleared. Again, in the highly organized political industrial systems of Germany, Russia, and now China, it has been possible in a short time to condition great masses to perform as desired. Social scientists observe that these are the facts, and they also devise theories and techniques to produce more facts like them, for the social scientists too are part of the highly organized systems.

A page later he describes the eighteenth-century notion of human nature as "referring to man's naturally sympathetic sentiments, his communicative faculties, and unalienable dignity. (Immanuel Kant immortally thought up a philosophy to make these cohere.)"

It was no accident that Goodman singled out C. Wright Mills as the modern exemplar of an environmentalist, neo-Marxist view of human nature. The controversy between the two men went back to the pages of Dwight MacDonald's *Politics* magazine. In July 1945 Goodman published in *Politics* a piece on "The Political Meaning of Some Recent Revisions of Freud," where he attacked Erich Fromm, Karen Horney, and their followers for believing in rational social authority, a situation in which the interests of society and of the individual become identical. "The method of Fromm and Horney is to empty out the soul and then fill it. It is filled with social unanimity and rational faith." Goodman proposed instead a conception of the rational ego as "the agent, the artist, the informant, and the social-interpreter of the instincts." The instincts, the unconscious, provide the *content* of spontaneity and freedom. "Social cohesion exists prior to the delegation of authority. Authority is delegated *pro tempore* whether to a man or to a system of institutions." The contemporary psychotherapist whom Goodman praised was Wilhelm Reich, who according to Goodman believed that instinctually satisfied people will not tolerate authority, dull work, or the representation of themselves by others.

Mills attacked Goodman's essay in the issue of October 1945. "He [Goodman] locates the dynamics of revolution in a tension between biology and institutions," Mills charged, "and rests his hope for revolution upon a mass biological release." The "gonad theory of revolution" did not apply to any revolution in history; if anything, revolutionaries tended to be sexual ascetics. "Leave Mr. Goodman with his revolution in the bedroom," Mills concluded. "We have still to search out the barricades of our freedom."

To this Goodman replied that when sexuality is free, "it is only one among several productive forces." The political energies of sexual ascetics "are precisely the energies that we see in the sadism and masochism of monolithic parties and in transitional dictatorships that become permanent." Marx, Goodman insisted, appealed to human nature against alienation, against "the collective conditions of work which exist under capitalism and which will continue to exist in any modern industrial society."

In *Politics* for December 1945 Goodman added a last word on "Revolution, Sociolatry, and War." Because of the affluence of modern industrial societies, he argued, we may

> act in a more piecemeal, educational, and thorogoing way. The results of such action will also be lasting and worthwhile if we have grown into our freedom rather than driven each other into it. Our attack on the industrial system can be many-sided and often indirect, to make it crash of its own weight rather than by frontal assault.

Goodman concluded: "we must—in small groups—draw the line and at once begin action directly satisfactory to our human nature."

A few months later (April and July, 1946) Dwight Macdonald contributed an essay called "The Root Is Man." Macdonald, who is now another supporter of draft resistance (and was named a "co-conspirator" with Paul Goodman, Noam Chomsky, and others, in the Spock draft conspiracy case), argued there that in the end one must depend not on the alleged laws of history but on man. "We are all in the position of a man going upstairs who thinks there is another step, and finds there is not." "The external process is working out, but the inner spirit is the reverse of what Marx expected. The operation is a success, but the patient is dying." This essay, a twentieth-century reaffirmation of the natural rights doctrine, was a sequel to Macdonald's "The Responsibility of Peoples" cited by Noam Chomsky in the opening and closing passages of his now-famous essay, "The Responsibility of Intellectuals."

In "The Responsibility of Intellectuals" Chomsky analyzes the arguments of both the liberal intellectuals who have helped design our Asian policy and the liberal intellectuals who have confined their criticism of it to a "responsible" discussion of means to certain ends but not the ends themselves. Both the defenders and the critics are adherents of the "end of ideology" ideology that would reduce all political questions to pragmatic ones and would con-

centrate all political power in the hands of those best equipped to make decisions—the technical elite or the "experts." That this ideology is self-serving Chomsky easily makes clear (here and in other essays) but he is concerned mainly with the argument (or lack of argument) behind it. The liberal intellectuals take the *aims* of American policy to be essentially what the government has announced them to be, and they bring their critical faculties to bear only on the *methods* employed to achieve them. This approach is defended as scientific and objective: it is "value-free" in the same way physics and astronomy are. Concerned only with technique, the intellectuals leave to others the choice of ends toward which the technique is employed. Any moral individual can ponder the ends of government policy, but only experts can determine the means; therefore only the means are worthy of serious intellectual labor.

Chomsky points out that the claim of the social sciences to expertise inaccessible to the intelligent layman is simply absurd, and that the exclusion of moral considerations as unworthy of serious thought is simply morally irresponsible. To so constrict the area of inquiry, Chomsky comes close to saying, to forbid the free examination of certain facts, claims, and purposes, is to make the intellect into a diminished thing, a passive manipulator of certain unquestionable givens. And it is to abdicate the responsibility of intellectuals to speak truth and expose lies.

In a long essay called "Objectivity and Liberal Scholarship" Chomsky reviews a liberal historian's book on the Spanish civil war, and shows a dozen ways the author distorts or ignores the vital role played by the anarchists and their betrayal by their supposed allies, the liberal democrats and the Communists. Chomsky concludes that this historian's version of the war is a phenomenon of "counterrevolutionary subordination" in scholarship, a result of the author's "underlying elitist bias" against mass movements (which he shares, ironically, with Communist historians of the same events). Liberal (and Communist) intellectuals, Chomsky claims, misunderstand and fear "revolutionary movements that are largely spontaneous and only loosely organized."

The burden of these two essays is essentially the same. The liberal intellectual elitist distrusts popular social movements for

some of the same reasons that he distrusts examination into the motives and moral assumptions of the U.S. government. Both represent, for example, incursions of the common man or mind into areas best left to experts. People are no more capable of governing themselves than intelligent laymen are capable of speaking about political "science." The historian of the Spanish civil war, furthermore, refuses to consider certain unpleasant (or incomprehensible) facts in the interests of his bias toward "liberal democracy" in the same way that apologists for the Vietnam war refuse to question certain comforting assumptions in the interests of their professional self-image and career.

The similarity between liberal elitists and Communist elitists Chomsky discusses in a short preface to the book review and in another article called "Knowledge and Power." He cites Bakunin's prediction that Marx's followers will establish a state governed by "a new privileged scientific-political estate," and Rosa Luxemburg's prediction that Lenin's organizational concepts will "enslave a young labor movement to an intellectual elite hungry for power." In both the U.S. and the U.S.S.R. bureaucratic elites have emerged with striking similarities between them, not the least being "the belief that mass organizations and popular politics must be submerged." By his criticisms of elites on both sides, and by his citations of Bakunin, Kropotkin, Luxemburg, and others in support of his views, Chomsky places himself solidly, if implicitly, in the tradition of the anarchists and libertarian socialists.

I have summarized Chomsky's well-known political views in order to draw out a few points that will relate clearly to something that is not so well known, Chomsky's theory of language. About a year ago, curious over what he was doing when he wasn't writing articles for the *New York Review of Books* (and *Liberation*), I sat down with five or six of his books and went to work. I am not trained in linguistics, but it soon became clear enough that Chomsky's work in the theory of language raises profound questions about the nature of man and man's mind. That his linguistic theory was also consonant with his political ideas dawned on me only after reading around in the history of philosophy and after some discussions with Staughton Lynd about the epistemological beliefs of the American Revolutionary and abolitionist thinkers.

Since then I came across an article in a back issue of the *Nation* that suggests the connection, and Chomsky himself has been fairly explicit in a recent speech called "Language and Freedom." What follows is an outline of his linguistic theory and its political implications.

The publication of Chomsky's little book *Syntactic Structures* in 1957 caused a major stir in the field of linguistics. In that book Chomsky presented his critique of the school of linguistics then predominant, the structuralists, and proposed his own theory, or model, which he called "generative" or "transformational" grammar. Trained in the techniques of structural linguistics by Zellig Harris, one of its most rigorous practitioners, Chomsky soon became dissatisfied with the piecemeal process of categorization that constitutes that approach. To the structuralists, language is "the sum of words and phrases by which any man expresses his thought" or "the set of finite inventories of elements and their relations." The business of the structural linguist is to investigate the occurrences of a language over a period of time, that is, "the talk which takes place in a language community." He takes the sample of recorded utterances and applies certain analytical procedures for "identifying all the utterances as relatively few stated arrangements of relatively few stated elements," elements being, crudely, irreducible units of sound (phonemes) and grammar (morphemes). These procedures, which are largely a matter of classification, have been uncharitably called "butterfly-collecting" in the manner of pre-Darwinian biology: they account for a detailed "external" description of each language (or what Chomsky calls "surface structure"), but they in no way account for the basic grammatical rules that each native speaker knows, consciously or not, and which enable him to produce and understand totally new sentences, not to mention the semantic structures that seem to underlie the syntactic rules, and the deep semantic and syntactic relations common to all languages (all of which are matters of "deep structure").

Chomsky's critique of this approach has two aspects. The more narrow and perhaps more rigorous is his proof that the descriptive procedures developed by structural linguists, the so-called "phrase-structure" rules (which Chomsky himself had helped for-

malize before developing his "generative" model of grammar) that break down larger units into smaller units, are not powerful enough to explain some of the most basic grammatical processes, like negation, interrogation, and passive-voice construction. More powerful rules are needed that manipulate elements into totally new arrangements, not just into the extensions or substitutions allowable under the weaker rules. Such rules Chomsky calls "transformational rules," and they, along with the phrase-structure rules, "generate" the grammar of a language.

The broader aspect of his critique deals with the broader assumptions of traditional linguistics. Chomsky disagrees with the implicit assumption that language is "behavior," that is, a set of externally observed acts. He claims rather that language is an abstract mental construct that enables a person to speak (or "behave" linguistically). In this he sides with Wilhelm von Humboldt, who claimed that language must not be considered "a dead product" but a living process. He also disagrees with the behaviorist assumptions regarding language-learning that are implied by the impoverished rules of structural linguistics. In his review of B. F. Skinner's *Verbal Behavior,* Chomsky thoroughly criticized Skinner's claim that a few external factors (stimuli) can account almost entirely for speech acts (responses), and that the contribution of the speaker to the process is trivial and elementary. Skinner did research with lower animals, like rats, and the stimuli which he isolated in his laboratory he simply extended to human beings. Chomsky claims that we need a far richer model of the human language faculty than Skinner's stimulus-response arcs in order to account for language learning and production, not only for the use of transformational rules, which are too complex to derive from conditioned reflexes, but for the use of new sentences never before uttered or heard by the speaker. "For about a hundred years," says Chomsky about this last point, "people were saying language was a habit system and nobody ever questioned it. Well, as soon as you ask 'How can you innovate by habit?' then the whole field collapses and takes some entirely new way." Another way to put it, perhaps, is that Skinner cannot account for the fact that monkeys don't talk (let alone rats) except that humans must be smarter, whereas Chomsky assumes that humans

have an innate mental structure fundamentally different from that of other animals, and he has taken a long first step toward characterizing it.

Chomsky is aware of the broader epistemological implications of his theory, and at a symposium he is as likely to debate a member of the philosophy department as the linguistics department (if he is not debating someone from the government department). His work calls into question the whole empiricist tradition (of which Skinner's behaviorism is an extreme development) that has prevailed in English and American universities almost since the days of Locke and Hume. For the mind to be powerful enough to master language (which a child does more or less by the age of six) it must be innately far more richly structured than a "blank slate" or "waxed tablet" with a few mechanical procedures. The mind must come with "innate ideas" (to use Descartes' now archaic phrase): dispositions or propensities or "germs of truth which exist naturally in our souls" (to use another expression of Descartes) that only need sensations to bring them to flower. Chomsky explicitly invokes the Cartesians, in fact, as well as Cambridge Platonists like Herbert of Cherbury (both of whom the empiricists Locke and Hume were explicitly out to refute), as his philosophical tradition. He has devoted a whole book, *Cartesian Linguistics,* to showing how the seventeenth-century rationalists and their successors were essentially on the right track, and that we have been off it (with a few exceptions like Wilhelm von Humboldt) ever since Locke.

In only one of his books on linguistics does Chomsky make an explicit statement on social or political matters, and this he does not in his own voice but through Humboldt, the linguist, political and educational reformer, friend of Goethe and Schiller, and practitioner of the ideas of Kant and the rationalists. In a long digression on his political and social theories in *Cartesian Linguistics* Chomsky describes Humboldt's opposition to the authoritarian state and his championship of intrinsic human rights, freedom, and spontaneity, and relates both his linguistic theories and his libertarian social theories to an underlying concept of human nature: rich and spontaneous, with innate dignity, and capable of profound self-realization if no mechanical obstacles are put in the way. In a footnote to this digression Chomsky compares Humboldt's views to Rousseau's critique of social institutions which strangle man's innate faculty of freedom.

After a long discussion with me about Chomsky, including the tantalizing digression, Staughton Lynd wrote to him asking to what extent he saw his own work as a basis for the kinds of extensions he cited in the work of Humboldt. Chomsky replied:

> I think that this work does show, at the level of scientific knowledge and explanation, that there is a given human structure of thought and expression that provides the framework for the specific kinds of spontaneity and creativity that are characteristically human, and that develop through experience but along lines determined by human nature. I would suppose that it is possible to transpose the same form of argument to the study of social relations and the study of human rights, and to develop a kind of natural basis for ethical judgment (including the evaluation of forms of social organization).

In a recent speech Chomsky has filled in more details about Rousseau, Humboldt, and Kant, but he has remained within the tentative and cautious limits of his letter to Lynd. He concludes his speech with a hypothetical program:

> I think that the study of language can provide some glimmerings of understanding of rule-governed behavior and the possibilities for free and creative action within the framework of a system of rules that in part, at least, reflect intrinsic properties of human mental organization. . . .
>
> Conceivably, we might in this way develop a social science based on empirically well-founded propositions concerning human nature. Just as we study the range of humanly attainable languages, with some success, we might also try to study the forms of artistic expression or, for that matter, scientific knowledge that humans can conceive, and perhaps even the range of ethical systems and social structures in which humans can live and function, given their intrinsic capacities and needs. Perhaps one might go on to project a concept of social organization that would— under given conditions of material and spiritual culture—best encourage and accommodate the fundamental human need—if such it is—for spontaneous initiative, creative work, solidarity, pursuit of social justice.

Just as Chomsky's model of the human mind includes the innate capacity to order and transform experience into concepts and patterns that transcend experience (because they are determined by the structure of the mind itself), so Chomsky's program of social research includes not only a wider range of data than the behaviorist social scientists now confine themselves to but also a set of principles for judging the ethical qualities of all data (because the principles are derivable, in theory, from human nature itself). We are not passive beholders of events, epistemologically or socially; we participate in them, and actively transform them, as we experience them. And our transformation is not altogether arbitrary—unless we fall to the common fate of manipulation, coercion, and oppression by our parents, educators, and rulers— but determined along lines that express our fundamental human nature. Serious thought about what that human nature is will give us—has already given us—clues to the nature of a truly human society.

Notes to Excursus

Marcuse's comment on Hume is from his *Reason and Revolution* (New York: Oxford, 1941; Boston: Beacon, 1960), 19–20. On the Dissenters, see Staughton Lynd, *The Intellectual Origins of American Radicalism* (New York: Random House, 1968; Vintage, 1969). The Kant quote on natural rights is cited approvingly by Marcuse in "The Struggle Against Liberalism in the Totalitarian View of the State" (1934), reprinted in *Negations* (Boston: Beacon, 1968).

The first Bakunin quote is from a collection of his writings edited by Kefanick, *Marxism, Freedom and the State* (London: Freedom Press, 1950), reprinted in Krimerman and Perry, ed., *Patterns of Anarchy* (New York: Anchor, 1966). The second Bakunin passage is from a collection edited by Maximoff, *The Political Philosophy of Bakunin: Scientific Anarchism* (Glencoe: Free Press, 1953), reprinted in Horowitz, ed., *The Anarchists* (New York: Dell, 1964).

The Goldman quote is from her *My Further Disillusionment in Russia* (Garden City: Doubleday, 1924), reprinted in Krimerman and Perry.

For the material on the Mills-Goodman debate I am indebted to Staughton Lynd.

Noam Chomsky's "The Responsibility of Intellectuals" and "Objectivity and Liberal Scholarship" are reprinted in *American Power and the New Mandarins* (New York: Pantheon, 1969). "Knowledge and Power" is in Priscilla Long, ed., *The New Left* (Boston: Porter Sargent, 1969). His major linguistics works are *Syntactic Structures* (The Hague: Mouton, 1957); *Current Issues in Linguistic Theory* (The Hague: Mouton, 1964), reprinted in Fodor and Katz, eds., *The Structure of Language* (New York: Prentice-Hall, 1964); *Aspects of the Theory of Syntax* (Cambridge, Mass.: MIT, 1965); *Cartesian Linguistics* (New York: Harper & Row, 1966); and *Language and Mind* (New York: Harcourt, Brace & World, 1968). Of these, the last two are the most accessible to the layman.

The four quotes from the structuralists are from (1) Whitney (an obscure article written in 1872 that Chomsky cites several times); (2) Hockett, *A Course in Modern Linguistics* (New York: Macmillan, 1958); (3) and (4) Harris, *Methods in Structural Linguistics* (Chicago: University of Chicago, 1951).

Chomsky's review of Skinner may be found in *The Structure of Language*. His quote on innovation is from Sklar, "Chomsky's Linguistic Revolution," *Nation*, September 9, 1968. His letter to Lynd is dated April 5, 1969.

For an extremely hostile view of Chomsky's linguistics, from what seems to be a Marxist-Leninist-Stalinist-Maoist perspective, see "The Reactionary Idealist Foundations of Noam Chomsky's Linguistics," *Literature and Ideology*, Winter 1969, 1–20.

CHAPTER SEVENTEEN

The Politics of Resistance

Resistance strategy had many interconnected aspects, ranging from cold-blooded calculations that bore not at all on individual experience to warm-hearted encounters that communicated a new social vision for everybody to share. Even the mechanical metaphors of machines and frictions derived from cranky individualists like Thoreau, who said, "Let your life be a counter friction to stop the machine," and from impassioned movement leaders like Mario Savio:

> There's a time when the operation of the machine becomes so odious, makes you so sick at heart, that you can't take part, you can't even tacitly take part. And you've got to put your bodies upon the gears and upon the wheels, upon the levers, upon all the apparatus, and you've got to make it stop.

It was the hope—not the confident deduction from political theory, but the hope—that the acts of returning a draft card and refusing all subsequent cooperation with the draft would multiply as the example became known until there were too many for the draft and court systems to handle. The initial stages of the snowball would be the most difficult, for those who led the movement could be certain of lonely prison terms and little support from friends. But they would have the comfort of knowing that their example gave others courage, and that as they languished in

277

prison others were refusing induction. The later phases of the snowball, or "lemming effect," would be easier, as the fear of being alone would vanish and the hope of being "effective" would grow. Eventually, perhaps when ten thousand acted, perhaps when fifty, the prisons would fill, courts would clog, and the resulting bureaucratic flap would bring pressure on the federal government to end the war, or at the very least the president would have to ask Congress for legislation to make new courts and prisons and so risk a reexamination of the war and its rising costs. Moreover, the existence of hundreds and perhaps thousands of young men in prison over a matter of conscience would exert a steady moral pressure on the American public. Even more than the American emigrants in Canada, our domestic exiles would trouble every American whose patriotism demanded he think well of his country's place in the world.

To encourage the snowballing effect, some Resistance groups drew up two kinds of pledges. For those—and they turned out to be in the majority—whose commitment to noncooperation was not dependent on strategic efficacy or on how many others he joined, there was an "unconditional" pledge: "I will return my draft card on October 16." For those who sought safety in numbers or at least comfort in solidarity there was a conditional pledge: "I will return my draft card on October 16 if 500 others do so too." (The number varied from place to place.) The groups that offered two pledges on October 16, such as the New England Resistance, found almost no takers for the conditional pledge, a fact which cheered the organizers, who were worried about the depth of commitment of the new joiners.* As Bill Dowling of New England Resistance put it, "The main purpose of the conditional pledge was to express our confidence that we might actually get 500 cards, and the confidence itself was contagious."

* This is not to say that no "lemming effect" operated. During the large turn-ins in Berkeley and Boston October 16, for instance, some men were no doubt moved by the example before their eyes to imitate it. At least in Boston some steps were taken to inject sobriety into the charged atmosphere of the Arlington Street Church but the religious drama was still powerful and attractive (even if not, as some have charged, a "revival meeting"). The curious are referred to the transcript of the Spock trial, especially the cross-examination of Rev. Coffin, Fr. Cunnane, and Michael Ferber.

Despite a general consensus that conditional pledges were only marginally useful, the New York Resistance for the April 3 turn-in introduced a new refinement, the "graduated pledge." Invented by David Osher, whose attitude toward it a year later was largely regretful but tinged with a fatherly pride, the graduated pledge was a device for escalating the numbers exponentially, a sort of higher-order snowball, or a domino theory of lemmings. Each resister was asked to put a check opposite the number in the company of whom he would return his card: 500, 1000, 2000, etc., all the way up to 15,000. The office receiving the pledges would keep a count of all the unconditional pledges, making daily phone calls to other groups to see how they were doing. When the lowest conditional figure was reached, all those who checked it would be told to get their cards ready, and their number would be added to the total. Since it was felt that the higher the conditional figure the greater the number who would check it ("Almost anyone would return his card with 10,000 others!"), it seemed that rapid growth would be easy. The numbers would grow until they reached critical mass, then the whole thing would go off like a bomb, blowing up the Selective Service System with it. Needless to say, it didn't work. About 1000 turned in their draft cards on April 3 around the country, almost no one in New York checked any number but number one (their own), the other groups would not or could not cooperate with the computer-like information-retrieval system the plan required, and the New York Resistance found itself on April 4 with thousands of beautifully printed graduated pledges, unchecked.*

Probably very few resisters turned in their cards or refused induction out of a mathematical calculation, and few believed that numbers alone would have an appreciable effect on the war. This was the most narrow view of Resistance strategy: "to make it impossible," in the words of an early CADRE leaflet, "for the

---

* Conditional pledges were so popular in New York that even support statements had boxes to check. The Faculty Support Group at Columbia circulated a statement pledging the signer to "support those Columbia students who decide to refuse cooperation with Selective Service." Though the language was mild and probably quite legal, there was space below the statement for checking a box with the number of colleagues the signer felt safe or effective signing among.

United States to fight a war in Vietnam by cutting into the pool of manpower from which the military draws the men it needs to fight." After nearly three years it is possible to detect slight steps toward this goal—some draft boards, partly because of resistance, have had trouble meeting their quotas, while the falling rate of reenlistments and the reluctance of some units to go into battle are partly due to the spirit of resistance exemplified by those confronting the draft—but the Selective Service System and the Pentagon have as yet encountered no real threat to their capacity to maintain as many as half a million men in Vietnam. The epidemic of noncooperation that some early organizers dreamed of never took place. A New York Resistance pamphlet dryly summed it up:

> In the foreseeable future it is probably not within the power of the draft resistance movement to impede Selective Service's ability to carry out successfully its manpower recruitment function, for its success in this realm is contingent only upon its ability to fill a fairly small quota every month.

A somewhat more realistic, though still ambitious, version of this numerical strategy was to so clog and confuse the Selective Service System that the draft itself would be abolished. The war might go on, but there would be limits to the size of the armies in Vietnam and elsewhere. As the war grew more and more unpopular, the government might find it more and more difficult to raise an army, now with inducement rather than induction as its recruitment method. And the spectacle of the vast bureaucracy of the draft being crippled by popular resistance would be an acute embarrassment to the warmakers in the government.

To determine the extent to which the draft itself has been hurt by the Resistance and other groups of noncooperators we must examine the statistics. Some of the statistics, unfortunately, can only be educated guesses, but the picture that emerges from them is impressive.

Just how many men have returned their draft cards is impossible to determine. Adding up the counts at all the Resistance rallies from October 16, 1967, to early 1970 gives a sum of only about five thousand, and of this total a substantial percentage has reneged (accepted new cards). But there are strong indications that the total is several times as high. No one knows how many have returned their cards privately, and no one has been keeping a count of those cards turned in, a handful at a time, at antiwar rallies across the country: two in Rochester, three in Fort Collins, Colorado, twenty-five in Missoula, Montana, etc. But a stunning revelation from the clerk of local boards 60 and 62 in San Jose, California, suggests that in some parts of the country we have seen only the tip of the iceberg. Under oath in a resister's trial she testified that during 1968 alone over two thousand men returned their cards to her two boards. (Of these, two hundred were classified "delinquent" and processed for induction.) San Jose is hardly typical of the country, but it is probably not simply a freak either.

The number of people who have burned their cards is uncountable. Hundreds of cards, maybe thousands, went up in smoke outside the Pentagon in October 1967, and burnings have been a regular feature of demonstrations ever since.

It ought to be easier to determine the number of draft refusals, since the army, Selective Service System, and Justice Department all keep records, but it is hard to collect reliable information. The Justice Department figures show a steady rise in prosecutions for draft offenses:

In the year 7/64— 6/65	380 prosecutions were begun
7/65— 6/66	663
7/66— 6/67	1,335
7/67— 6/68	1,826
7/68— 6/69	3,305
and in the half year 7/69—12/69	1,785.

But there is no question that the number of prosecutions has fallen far behind the number of refusals. Between July 1, 1968 and June 30, 1969, 27,444 draft cases were reported to U.S. Attorneys. While over 3,000 prosecutions were initiated, prosecution was declined in 21,500 cases, usually because the men went into the armed forces or corrected their delinquency but sometimes, no doubt, because they emigrated.

Prosecution policies vary widely from place to place. . . . Some prosecutors let many complaints pile up undecided; others did not. In the Northern District of California (San Francisco), about 1300 of the 5038 complaints received during fiscal 1967, 1968, and 1969 were undecided last July 1. In the Central District of California (Los Angeles), only about 300 of the 9503 complaints were not taken care of either by starting or declining prosecution. The Eastern District of New York (about 900 cases) and the Eastern District of Pennsylvania (about 500 cases) also had huge backlogs of draft cases awaiting decisions by U.S. Attorneys.

Between the fall of 1968 and spring of 1970 some four hundred men had refused induction in Boston and (as of March 1970) not one had been indicted, a fact for which no one has offered a good explanation. In the fall of 1969 there were ninety-three indictments in Puerto Rico, but many hundreds more have refused. Kerry Berland and Jeremy Mott (of CADRE and the Midwest Committee for Draft Counseling) cite Minneapolis as one of the few urban areas where prosecutions have kept pace with draft refusals and in that city over 50 percent of all federal prosecutions are draft cases.

On June 30, 1969, 2,893 Selective Service cases were pending in the federal courts. Some were proceeding to trial, some were on appeal, some were being held up for decisions of higher courts. But probably about half these cases represent men who have left the country. Apparently most draft emigrants have not yet been indicted, though most who return can expect prosecution if they will not go into the army. The government need not hurry to indict those who have left, since the statute of limitations does not protect men who leave the country to avoid prosecution. Nevertheless, many federal courts are overburdened with draft refusers. During 1969, more Selective Service prosecutions were begun in the federal courts than any other group except auto theft, immigration, and illegal drugs.

Draft refusal in California has become a mass phenomenon. The March 1970 newsletter of the East Bay Resistance reported that "since 1967 when the Resistance first started, over 7000 men have refused induction in Oakland alone." Many thousands more simply fail to appear. According to a UPI report, May 3, 1970, only one-third of the men ordered for induction at Oakland, California actually go into the armed forces. During the six months which ended March 31, 1970, 4,463 men were ordered to report for induction. Of these about 5 percent refused induction, 7 percent were rejected, 35 percent joined the military, and 53 percent did not report.

Certainly far more men refuse induction at Oakland than at most induction centers. San Francisco's U.S. Attorney, James Browning, said that 822 men refused there during 1969—more than one third of the 2,140 who refused induction nationally. In many cities, however, large numbers of men don't report for induction. A draft file recently . . . revealed that a Chicago board ordered 13 men for induction one day in June, 1969. Of these, 1 transferred induction elsewhere, 1 refused induction, 4 accepted induction, and 7 didn't show up. We do not know how many of those not reporting eventually join the military, how many hide for long periods, how many leave the country, or how many await trial.

Published figures do not show how many men refuse to perform civilian work as conscientious objectors or commit other violations of draft law.

Nonregistration by eighteen-year-olds is also on the rise, but of course there are no figures. Berland and Mott guessed (February 1970) that there were between fifty and one hundred thousand nonregistrants.

To these figures we might add the ultra resistance and its anonymous imitators. As of March 1970, ninety people have publicly acknowledged their participation in raids against draft boards. They are responsible for the destruction or damage of perhaps half a million records, and some entire draft boards have been unable to function for several months after such a raid. In addition many boards have been badly damaged or burned to the ground by unknown raiders. By early 1970, for example, it was estimated by Minneapolis–St. Paul activists that about 40 percent of the files in Minnesota have been destroyed. Of course, many of the files can be reconstructed, but the process is very long and expensive, and never complete.

Perhaps we should also add the rising figures of legal or quasi-legal evasion, for which draft counseling groups were a direct cause, and the Resistance therefore an indirect cause. In the two years between October 31, 1967, and October 31, 1969, according to statistics in *Selective Service* monthly newsletters there was a net increase of approximately 737,000 men in the 1–Y category, while the number of men examined rose only slightly. In the same two years declared delinquencies more than doubled, from roughly 15,600 to 31,900. Delinquencies reached an all-time high of 34,492 in January 1970, dropping off after the Supreme Court struck down the delinquency procedures. The total number of conscientious objectors *recognized* by Selective Service grew by half, from 23,800 to 34,500, while the number of men *applying* for conscientious objector status, Berland and Mott guessed, has probably trebled or quadrupled.

At the top of a list of figures like these Bob Freeston of CADRE headed a leaflet, "The Draft Is In TROUBLE!" It would seem so.*

Another strategic context in which resisters put their tactics was that of the domestic costs of a prolonged war. The hope was to "bring the war home" to such an extent that the policy-makers

---

* As the leaflet points out, it is in trouble also because of its own bureaucratic problems, such as the lottery, and because of constraints imposed by the Supreme Court.

In early 1970 the Supreme Court made a series of decisions that limited the powers of draft boards. The Gutknecht and Breen decisions in January forbade the boards to punish delinquents by speeding their induction and gave to the registrant the possibility (previously denied) under some circumstances to go to court against his board before he refuses induction. The Toussie decision in March, though ambiguous, offered some comfort to nonregistrants who make it past twenty-three without being caught.

The Welsh decision in June widened the definition of conscientious objector to include those whose refusal to join the armed forces has only a moral or ethical basis. According to SSS National Headquarters, there were more than 14,000 claims for conscientious objector status filed in the month of the Welsh decision.

would consider it more prudent to end the war than continue it. This goal, intermediate between the doubtful one of destroying the draft and the incalculable one of long-range ideological and cultural change, had a measure of certifiable success. Of course, the war has not ended any more than the draft has, and if one's analysis has been cramped by repeated use of the slogan "End the war now" he will not see any success at all. But some real shifts of policy occurred, and they occurred in large part because administration officials feared the domestic consequences of continuing as before. In their considerations the antiwar movement, and draft resistance in particular, loomed large.

In March 1968 President Johnson rejected General Westmoreland's request for 206,000 additional soldiers and decided instead to reduce the area of bombing over North Vietnam, initiate peace talks, and retire from politics. After so many years of death and destruction Johnson's act was feeble and unsatisfying. Certainly the denouement drags on unconscionably. But however poor the military and political establishment may be at dramatic presentation, they know how to measure audience response. The public opinion polls were forecasting widespread disaffection with the war—and massive draft resistance. Walter Lippmann (only a week before the announcement) was writing:

> The Johnson administration is acting on the unexamined assumption that men can be drafted for war wherever the Government decides to wage it. This is a huge fallacy. . . . The President is confronted with the resistance, open or passive, of the whole military generation, their teachers, their friends, their families. The attempt to fight a distant war by conscription is producing a demoralization which threatens the very security of the Nation.

This was the first twentieth-century American war, concluded Lippmann, "when it was fashionable not to go to a war and entirely acceptable to avoid it."

Lippmann's column was one among many indications of rising opposition to the war and to the draft which American policymakers must have weighed when they decided not to escalate the war. A poll of Harvard seniors in January 1968 revealed that ninety-four percent disapproved of United States policy in Vietnam; fifty-nine percent intended "to make a determined effort to avoid military service"; and twenty-two percent declared that they would go to jail or to Canada rather than serve in Vietnam. What would have happened had the government decided on escalation is suggested by a Lewis Harris poll released in May 1968. According to Harris, twenty to thirty percent of the college students called in the following few months would "seriously contemplate" induction refusal. Harris stated:

> It is likely that many of them when faced with an actual call-up to service will not be pleased but will serve. But even if as many as 25,000 choose to go to prison or one of the other courses of refusing to serve, the size of the crisis surely will exceed any this nation has ever faced in terms of resistance to the draft.

The government chose not to take the steps which might have called this mass of resisters into being. Draft calls were kept low during the summer of 1968, and the percentage of college students among those drafted rose only to 16 percent as of October 1968.

The best available account of the Johnson administration's reappraisal is that by former Air Force Undersecretary Townsend Hoopes. He describes a memorandum prepared by Phillip Goulding, Assistant Secretary of Defense for Public Affairs, in which domestic considerations took primacy. Goulding (in Hoopes' words) noted that there had been absolutely no preparation of public opinion for such a large-scale mobilization. The official line had stressed our ability to fight in Vietnam and at the same time to meet commitments elsewhere without undue strain; it had held that we were winning the war and, specifically, that we had emerged victorious from the Tet offensive; it insisted that ARVN was improving every day. Now suddenly 250,000 American Reservists were to be separated from their families and careers and another 200,000 men drafted—all in the absence of any new or palpable national crisis.

Goulding argued that the shock wave would run through the

entire American body politic. The doves would say the President was destroying the country by pouring its finest men and resources into a bottomless pit. The hawks would cry that the Administration had no moral right to disrupt the lives of all these young men and still insist on waging a war of limited objectives, limited geographical boundaries, and limited weapons. They would demand, Goulding wrote, that the Administration "unleash . . . hit the sanctuaries . . . if necessary invade." The antiwar demonstrations and resistance to the draft would rise to new crescendos, reinforced by civil rights groups who would feel the President had once again revealed his inner conviction that the war in Vietnam was more important than the war on poverty.

McGeorge Bundy, one of the chief architects of the Kennedy-Johnson policy in Southeast Asia, made some equally revealing remarks on several occasions shortly after he left the administration and shortly before the bombing halt. Speaking at De Pauw University on October 12, 1968, for example, Bundy said he now believed the domestic costs of the war to be "plainly unacceptable." He cited "the growing bitterness and polarization of our people," and then added: "There is a special pain in the growing alienation of a generation which is the best we have had, so we must not go on as we are going."

Thus a strong case can be made that draft resistance set limits on the escalation of the Vietnam war. Even more clearly, it has limited the government's capacity to wage future wars by critically delegitimizing conscription in the eyes of America's youth. As of the summer of 1968, a Harris poll revealed that "Americans favor the present draft system by a margin of 53% to 36%, the smallest majority in the history of the polls." Only a year later, in September 1969, 65 percent of young people sixteen to twenty years old and 53 percent of young people in their twenties believed that the military draft was "wrong because it forces young men to fight in a war they don't believe in." If, as most resisters believe, American imperialism requires conscription so that it can rapidly increase the size of its armed forces to fight more than one Vietnam-type war simultaneously, then the fact that a majority of those who will be asked to serve condemn the draft significantly limits the maneuverability of American imperialism.

The ideological and cultural shift that the draft resistance movement helped effect is not measurable in statistics or describable in terms of positions on issues. It has a profounder meaning. It has to do with the weakening of the authority principle on which law and order, in their conventional definition, are based. The Quaker social philosopher Kenneth Boulding takes conscription as characteristic of states that lose the voluntary allegiance of their citizens.

> The draft may well be regarded as a symbol of a slow decline in the legitimacy of the national state (or of what perhaps we should call more exactly the warfare state, to distinguish it from the welfare state which may succeed it), that slow decline which may presage the approach of collapse. In the rise and decline of legitimacy, as we have seen, we find first a period in which sacrifices are made, voluntarily and gladly, in the interests of the legitimate institution, and, indeed, which reinforce the legitimacy of the institution. As the institution becomes more and more pressing in its demands, however, voluntary sacrifices become replaced with forced sacrifices. The tithe becomes a tax, religious enthusiasm degenerates into compulsory chapel, and voluntary enlistment in the army becomes a compulsory draft. The legitimacy of the draft, therefore, is in a sense a subtraction from the legitimacy of the state. It represents the threat system of the state turned in on its own citizens, however much the threat may be disguised by a fine language about service and "every young man fulfilling his obligation." The language of duty is not the language of love and it is a symptom of approaching delegitimation. A marriage in which all the talk is of obligations rather than of love is on its way to the divorce court. The church in which all worship is obligatory is on its way to abandonment or reformation, and the state in which service has become a duty is in no better case. The draft, therefore, which undoubtedly increases the threat capability of the national state, is a profound symptom of its decay.

The decay of the state is due not to a simple reflex of its bad policies but to the initiative and determination of its citizenry to resist it or refuse to cooperate altogether. Awakened, no doubt, by particular outrages from those with power, America's young people have begun to question the existence and location of power itself. Some of them, even those who shout "Power to the people!," will fall into new authoritarian situations. But there remains a growing trend toward liberation from all repressive centers of authority, personal and political, left, right, and corporate liberal. We are seeing a revival of anarchist and libertarian socialist theory and practice. An idea now only dimly felt is growing brighter and clearer: that states have power only because we allow them to. At the same time we are seeing something new in the history of social revolution: a simultaneous spiritual or psychological revolution that is merging with the political revolution.

Notes to Chapter Seventeen

Most of the statistics quoted in this chapter are from the May 1970 issue of the *Draft Counselor's Newsletter* published by the Midwest Committee for Draft Counseling, regional office of the Central Committee for Conscientious Objectors. They in turn were taken from government sources.

Walter Lippmann's column, "This Draft Is Difficult to Justify," appeared in the *Washington Post*, March 24, 1968 and was called to our attention by Paul Lauter. The various polls are summarized in *Resist*, January 19 and June 10, 1968 and the *Chicago Daily News*, Sept. 8, 1969. Townsend Hoopes' article, later expanded into a book, was published in the *Atlantic*, October 1969. The figure for the percentage of students among those drafted in October 1968 is from the *New York Times*, Dec. 1, 1968. The Bundy quote was cited by Noam Chomsky in his "The Menace of Liberal Scholarship," *New York Review of Books*, January 2, 1969. The connection between conscription and the government's power rapidly to expand its military involvements is discussed in Rick Boardman, "Draft Resistance and American Imperialism," March 1969; David Greenberg, "Vietnam Is Not an Accident," May 1969; and John M. Swomley, "Conscription and Foreign Policy," papers privately circulated

CHAPTER EIGHTEEN

Epilogue: UNDO

May 1970 was the month of the Cambodia invasion and the Kent, Augusta, and Jackson State murders. An antiwar movement which the Nixon administration had been fairly successful at suppressing by federal indictments, defusing by a program of slow withdrawals from Vietnam, and diverting by the ecology issue, now suddenly enjoyed a ten-fold growth in numbers and energy. It was no less amazing to movement organizers than it was to Nixon, and while he was losing sleep and holding consultations at the White House they were rushing about trying to give some shape to the spontaneous outpouring of activity.

Although it was overshadowed by the first nationwide student strike in America's history, by the massive demonstrations, and by the teams of Congressional lobbyists, the draft resistance movement had a resurgence of its own, and was as hard pressed as the larger movement in coming to a focus. During the first two weeks of May over ten thousand draft cards and card-pledges were turned in around the country. By Monday May 4—Nixon's speech was April 30—some three hundred fifty Princeton men had handed in their cards and by Wednesday over three thousand nationwide had signed up as charter members of a new multi-tactic umbrella group called Union for National Draft Opposition (UNDO). Its breathless organizers were given the university computer, office space, and lots of money, and with these assets it went about "coordinating" the antidraft activity across the country. By Thursday there were eleven UNDO chapters outside Princeton, by the next Monday there were fifty.

The chapter at Union College in Schenectady, New York, assumed the task of coordinating the card turn-ins, leaving to the Princeton computer the larger job of processing and repackaging all other (largely legal) forms of antidraft work. Calling itself National Center for Draft Resistance (NCDR), Union College UNDO was on the phone every day, keeping groups throughout the country up on the latest figures. On Tuesday, May 12, NCDR announced the national total of cards and pledges had reached 10,650, at least six thousand of which came from California. Several thousand more came in during the next two weeks.

Meanwhile Princeton claimed over 150 chapters and called a "convocation"—at Princeton—to make national decisions and set up a national governing body. One of the matters to be settled was what to do with all the draft cards. Most groups were holding theirs, some had sent them to NCDR, and many were bound by a conditional figure (most often fifty or one hundred thousand) that had to be reached nationwide before their local pledge cards could be transformed into real draft cards.

At the conference (May 19 to 21) the nearly four hundred delegates voted by a narrow margin to set the national figure at one hundred thousand. If that number were reached all the pledges would be exchanged for draft cards and the huge bundle would be taken to Washington. Those draft cards which had already been relinquished without strings were to be gathered by NCDR and delivered to Nixon on June 10. They projected about ten thousand cards for that bundle.

During the same month there were militant but nonviolent demonstrations at draft boards and army bases across the country, some of them involving UNDO groups, but most arising from *ad hoc* committees after April 30. In Massachusetts, for example, a coalition of student and community groups from Worcester so surprised the SSS and the police with their numbers and determination that the local board closed for two days in a row. On the third day over two hundred fifty were arrested, the largest number in Worcester's history. In Boston, buses of inductees or pre-inductees were delayed twice in a week by several hundred who sat in the army base entrance. Hundreds were arrested, including three pre-inductees who got off their bus to join the demonstration. The Newton draft board, harried for a week by local groups, received the attentions of the army base demonstrators for a day, and as a result one hundred seventy were arrested, the largest number in Newton's history. Meanwhile the Early Morning Show of BDRG was revived by another group, a third group (called the Black Thursday Coalition) set to work hassling draft boards in a variety of little ways, and a fourth began trying to induce draft board members to resign. Comparable stories came in from all parts of the country.

By the end of May, naturally, the hothouse atmosphere began to cool off. Many students went home. People with one misdemeanor charge hesitated to add a second. Draft card returns slackened. Princeton's computer hummed a little less. The cumbersome national machinery set up by UNDO was left to do its thing (useful for communications but clumsy and coercive for decision-making) while the delegates returned to their groups to see what could be done to preserve momentum through the summer. Many UNDO chapters folded, some continued a paper existence. Resistance groups like CADRE, Philadelphia, Palo Alto, who sent delegates, remained stable centers of experience and long-range action. After the deluge, which proved the enormous size of resistance sentiment, most organizers went home to deepen their roots, and so to make possible the enormous work yet to be accomplished.

Notes to Chapter Eighteen

This epilogue was written by Michael Ferber, who worked with Boston UNDO and had numerous phone conversations with Princeton and Union. He also talked with the Harvard delegates to the Princeton convocation and with Lee Swenson (of the Institute for the Study of Nonviolence in Palo Alto) who also attended.

The number of draft cards returned between April and August 1970 was estimated at 11,000. As of November 1970, "close to 25,000" were estimated to have returned their cards or signed the UNDO pledge (David · McReynolds, "Striking the Draft," *WRL News,* Nov.–Dec. 1970).

Index

Algerian war, influence of on American Resistance: 2–3, 16, 34, 59, 117–118, 245

Angert, Dan: 55, 58

Ann Arbor Resistance: 36, 58, 140, 245–246

April 3 Movement (at Stanford): 234–238

Arlington Street Church (in Boston): 108, 157, 188–189, 224, 258, 278*n*

Arlook, Ira: 78, 81

BDRG. *See* Boston Draft Resistance Group

Bell, Tom: 55,. 56, 68–76, 131, 136

Berkeley Resistance: 248, 278*n*. *See also* East Bay Resistance; San Francisco Resistance

Berland, Kerry: 97, 98, 282, 283, 284

Berrigan, Daniel: 22, 202, 203, 205, 207–208, 211–212, 214, 217–219

Berrigan, Phillip: 201, 202, 203, 207, 209, 218

Bevel, James: 30, 59, 98, 119

Boardman, Rick: 96–97, 101, 215, 223, 224

Booth, Paul: 10, 35, 36, 38, 41, 55, 58, 59

Boston Draft Resistance Group (BDRG): 63–64, 104, 106, 109, 157, 169–178, 293

Boston Resistance. *See* New England Resistance

Buffalo Resistance: 192–193, 222, 223

CADRE (Chicago Area Draft Resisters): 62, 94–103, 150, 222, 223, 244, 279–280, 282, 284, 293

Calvert, Greg: 1, 61, 127, 130–132, 139–140, 164–166, 183

Camus, Albert: 2, 10, 242

Carmichael, Stokely: 33, 41

Catholic Worker (newspaper or group): 6, 19, 21–27

Catonsville Nine: 161, 202, 204, 207, 209, 214, 215, 217

Chandler, Jody: 178*ff*

Chicago Area Draft Resisters. *See* CADRE

Chicago Fifteen: 202, 208, 216

Chicago Resistance. *See* CADRE

Chomsky, Noam: 110, 184, 258, 268–278

Coffin, William Sloane: 108–109, 111, 124, 166, 189–190, 259, 278*n*

Committee for Nonviolent Action (CNVA): 11, 17–18, 19, 22, 48–50, 51, 85, 158

Congress Of Racial Equality (CORE): 18, 23, 30, 59

Cornell, Tom: 17, 21–27

Corporations, as Resistance target: 209–211, 222–241

Dancis, Bruce: 70, 72, 74, 75

Davidson, Carl: 127, 131–132, 164, 167

Davis, Rennie: 36, 184
Day, Dorothy: 22, 24
Dellinger, David: 3, 6, 49, 140
Detroit Resistance: 57–58, 223
Dolan, John: 96, 100
Dowling, Bill: 105*ff*, 278
Draft cards: burned, 21–27, 47–48, 72–76, 136–137, 281; turned in: 3–4, 12–16, 102–103, 105–114, 135, 142–143, 174–175, 222, 224, 241*n*, 277*ff*, 280–281, 291–292

East Bay Resistance: 283. *See also* Berkeley Resistance; San Francisco Resistance
Egleson, Nick: 110, 112–114, 170, 172
End The Draft (ETD): 7, 18–21, 35, 50

Falk, Jeff: 97, 98
Ferber, Michael: 94, 124, 128, 130, 135, 166, 230, 278*n*, 293*n*
Forest, Jim: 207–208, 213
Freeton, Robert: 98, 284

Gardner, Tom: 126–127
GI Resistance: 61, 137–140, 145–146, 173, 179–180, 186–199, 227–228, 231–232
Ginsberg, Allen: 108, 122
Gittlin, Todd: 10, 34
Goodman, Mitchell: 120, 121, 123, 124, 166
Goodman, Paul: 43, 75, 123, 265–268
Greenberg, David: 100, 103, 234
Grizzard, Vernon: 167, 170, 176, 177–178

Hamilton, Steve: 1, 78, 79, 88–90, 127, 140–141
Harney, Jim: 107, 109, 111, 205

Harris, David: 1, 78–91, 105, 128, 130, 135, 141–143, 215, 243
Hartzog, Bill: 38, 127
Hawaii Resistance: 193–199
Heller, Lennie: 1, 78, 79, 88–90, 99, 104–105, 128, 146, 243
High-school Resistance: 141, 151, 173, 179, 228
Honeywell Project: 238–240. *See also* TCDIC

Irons, Peter: 10–16, 35, 72, 79

Jack, Alex: 105*ff*, 153–154, 251
Jezer, Martin: 48, 63, 64, 74, 75, 137

Kepler, Roy: 88, 120
Kramer, Brent: 42, 43, 59
Kugelmass, Joel: 78, 224

LaPorte, Roger: 25–26
Lauter, Paul: 42, 57, 136
Lester, Julius: 134–135
Los Angeles Resistance: 222, 282
Lynd, Staughton: 54, 59, 94, 117, 118–119, 270, 274

Macdonald, Dwight: 2, 3, 4, 268
McReynolds, David: 21, 24–26, 71
Maher, John: 167, 169, 170, 176
Marcuse, Herbert: 11, 133, 256–257, 258
Meyer, Karl: 10–11, 16
Miller, David: 22–24, 26–27, 36, 49, 65
Milwaukee Fourteen: 107, 109, 161, 202, 205, 206, 207, 208, 211–214, 215
Minneapolis–St. Paul Resistance. *See* Honeywell Project: TCDIC
Mitchell, David: 7, 17–21, 59, 65, 98
Moses, Robert Parris: 30, 31, 242

Mott, Jeremy: 96–97, 282, 283, 284

Mungo, Ray: 50, 110, 157

Muste, A.J.: 3, 12, 22, 24, 48–49, 72, 116

National (Resistance) conferences: 160, 174, 223, 230, 233

Nelson, Bruce: 162, 234

New England Resistance (NER): 94, 104–114, 153–155, 157, 158–159, 160, 175, 191, 222, 223–230, 278, 282

New York City Resistance: 133, 159, 222, 223, 230–233, 279, 280, 282

Oglesby, Carl: 35, 36, 37, 41, 118–119, 184

Omega symbol: 251–252

Osher, David: 159, 279

Palo Alto Resistance: 78–91, 157, 160, 223, 233–238, 293

Peacemaker (newspaper or group): 6, 7, 11, 18, 48–50

Philadelphia Resistance: 151, 152, 156–157, 175, 222, 282, 293

Phillips, John: 48, 208, 216

Progressive Labor Party (PLP): 42, 50–51, 106, 176–177

Rader, Gary: 75, 94–96, 99, 101, 105, 121, 139

Randolph, A. Philip: 5, 117, 118

Raskin, Marcus: 120, 121, 124, 166

Reed, David: 47–49

Resist: 122, 123, 135, 165, 180

Robertson, Neil: 107, 224, 225, 226

Rupert, Paul: 78, 80, 137, 223, 235–236

Rustin, Bayard: 3, 5, 117

Samstein, Mendy: 38, 81–82

Sanctuary: 161, 225–227, 188–199

San Francisco Resistance: 222, 223, 224, 231–232, 282. *See also* Berkeley Resistance; East Bay Resistance

Savio, Mario: 89, 277

Segal, Jeff: 59, 63, 100, 144, 167

Shero, Jeff: 36, 55, 56

Sherzer, Joel: 11–12, 15–16

Shurtleff, Jeff: 78, 81, 82, 83, 87, 246–247

Silbar, Earl: 40, 42

Spock, Benjamin: 2, 111, 120, 121, 123, 124, 166, 174, 188, 214, 278*n*

Stop The Draft Week (STDW): 135–136, 140–147

Student Nonviolent Coordinating Committee (SNCC): 12, 18–19, 21, 29–33, 50, 57, 58, 81–82, 98, 101, 126–127, 132, 134, 158

Student Peace Union (SPU): 10–16, 17, 19, 35

Students for a Democratic Society (SDS): 1, 33–44, 47, 50, 51, 52, 53, 54, 57, 59–63, 100, 111, 114, 127*ff*, 141–142, 158, 249–250; attempts to use draft in community organizing, 164–184; Cornell chapter, 68, 70; endorses draft resistance, 60–61; Harvard chapter, 109, 128; Hawaii chapter, 193, 194; New York City chapter, 169; Stanford chapter, 234–238

Sweeney, Dennis: 1, 78–91, 130, 141–142, 224

Swinney, Dan: 180–181, 182–183

Talmanson, Robert: 105, 107, 188–189, 225, 226

TCDIC (Twin Cities Draft Information Center): 150, 151, 222,

282, 283–284. *See also* Honeywell Project

Ultra resistance: 201–221, 234,
283–284
Union for National Draft Opposition (UNDO): 291–293

War Resisters League (WRL): 19,
21, 71
Washington   (D.C.)   Resistance:
169, 223

Waskow, Arthur: 120, 121, 218
Webb, Lee: 36, 38
Williams, Chris: 11–12, 15–16
Wisconsin Draft Resistance Union
(WDRU): 99, 133, 178–184
Women's liberation: 54–55, 159–
160
Wood, Dan: 55, 57–58
Working-class   Resistance: 113,
141, 164–184, 187, 227

Zevin Robert: 119–120, 122
Zinn, Howard: 30, 110